Reports of the Research Committee of the Society of Antiquaries of London, No. 60

EARLY INCISED SLABS AND BRASSES FROM THE LONDON MARBLERS

This book is published with the generous assistance of
The Francis Coales Charitable Trust.

EARLY INCISED SLABS AND BRASSES FROM THE LONDON MARBLERS

Sally Badham and Malcolm Norris

The Society of Antiquaries of London

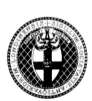

First published 1999
by
The Society of Antiquaries of London
Burlington House
Piccadilly
London W1V 0HS

© The Society of Antiquaries of London 1999

ISBN 0 85431 272 2

ISSN 0953-7163

British Library Cataloguing in Publication Data
A CIP catalogue record for this book is available from the
British Library

Designed and laid out by Chuck Goodwin, London W2 5DA
Printed in Great Britain by Redwood Books, Trowbridge, Wiltshire

Dedication
In memory of Frank Allen Greenhill MA, FSA,
FSA (Scot) (1896 to 1983)

In carrying out our study of the incised slabs and
related brasses from the thirteenth- and fourteenth-
century London marblers' workshops, we have
drawn very heavily on Greenhill's records. His
rubbings of incised slabs, mostly made in the 1920s
and 1930s, often show them better preserved than
they are now and his unpublished notes provide
much invaluable background information. Without
access to his material, our study would have been less
complete. For this reason, we wish to dedicate this
volume to Greenhill's memory.

Contents

Foreword

This work is dedicated, rightly, to the memory of Frank Allen Greenhill. Sixty years of his leisure time was spent in researching and recording incised slabs. This he did in his meticulous and indefatigable manner and he would not be deflected from his path. Apart from two or three nineteenth-century publications, here was a field of research wide open and just waiting to be tackled by a medievalist.

He was born in 1896 and before the First World War had already become an avid brass rubber. Early on, in two separate churches, he espied fine incised slabs and at once realized that here was something to which he could devote his life. In Rouen, during the 1914–18 war, he observed the vast quantities of slabs remaining in the cathedral and other churches of that city; this spurred him on even more.

Greenhill appointed Malcolm Norris, one of the co-authors of this monograph, together with myself and one other friend, to be his executors. As Malcolm died unexpectedly in 1995, it now falls to me to write this note.

Fortunately, Greenhill's profession took him to various parts of England and also to Scotland, enabling much work recording incised slabs. His first work, *The Incised Slabs of Leicestershire and Rutland*, was published in 1958; this dealt with each effigial slab in considerable detail, as regards both costume and life of the deceased person commemorated. About this time he retired. Thereafter he spent much time on the Continent researching in national archives as well as making rubbings in important churches; during this work he encountered foreign antiquaries, many of whom became personal friends.

His research reached its apogee with the publication on his eightieth birthday of *Incised Effigial Slabs: a Study of Engraved Stone Memorials in Latin Christendom, c 1100 to c 1700*, in two volumes, one of text and the other of illustrations and lists arranged by country.

But apart from incised slabs, various scholars were studying the well-known early brasses, notably knights, especially those of the d'Abernon family at Stoke d'Abernon, Surrey; the Trumpington family at Trumpington, Cambridgeshire; the de Bures family at Acton, Suffolk, and the Septvans family at Chartham, Kent. In 1965 J C Ward published a paper on the life of de Bures, showing that he died in 1331 instead of the previously accepted date of 1302; this was followed by S D T Spittle in 1970 with a similar analysis of the Trumpington brass, dating it to *c* 1326 as opposed to the standard date of 1289. As a result, others took up the cudgel. For their centenary in 1987 the Monumental Brass Society published a volume entitled *The Earliest English Brasses*, in which Nicholas Rogers, Paul Binski and John Blair presented their researches, throwing established dating to the winds.

This present work, *Early Incised Slabs and Brasses from the London Marblers* by Sally Badham and Malcolm Norris, combines the stylistic analysis adopted in *The Earliest English Brasses* with incised slabs – a line of research not previously attempted. Yet again we have a new aspect.

Words are inadequate to express the gratitude that Greenhill would have felt that part of his researches proved of value and were used and appreciated by scholars of a later generation. Greenhill wrote in *Incised Effigial Slabs* that he had but scratched the surface of the subject. Everybody disagreed – but he was, as always, correct. During one week alone in France in 1995 the best part of fifty incised slabs quite unknown to Greenhill were found.

So the task goes on. It will never be complete.

JOHN COALES
August 1998

Acknowledgements

In carrying out this study we have received considerable help both from colleagues in the Monumental Brass Society and from other friends. Our greatest debt is, of course, to the late Frank Greenhill, to whom this monograph is dedicated. Father Jerome Bertram FSA, Dr John Blair FSA, Brian Gittos and Moira Gittos and, above all, John Coales FSA have offered generous help, advice and information. They, together with Jon Bayliss, Nicholas Rogers, Professor Nigel Saul FSA and Tim Sutton, have all read this monograph in draft and contributed many useful suggestions for improvements. Bernard Nurse and Adrian James of the Society of Antiquaries have been unfailingly patient and helpful in response to our many demands throughout. We are also grateful to Portia Askew, Claude Blair FSA, Derrick Chivers, Paul Cockerham FSA, John Goodall FSA, Jane Houghton, Philip Lankester, Dr Nigel Ramsey FSA, Frank Robson, Les Smith and Martin Stuchfield for help given. Additionally, we owe a debt of gratitude for their co-operation and assistance to the incumbents of the many churches in which we have examined monuments.

In May 1995, Malcolm Norris, one of the authors of this monograph, died unexpectedly. The manuscript was in an advanced state of completion, but not finalized. Sally Badham would like to express her very warm appreciation to Malcolm's widow, Laurie, for all her help, at a very difficult time, in making it possible for all the material relating to this work to be brought together, thus ensuring that publication of this final contribution to Malcolm Norris's distinguished record of scholarship was not delayed by his untimely death.

PART 1

THE ORIGINS AND DEVELOPMENT OF THE INDUSTRY

CHAPTER 1

INTRODUCTION AND METHODOLOGY

Although the objective of the Monumental Brass Society is to promote the study both of monumental brasses and of incised slabs, research on the two media has proceeded along separate and largely independent lines. As the volumes of the *Transactions of the Monumental Brass Society* attest, attention has focused mainly upon brasses; they have been widely studied in the context of various disciplines and copiously illustrated. In contrast, were it not for the work of Creeny in the last century and, above all, Greenhill in this, there would be little in print on incised slabs, other than a handful of county studies. Greenhill's pioneering work, in particular, has provided the opportunity for others to discover the volume and quality of slabs both in this country and on the Continent. Too often, however, English incised slabs have wrongly been dismissed as an inferior art form.

Like brasses, incised slabs are susceptible to stylistic analysis to identify workshop groupings and it is therefore surprising that so little typological work has been carried out on slabs, even on the early London products. As long ago as 1958, Greenhill suggested that the makers of early marble tombs may have produced both incised slabs and brasses.[1] This may be seen as a logical conclusion: there is ample evidence (set out in Chapter 2) that in other workshops, both in this country and on the Continent, the same men made both brasses and incised slabs. Some other writers have touched upon this point in relation to the London workshops, but hitherto no attempt has been made to follow this up systematically. We have sought to remedy this omission by identifying existing and recorded Purbeck marble incised slabs from the pre-Black Death London workshops and comparing their designs with those of contemporary brasses.

In the course of our study, we have examined all 170 effigial incised slabs in England and Wales listed by Greenhill and given dates in the span 1250 to 1400, together with the handful of such slabs that have come to light since Greenhill's death. Many were quickly discounted, being readily identifiable as originating from sources other than London. (A brief survey and a discussion of these slabs are in Chapter 3.) Having eliminated incised slabs of clear overseas or regional origin, we were left with twenty-eight effigial slabs which appear to have come from the London workshops. Since it transpired that all of these were of Purbeck marble, we next examined all non-effigial Purbeck marble slabs with incised inscriptions which had been rubbed by Greenhill, listed by Dru Drury, Leach, Sadler or John Blair, or were otherwise known to us.[2] As we explain in Chapter 4, for some both the early date and the style of the inscription suggested that they had been made by the marblers at Corfe. However, twenty-four had incised lettering which linked stylistically with that on the effigial Purbeck marble incised slabs which we had already identified as likely London products and a further eight appeared to be related to them. Most of these were relief cross slabs, but some were simple slabs, usually coffin-shaped, with just an incised inscription. A further six Purbeck marble slabs had other types of incised detail pointing to a

1.1 Distribution map of incised slabs from the London marblers.

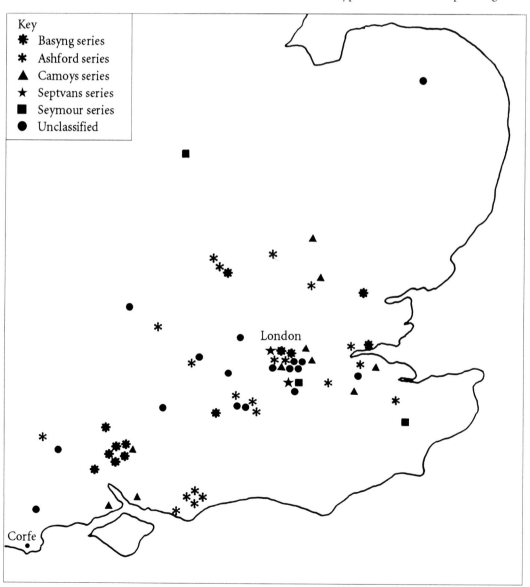

Key
✸ Basyng series
✳ Ashford series
▲ Camoys series
★ Septvans series
■ Seymour series
● Unclassified

London

Corfe

London origin. This survey gave a total of sixty-six products of the London marblers that included incised detail. (The incised slabs are listed in Appendix A.) The majority of the incised slabs were in London or the surrounding counties of Middlesex, Kent, Essex, Hertfordshire, Bedfordshire, Buckinghamshire, Hampshire, Sussex and Surrey, with a handful further afield in Wiltshire, Dorset, Oxfordshire, Northamptonshire, Cambridgeshire and Norfolk (Figure 1.1). Brasses and other monuments from the same workshops appear to have had a wider distribution (Figure 1.2). (They are listed in Appendix B.) Throughout this monograph all county references are on the basis of pre-1974 boundaries, for compatibility with gazetteers listing brasses and incised slabs.

In view of the persuasive evidence put forward by Claude Blair that the Corfe marblers produced some effigies and sculptures in other freestones in addition to their Purbeck marble wares,[3] we examined other non-effigial incised slabs with inscriptions known to us, but none appeared to share the stylistic characteristics of the Purbeck marble slabs referred to above. However, one of the incised inscriptions on a Purbeck marble slab included in the analysis in the previous paragraph, at Little Shelford, Cambridgeshire, is set in the back of a tomb recess housing a freestone effigy attributed to the court workshop. Finally, we also looked beyond Greenhill's definition of an incised slab[4] at the few carved Purbeck memorials

1.2 Distribution map of other monuments assigned to the Basyng, Ashford, Camoys, Septvans, Seymour and Hastings pattern series from the London marblers.

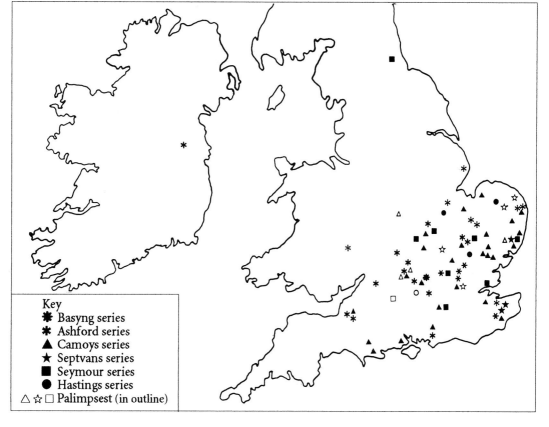

Key
✳ Basyng series
✱ Ashford series
▲ Camoys series
★ Septvans series
■ Seymour series
● Hastings series
△ ☆ □ Palimpsest (in outline)

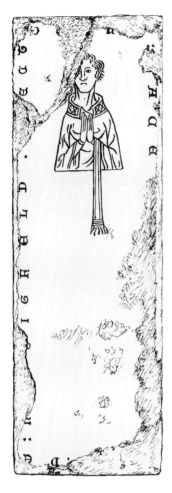

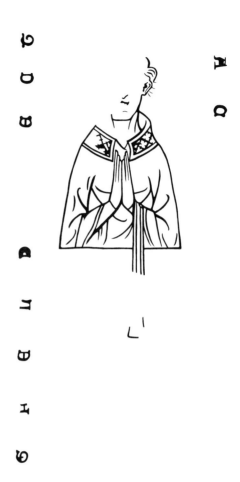

1.3 (above) West Wickham,
Kent III: John de
Huntingfeld, ob 1362.
London A incised slab.
Early nineteenth-century
drawing by T Fisher,
Society of Antiquaries,
'Kent Illustrations: Prints
and Drawings' collection,
3, fol 61.

1.4 (above, right) West
Wickham, Kent III: John de
Huntingfeld, ob 1362.
London A incised slab.
Tracing of 1837 dabbing by
J Waller, Society of
Antiquaries collection.

which incorporate incised or brass-inlaid inscriptions, but we found only two monuments with relief effigial representation which can conclusively be linked with the incised slabs that are the subject of this monograph, suggesting that most were made in other workshops, probably in Corfe. Although we are confident of having examined all surviving effigial incised slabs which fall within the period of study, the same is not true of incised cross and inscription slabs, examples of which in southern England, with the exception of Dorset, Lincolnshire, Northamptonshire and Oxfordshire,[5] have yet to be systematically recorded and listed. Once such *corpora* have been compiled for the remainder of southern England, more products of the London marblers will undoubtedly come to light, enabling others to add to our findings.

Having identified those slabs of probable London origin, we have endeavoured to check as comprehensively as possible both their existing appearance and records of their earlier state. Our main historical source has been Greenhill's rubbings, recently deposited in the library of the Society of Antiquaries of London, and his unpublished notes, currently in the custody of John Coales.

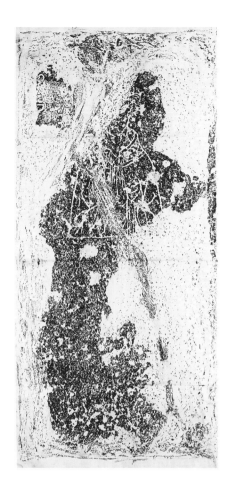 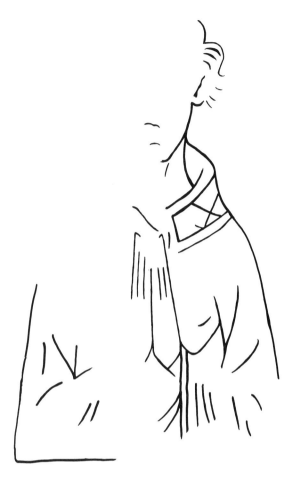

Additionally, the Society of Antiquaries' main collection of incised slab rubbings, including some extremely valuable nineteenth-century ones by Waller, and other antiquarian notes and drawings have helped to fill out the picture.

It quickly became apparent in the course of this historical study how rapidly these slabs are deteriorating and being destroyed. The most telling illustration of this is the series at West Wickham, Kent. On first visiting the church, it was difficult to find any trace of either the 1344 Cestreford slab or the 1362 Huntingfeld slab listed by Greenhill, though after a thorough search very worn traces of the latter were discovered. Greenhill's unpublished notes revealed that two fragments of the Cestreford slab remained outside the south porch; one is now completely effaced and on the other only faint indents of a few letters remain visible, all evidence of the incised figure having been completely worn away. It was only after searching the Society of Antiquaries' rubbings, prints and drawings collections that a better understanding of the original appearance of these slabs was gained and the former existence of a third slab was revealed. Figures 1.3 to 1.6 illustrate how the Huntingfeld slab

1.5 (above, left) West Wickham, Kent III: John de Huntingfeld, ob 1362. London A incised slab. 1947 rubbing by F A Greenhill, Society of Antiquaries collection, photograph by A C Cooper Ltd.

1.6 (above) West Wickham, Kent III: John de Huntingfeld, ob 1362. London A incised slab. Tracing of detail from 1989 rubbing by S F Badham showing present condition.

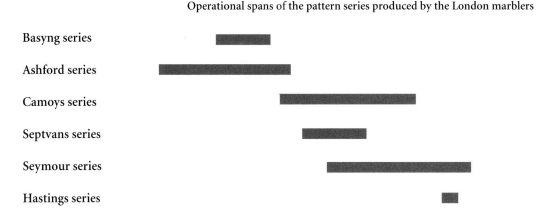

Operational spans of the pattern series produced by the London marblers

1.7 Diagram showing the operational spans of the pattern series produced by the London marblers.

has deteriorated over the past 200 years. By the time another generation has passed, all vestiges of a once fine series of slabs will probably have gone.

West Wickham is not an isolated example. Few slabs discussed in this monograph have remained undisturbed or been well protected. Many were buried or reused as building material and subsequently rediscovered. Often, however, these are in better condition than slabs left open to view since they were first laid down. Slabs at Cliffe-at-Hoo, Kent, Salisbury, Wiltshire, Romsey, Hampshire, and Tilsworth, Bedfordshire, have virtually worn out. The surface and consequently the incised detail of the lady at Sawbridgeworth, Hertfordshire, is crumbling away and it has now been permanently carpeted over. Fixed pews were built on the slab at Horton Kirby, Kent, in the 1930s, thus rendering it inaccessible. One of the slabs at Great Bookham, Surrey, has been reburied in a buttress. Pipes obscure the incising on the fragment at Harrow, Middlesex. A fixed long-case clock and bench cover most of the slab at Wimborne Minster, Dorset. Slabs at Lesnes Abbey, Strood and Snodland, all in Kent, and five fragments at St Bartholomew the Great, London, have disappeared. Incised slabs have probably been even less well protected than brasses over the centuries. The threats represented by the Reformation of the sixteenth century, the Civil War of the seventeenth and the church restorations of the nineteenth are well known to students of brasses and incised slabs, but slabs were at risk even before then. There is evidence in London, certainly as far back as 1456, of churchwardens selling off old marble gravestones to make way for new memorials.[6]

In the light of this evidence of past and present depredations of incised slabs, three points impressed themselves upon us. First, in a study such as this, the use of antiquarian sources is not just desirable, but a necessity. Second, it is now a priority to illustrate what remains of these monuments. Third, in carrying out this study we are trying to reconstruct a picture from just a few tiny fragments of the whole; this is also true of early brasses and for both studies only limited conclusions can be reached with certainty.

However, in considering the evidence presented by the incised slabs alongside the evidence already published on brasses, we have been able to reconstruct a fuller picture than has previously been available of the operations of the London marblers before the Black Death. In particular, we suggest that in the late thirteenth century production was on a larger scale than previously believed. We also provide evidence to suggest that more than one workshop was producing brasses and incised slabs in London for much of the period covered by this study, their spans of operation being set out in Figure 1.7. Finally, our findings also throw fresh light upon the recent reappraisal of the dating of early brasses and, indeed, on the wider problem of dating monuments of the Decorated period.

CHAPTER 2

COMMON SOURCES OF BRASSES AND INCISED SLABS

A perception of monumental brasses in Britain as the particular and exclusive product of certain English craftsmen has become well established. This view has in fact been encouraged by a too exclusive interest in the brasses themselves, but was also given credibility by the successful and prolific development in the fifteenth century of incised slabs in alabaster by the Derbyshire, Nottinghamshire and, later, Burton-on-Trent workshops.[1] These craftsmen in this period made notably little use of brass inlays, only those originally set in a slab of 1498 at Stanford-on-Soar, Nottinghamshire, having so far been recorded.[2] Furthermore, where brasses are associated with alabaster high tombs, as for example at Chesterfield, Derbyshire, the work for which was contracted to Henry Harpur and William Moorecock of Burton, the metal elements and the slab in which they are set were very clearly the consequences of subcontract work.[3] The scepticism of Trivick that 'the technique of incising a stone slab is not the same as incising on metal plate – it is very doubtful if the same craftsmen would execute both'[4] reflects a widely held assumption, which has successfully, if unfortunately, divorced the study of engraved brasses from that of incised slabs, contributing to the neglect of the latter. It is possible that an individual craftsman who specialized in engraving brasses would not also have produced incised slabs, but that does not mean that the two types of monument were not made in the same work-shop, to the same patterns and under the direction of a single master.

Greenhill, after sustained research, suspected a common origin for the two, stating that 'the close resemblance of the early incised effigies depicted on marble slabs to those of contemporary brasses can hardly be a chance one, and indicates that either the makers of marble tombs worked in both media or the drawings for both types were supplied from a common source'.[5] It is this view that is developed in the examination that follows. There is nothing surprising about this conclusion. A brief survey of the inter-relationship of these two monumental forms in northern Europe leaves little room for doubt that designers worked concurrently in both media. Moreover, there is evidence to indicate that some regional brass-engraving workshops in England also produced incised slabs. From this it may be presumed that the London marblers of the late thirteenth and early fourteenth centuries also produced both incised slabs and brasses, and that the evidence of the design of the former must be of relevance to the latter.

In the thirteenth and fourteenth centuries the most prestigious centres of brass engraving lay in the workshops of northern France and the Franco-Flemish borderland, most notably in Paris and Tournai.[6] In both these centres craftsmen evidently worked in both media. Very few French brasses survive, but the drawings of Boudan and others for de Gaignières[7] reflect a common source of design in brass and stone. In many French incised slabs marble, composition or brass inlays were inserted, of which a few fifteenth-century examples of brass survive. Notable cases are those of an armed figure of 1459 at Boncourt and Toussaint de la Ruelle's slab of 1470 at the collegiate church of St Omer.[8]

In Tournai and Ghent the evidence is more comprehensive, not only in including a range of slabs employing a variety of inlays, of which outstanding examples are that of a subdeacon of *c* 1320 at Noyon,[9] and the 1488 slab to Joos de Bul at the St Joos Hospital, Bruges,[10] but also in documentary evidence of craftsmen working in both media. Amongst the destroyed archives of Tournai was a contract, dated 1301 or 1311, for the making by Jacques Couves of Tournai of a memorial to Jean de Mur, which had a design partly incised, partly inlaid in brass and partly inlaid in alabaster.[11] Surviving examples of such treatment include the Noyon subdeacon and fragments illustrated by Page-Phillips.[12]

Extensive contract evidence records the work in Tournai of, amongst others, members of the families of Hanette, Escamaing, Génois and Bidet, and in Ghent of those of Van Meyere and Goethals. All of these apparently worked in both media, extending, as Nys has recently shown, to the making after the mid-fourteenth century of both incised and mural tablets.[13] Jan d'Escamaing, a maker of many brasses, is recorded as having re-engraved a slab to the Camphin family in 1350,[14] and Alain Génois, equally associated with brasses, completed the inscription of a stone tablet in 1474.[15] In Britain, surviving slabs of Tournai marble, such as those at Barton-upon-Humber and Boston, Lincolnshire, register the same composition of materials, though the brass, alabaster or composition inlays have now entirely gone. Comparability of design is very close, as between the 1349 Walsokne brass at St Margaret's, King's Lynn, Norfolk, and the 1340 incised slab of Wessel called Smalenburgh at Boston, Lincolnshire.[16]

Turning from France and the Low Countries to the east, there is, as yet, no evidence from the Rhineland reinforcing this association. Indeed, a known brass engraver at Köln, Willem Loeman, was associated with other metal workers, rather than marblers.[17] Further north and eastwards, however, the close association of incised slab production with brass engraving is confirmed. Several locally engraved brasses in and around Lübeck have a coarse simplicity that relates them to contemporary incised slabs, both in execution and in peculiarities of design. Notable examples are a large brass of 1432 at Gadebusch to a Queen of Sweden, and the 1445 slab of Sir Mathias Axcow and his wife at Doberan,[18] in which the style and the arrangement of the women's dresses are remarkably similar. At Bardowick the 1406 brass of Herman Schomekers[19] belongs to a long series of memorials of Lübeck origin. It shows the figure blessing the chalice and host, and dressed in processional vestments without a cope, the almuce having been drawn over the head. Closely comparable incised slabs include that of 1417 at Riga to Johann Sobbe, and at Lübeck those of 1464 to Nikolaus van der Molen, of 1514 to Johannes Cordes and of 1521 to Heinrich Lunt.[20] In the case of the Schomekers brass, the entire canopy is in stone, an arrangement also used at Poznan Cathedral, Poland, for the *c* 1380 brass of a priest, which includes incised background ornament and head cushion.[21]

Within central Germany, the engraving of brasses flourished from the mid-sixteenth century in Nürnberg, the Vischer family being the leading makers. Brasses co-existed with the production of many incised and relief slabs, some of which contain metal inlays. These are in some cases engraved, in others in relief, as is well illustrated at Erfurt Cathedral in the slabs of 1481 to Heinrich Gassmann and of 1542 to Johann von Mengershausen.[22] Whether stone and metalwork were completed within the one workshop or represent the association of different workshops is a matter of conjecture. The Gassmann slab has the aspect of an integrated work, as, to a lesser extent, does that of Mengershausen. However, the engraved half effigy on Johann von Heringen's monument of 1505 at Erfurt Cathedral[23] appears to have been inserted with little regard for the stone elements, the border and the metal design being complete. What may be confidently claimed is that the craftsmen in both media worked in very close association, and it is likely that some composite memorials were made in the one workshop.

Yet further east, the large and highly unusual brass of *c* 1475 at Wielgomlyny, near Radomsko, Poland, showing three armed figures of the Koniekpolski family, relates directly in design to Polish incised slabs.[24] The arrangement of the figures, their stance and the particular representations of their hands were all represented in the lost slab to Jan Kovilenski, formerly in the Augustinian church at Kraków,[25] and highly comparable with the mutilated slab of *c* 1475 of Jan of Sprowa at the Cistercian monastery of Mogila, near Kraków.[26] Finally, to the south west, in Silesia, Kębłowski has explained how one of the highly important and early series of brasses at the monastery of Lubiąż, that of Duke Konrad of Zagán, who died in 1304, is inlaid in a reused effigial incised slab.[27] We can only speculate as to whether this was an earlier memorial to Duke Boleslaus, who was subsequently commemorated by a brass as Kębłowski argues, or no more than the use of a rejected memorial, though the original figure was certainly represented with the Silesian eagle on a shield. Whatever the explanation, a close association between the two crafts may, once more, be inferred.

Focusing then again on the English memorials, it is not surprising from what has been noted that a dichotomy between engraved brasses and incised slabs cannot be sustained. In the seventeenth century, the renowned master masons Epiphany Evesham, Edward Marshall and Nicholas Stone all worked in both media, as well as producing relief tombs. At Marsworth, Buckinghamshire, the high tomb of Edward West, who died in 1618, contains incised elements wholly consistent with the work of Evesham and includes a brass with the signature of this master.[28] The fine slab of 1630 at Hintelsham, Suffolk, to Captain John Timperley has the pose, style and ornament consistent with the workshop of Marshall.[29] He signed the 1629 Filmer brass at East Sutton, Kent, and is accredited with many other memorial brasses. Nicholas Stone's notebook and account book contains items referring both to brasses and to incised slabs.[30] Additionally, Anne Reade's slab of 1624 at Faccombe, Hampshire, is one of the incised slabs attributed to Francis Grigs,[31] who signed brasses of 1640 at Upton Cressett, Shropshire,[32] and of 1647 at Bradfield, Yorkshire.

In the fifteenth and sixteenth centuries the particular association of alabaster craftsmen provides evidence of the relationship between the incising of slabs and sculpture throughout the Midlands. There is no similar link with brass engraving[33] other than in very isolated instances. One such is the 1585 Saunders monument by Garrett Hollemans at Welford, Northamptonshire, which combines a brass plate having figures engraved on it with a polished limestone slab on which an inscription is incised, all incorporated in an alabaster wall tablet.[34] There is no reason to believe that these conditions applied elsewhere. Analysis of the Lincolnshire incised slabs gave rise to presumptions of common origins with brasses of the north east, a relationship demonstrated by Badham.[35] More recent work has indicated a link between brasses and incised slabs in Yorkshire.[36] The study that follows accordingly attempts no more than to extend such analysis to an earlier period of development of these crafts within the London workshops. Its surprises lie not in the demonstrated association of these memorials, which should be anticipated, but in the specific conclusions to which the comparisons lead.

Chapter 3

The development of effigial incised slabs to 1400 in England and Wales

The London-made Purbeck marble incised slabs that are the main focus of this monograph were produced in the period *c* 1280 to *c* 1360. By this time effigial incised slabs were an established monumental type. They had been produced from at least the early twelfth century, although only a handful survive from before the mid-thirteenth century. Two of the earliest listed by Greenhill, at Llanveynoe, Herefordshire, and Heath, Derbyshire, are probably not strictly monumental, the first showing a crucifixion and the second a king and two subsidiary figures. These are perhaps more closely linked with pre-Conquest Christian monuments, some of which have figural representation, such as the panel set into the exterior wall of St Gwyndaf's church, Llanwnda, Pembrokeshire.[1]

The earliest post-Conquest monumental Purbeck marble slab showing effigial representation of the deceased is the bas-relief slab with a single hollow-moulded chamfer from St Frideswide's Priory, Oxford, now in the Ashmolean Museum, dated by John Blair to *c* 1080 to *c* 1130.[2] The top surface displays stylized crosses formed by groups of concentric semicircles, with a rudimentary face at the top. Other Purbeck marble slabs likely to date from the first half of the twelfth century are the peculiar incised slab at Shillingstone, Dorset, now mostly effaced, but which appears to show a naked man with a sun and moon either side of his head, and the rather crude incised figure of an abbot in mass vestments at Carisbrooke on the Isle of Wight.[3] Another very early survival is the incised slab of brown sandstone at Selston, Nottinghamshire, showing a priest holding a chalice and with a book, undoubtedly a bible or a missal, by the side of his head.[4] He is shown wearing the processional chasuble, which antedated the cope, indicating that the slab probably cannot be much later than *c* 1100.

The St Frideswide slab is essentially a cross slab, with effigial representation incorporated in the design; other early effigial slabs also betray the developmental origins of effigial incised slabs in cross-slab design. Two weathered portions of the sandstone slab of a priest at Gainford, Co. Durham, are built into the north porch and external north wall; the composition has been reconstructed by

Ryder from rubbings and an 1847 description by Walbrun.[5] The upper portions showed a priest holding a nimbed cross, as if elevating the Host, and the lower fragment showed a three-stepped calvary base and the shaft of a cross overlapped by a human foot. A thirteenth-century slab at Sollers Hope, Herefordshire, has a full-length, sideways-turned knight carrying a shield and wearing a flat-topped pot-helm.[6] At the top of the slab is a nimbed cross head of the cross patée type. In this case the figure is incised, but the cross is in low relief. Later English slabs which combine elements of cross-slab design with effigial representation include the slab at Curry Rivel, Somerset, attributed to Walter d'Albini, *ob* 1275, which shows the head of a priest above a cross, with traces of a single canopy over all;[7] the slab of likely mid-fourteenth-century date at Hawkridge, Somerset, with two kneeling civilian figures under canopies on either side of a cross;[8] the slab to Bew Fitzwarren, *ob* 1361, at Monkton Farleigh Priory, Wiltshire, which shows the half-effigy of a civilian in a quadrilobe opening from the top of a cross; the 1369 slab at Hemsworth, Yorkshire, which depicted the heads of Simon and Cecilia de Wudston above two crosses;[9] and the half-effigy of the wife of William de Staunton above a cross at Staunton, Nottinghamshire.

In the period *c* 1250 to *c* 1400, only two workshops producing incised slabs for sale in England had other than a relatively local marketing zone, but their pre-eminence was considerable. Between them they produced more than one third of the effigial slabs of this period now surviving. One was the London-based workshops of the Purbeck marblers that are the main focus of this monograph and whose brasses, cross slabs and other products, as well as their incised slabs, had a widespread distribution in southern and eastern England. Indeed, for much of the area in which these slabs are found, there are no surviving effigial slabs of evident regional origin, suggesting that the London workshops operated a virtual monopoly over a significant portion of the country. The second source was the Tournai marblers of Flanders, who exported their products throughout much of Europe, including England. In the eastern counties, and to a lesser extent the Midlands, a large number of slabs are of Tournai marble and often combine incising with brass or other inlays; they are clearly recognizable from their distinctive appearance and are well documented. Examples are most numerous in Lincolnshire, notably the fine series of twenty-three slabs at Boston.

Once the products of the London and Tournai workshops are discounted, there are only just more than one hundred surviving effigial incised slabs in England and Wales from the period *c* 1250 to *c* 1400. Although most counties have at least one such slab, strong regional concentrations are rare. We have not been able to identify cohesive pattern series for thirteenth- and fourteenth-century regional workshops like those attributed to the London marblers, but this does not mean that there were no specialized workshops producing incised slabs in the provinces. Moreover, although the quality of design and workmanship of the regionally produced incised slabs varies enormously, it would not be true to say that all such products are inferior in comparison with London- and Tournai-made incised slabs. On the contrary, some, such as the unknown knight at Bromyard, Herefordshire, Richard de Gaynisburgh's slab at Lincoln Cathedral and John de la Launde's slab at Arnold, Nottinghamshire, are clearly highly accomplished products. None of these three can be firmly linked with other surviving incised slabs, but it is inconceivable that they were one-off products of a craftsman not specializing in this medium. A more likely explanation is that they are the sole survivors of established series of some importance.

It is almost certainly the case that only a tiny proportion of the slabs originally laid down have survived. We have already shown in Chapter 1 how even in the last fifty years the stock of London-made incised slabs has deteriorated. How much more loss and destruction must there have been over the previous centuries, when conservation was even less of a priority than it is now? Cross slabs are undoubtedly by far the most numerous type of incised memorials surviving, but many have been reused as building material in the walls of churches. Many incised effigial slabs must have suffered the same fate, or been turned over and reused as paving. Ryder has suggested that the surviving total of cross slabs represents less than 10 per cent, and possibly as little as 2 to 3 per cent, of the original numbers laid down.[10] In these circumstances, it is hardly surprising that it is so difficult to identify workshop groupings amongst the surviving regionally produced effigial incised slabs discussed below.

Of the slabs we rejected as of other than London origin, a small number were of Purbeck marble. Two of these were of thirteenth- or fourteenth-century date and are located in Dorset, close to the Purbeck marble quarries at Corfe. The lower portion of a slab to an unknown abbot at Milton Abbas, Dorset, is competently executed, but neither the figure nor the style of Lombardic lettering are at all like the London products.[11] The use of Roman forms amongst the Lombardic lettering suggests that it might have been produced before the marblers established a base in London. The surface of the four-teenth-century slab at Church Knowle, Dorset, of a priest in academic dress has badly exfoliated, but sufficient remains to show a very angular design, again very different from London pattern types. The Corfe marblers' production of cross slabs remained prolific even after some of their colleagues set up workshops in London and it is evident that they also produced some incised effigial slabs for the local market.

The Corfe quarries were not the only source of incised slabs in south-west England. Bristol was an important centre for the carving of effigies from *c* 1240, though the full extent of its influence is debatable.[12] It seems likely that a number of incised slabs were produced in the same workshops. This may well include the fine slab to John le Botiler at St Bride's Major, Glamorganshire, recently redated to the 1330s, which is clearly outside the Welsh monumental tradition.[13] It is just across the Bristol Channel from Bristol and has an affinity with an unusual slab, carved from the lower lias limestone of the quarries at Keynsham, near Bristol.[14] This slab, identified by the heraldry as commemorating a knight of the de Button family, was found during excavations immediately to the south of the church at Bitton, Gloucestershire.[15] The sword and shield of this figure are in low relief, the head is in fuller relief and the remainder of the figure is incised. The drawing of the lower part of the figure is like the St Bride's slab, though the equipment shown, notably the spurs, is later in date. The Bitton slab has traditionally been attributed to an early thirteenth-century member of the de Button family, usually Sir Walter, who died in 1227.[16] There is no sound basis for this attribution and a date in the latter part of the thirteenth century seems much more likely. It may have commemorated Adam de Button, who was alive in 1294 and for whom a chantry was established at Bitton in 1299 by his son, Thomas de Button, Dean of Wells and Bishop of Exeter.[17] A blue lias slab of apparently similar design, to Thomas le Despenser, is under the organ at Toppesfield, Essex; conceivably this might also have come from the same workshop.[18]

A number of the early slabs from the Bristol region show quite strong French influence. The earliest of these is the blue lias slab in Wells Cathedral, Somerset, to Bishop William Bitton II, who died in 1274.[19] Another lias slab at Chelvey, Somerset, shows a bareheaded knight carrying a lance, probably dating from the fourteenth century.[20] This may have come from the same workshop as the unusual, but fine, slab of a knight wearing a kettle-hat over his mail coif, with an inscription in Lombardic lettering, formerly at Ashington, Somerset.[21] In addition, a lost fragment of a lady of *c* 1300 from St Mary Redcliffe, Bristol,[22] an unknown lady at Painswick, Gloucestershire, and a canon of *c* 1390 at Wells Cathedral, Somerset, may have originated at Bristol, albeit over an extended period. A group of three slabs at Iron Acton, Gloucestershire, from the late fourteenth century and the beginning of the fifteenth century, appear more crudely incised and may have originated else-where.[23] The unusual limestone slab to Bew Fitzwarren at Monkton Farleigh Priory, Wiltshire, is another possible Bristol product, although a more local origin, perhaps from Bath, is more likely.

There are no other regional concentrations in the south west, though there are isolated examples of regionally produced effigial incised slabs. The *c* 1300 Ham stone slab to an unknown lady at East Coker, Somerset,[24] and the lias slab to Walter d'Albini, who died in 1275, at Curry Rivel, Somerset, are simpler products than the Bristol-made slabs. The former was probably carved in the Ham Hill quarries near Yeovil, Somerset. In Wiltshire, a striking slab of a civilian under a canopy at Odstock[25] and fragments of a slab to a lady at Bishopstone near Salisbury are both of sandstone and probably originated at Salisbury. Some aspects of the drawing of the figure on the Odstock slab are like the Purbeck marble Ashford-style slab at nearby Steeple Langford (discussed in Chapter 13) and it is tempting to speculate that it might have served as a model for the Odstock slab. However, the treatment of the canopy is very different from anything else we know and suggests direct imitation of a florid, three-dimensional canopy by someone inexperienced in two-dimensional representation. A small fragment at Avebury shows a well-cut dog nestling at the foot of a lady's gown; what little remains suggests that this was once a high-quality slab. Finally in the south west, the coffin-shaped slab at Hawkridge, Somerset,[26] has been linked with the 1322 slab at Mortehoe, Devon, to Sir William Tracey,[27] though we do not find the parallels totally convincing.

Herefordshire and Shropshire contain a number of slabs of clearly local origin. The earliest and one of the most striking is the knight at Bromyard, Herefordshire, traditionally dated *c* 1260, but possibly some decades later.[28] Another extremely fine composition is the elegantly drawn figure of a lady at Little Hereford; this slab is now almost completely covered. Amongst early fourteenth-century examples, the lady holding a heart at Tong, Shropshire, has some features, notably the drawing of the hands, in common with the slab to Maud de Eddefen at Edvin Ralph, Herefordshire.[29] The most interesting Herefordshire group, however, dates from the second half of the fourteenth century. It features sandstone slabs with the effigies inlaid in white cement or plaster of Paris, which is incised with the details of the design. The finest and most complete is the slab to Sir Andrew Herley and his wife at Allensmore. Other examples include two in Hereford Cathedral commemorating an unknown priest and a knight and lady, and others at Canon Pyon to a civilian and wife and at Dilwyn to a civilian and priest. Slabs with similar inlays are also found in Gloucestershire, for example at Miserden, but they do not include effigial compositions.

In the Midland counties there is a variety of effigial incised slabs. From the fifteenth century the products of the alabasterers dominated incised slab production in this area, but only two slabs from the late fourteenth century are of this stone. The *c* 1380 slab at Ticknall, Derbyshire, shows an armed figure commemorating John Franceys; it was discovered in 1820 and is in excellent condition for the most part, though there has evidently been a limited amount of recutting, especially of the face and parts of the marginal inscription. The alabaster slab of *c* 1400 at Elford, Staffordshire, to a lady of the Huddylston family has been more extensively and crudely recut. Two of the earliest slabs in the Midlands are both sandstone coffin-shaped slabs, which combine incising with sunk-relief carving. At Catthorpe, Leicestershire, the slab of *c* 1300 has the head and hands of a lady of the Chaynel family carved in sunk relief.[30] This standard quarry product has been embellished with additional incising to show the rest of the figure and to include a perimeter inscription in Lombardic lettering, though the surface is damaged and little of the effigial incising can still be seen. Another variant on this theme is the slab at Willey, Warwickshire, where the figure of a priest in mass vestments is seen through three ogee quatrefoils, the shape of which suggests a date in the mid-fourteenth century.[31] The head and hands are carved in relief in the uppermost aperture, with the remainder of the figure, as seen through the other apertures, being incised.

The remaining Midlands slabs all feature full-length figures, but they vary, both in type and in quality. The finest, though it is now rather worn, is undoubtedly the slab at Arnold, Nottinghamshire, commemorating John de la Launde, who died in 1349.[32] This is a most unusual iconographic type, which shows a kneeling nimbed figure, perhaps representing St John, supporting a statue of the Virgin and Child on a canopied corbel.[33] The slab forms part of a decorative scheme in the chancel, including an Easter sepulchre, sedilia and a double piscina, which was probably carried out in John de la Launde's lifetime, perhaps in the late 1330s.[34] Possibly contemporary with this slab is the fine slab at Staveley, Derbyshire, to Prior John de Warsop. He is shown holding a crosier, the background of which is cut away, and the marginal inscription is finely carved with foliated flourishes, features suggesting French influence. Slightly earlier in date is a well-preserved slab at Mansfield, Nottinghamshire, to an unknown priest. A chalice is shown, lying on the chest and stomach in the fashion of French and Flemish slabs. Less impressive are slabs at Southwell Minster, Nottinghamshire, to two unknown ladies; the very worn half-effigy of a lady with a cross beneath at Staunton, Nottinghamshire; and a virtually effaced half-effigy of a lady on a bracket at Madeley, Staffordshire. The remains of a late fourteenth-century knight at Handsworth, Warwickshire, are very fragmentary, but appear to be from a good-quality slab.

Lincolnshire has over forty pre-Black Death effigial incised slabs, but the vast majority were imported from Tournai. Most of the remainder were probably produced in Lincoln, which was also an important brass-engraving centre from *c* 1270 to *c* 1340.[35] The *c* 1300 priests at Harpswell and Buslingthorpe and a fragment of a *c* 1325 civilian in Lincoln Cathedral, all apparently in Ancaster stone, are probably by the same hand and may be related to two early fourteenth-century fragments of similar stone at Tetney.[36] It should be noted that the foliage at the foot of the Harpswell and Lincoln Cathedral figures is very similar to the foliage on an incised cross slab at Patrington, Yorkshire, just across the Humber.[37] The slab, probably dating from the second quarter of the fourteenth century, to William de Wermington, mason, at Crowland Abbey, is of a different style.[38] It appears to be of Barnack stone and may have come from somewhere in south Lincolnshire, perhaps Boston. The beautiful, but almost effaced, slab in Lincoln Cathedral to

Richard de Gaynisburgh, *ob* 1350, is another likely Lincoln product, though no other local slabs of that period survive for comparison.[39] Fragments of another fourteenth-century slab are at Easton-on-the-Hill, Northamptonshire. They depict a lady in a flowing gown under a canopy, with a perimeter inscription in Lombardic letters of curious design, arranged in retroscript.[40]

In Yorkshire, there are nine effigial incised slabs dating between *c* 1250 and *c* 1400, all apparently local, but of a variety of dates and styles. The sandstone slab to William de Malton, *ob* 1279, at Watton is a well-designed monument, showing the prior under a canopy, above which are two censing angels.[41] Thomas de Blande's late fourteenth-century slab at Startforth was probably originally a fine composition, but is now sadly worn.[42] In far better condition and indisputably of the finest quality is the elaborate alabaster slab at Harpham to Sir William de St Quintin, who died in 1349, and his wife, who died in 1384.[43] It was probably set up by the couple's son, Anthony de St Quintin, at the beginning of the fifteenth century, at the same time as he prepared his own tomb at Hornsea, where he was rector. The figure on his slab is defaced, but traces of the incised canopy survive; they bear a close resemblance to the canopy at Harpham.[44] The remains of Alice Tiasse's slab at Burgwallis[45] are too fragmentary, and those of the military slab at Holme on Spalding Moor too worn, for any thorough assessment to be made of them. The remaining three slabs, however, have parallels with contemporary York-made brasses.[46] The beautiful fragment recently discovered at Welwick[47] has an incised crosier and indents for brass letters of a style which probably links to an indent at Burnby, letters from Middleham Castle and the lost Langton monument from York Minster, all in Yorkshire.[48] The 1369 slab at Hemsworth has isolated heads, of a form paralleled on Yorkshire Series 0 brasses.[49] Additionally, details of the worn slab of *c* 1390 to a civilian at Holy Trinity Goodramgate, York, particularly the sideways-turned hands, suggest a link with Yorkshire Series 1 brasses.[50]

Relatively few effigial slabs of local origin can be found in the most northern counties of England. The tiny chrysom at Auckland St Andrew, Co. Durham, is difficult to date, but is unlikely to be earlier than the late fourteenth century and may well be considerably later.[51] There are two slabs at St Bees, Cumberland, but of very different styles and dates. The broken, but nearly complete, early fourteenth-century slab to Prior Thomas de Cotyngham, evidently prepared in his lifetime,[52] shows a rather naïvely drawn figure, surrounded by a Latin inscription in Lombardic lettering, the individual words separated by serifs, rather than the conventional stops.[53] The 1369 slab to Joan de Lucy shows a grim-faced and somewhat ill-proportioned lady, but the detailed drawing of the hair and the drapery are well executed.[54] Both slabs are probably from a local source. In Northumberland there is just one slab, an unusual but boldly drawn figure at Cambo of an unknown civilian wearing a sword and with his arms raised.[55]

Purbeck marble is rarely found in Wales; the only examples dating from before *c* 1400 known to us are the Lady Chapel window shafts at Llandaff Cathedral, Glamorganshire, the effigies to Bishop Anselm, *ob* 1247, and Bishop Thomas at St Davids Cathedral, Pembrokeshire, and the font at St Davids. It is therefore hardly surprising that no Purbeck marble incised slabs have been found in Wales. As Gresham has argued, while north Welsh stone carving shows some influence from contemporary English work, it nonetheless impressed on its products a characteristic and often unusual style, derived from the strong native tradition.[56] Effigial incised slabs are rare, a more frequently found composition being heraldic slabs, showing a shield with an inscription in false-relief Lombardic letters round the border, with a diagonally placed sword behind, which is sometimes grasped by a hand, as at Gresford, Denbighshire.[57] Of the effigial slabs that survive in north Wales, only that at Rhuddlan, Flintshire, to William de Freney, Archbishop of Edessa, is in the English style; it may have been made by craftsmen from across the border.[58] This contrasts with a group of highly decorated monuments evidently originating from a single Welsh workshop in the last quarter of the fourteenth century. They show full-length figures, each under a cusped canopy with foliage decoration in the corners between the canopy arch and the perimeter inscription. Slabs of similar design and clearly common origin are found with carved effigies and with effigies in very low relief; in the case of this group, it is difficult to determine where to draw the boundaries in determining what is an incised slab and what is a relief figure. Examples which probably fall within Greenhill's definition of an incised slab are at Bangor Cathedral, Carnarvonshire, to Eva, wife of ...anwel,[59] at Northop, Flintshire, to Lleucu ..., *ob* 1382,[60] and votive offerings at Llaniestyn, Anglesey, showing St Iestyn[61] and at Llanbabo, Anglesey, showing St Pabo in royal robes,[62] though the second of these was not listed by Greenhill. Possibly also related to this group is a late fourteenth-century slab at Cilcain, Flintshire, with a half-effigy to Marred, daughter of Ierwerth,[63] though another slab at Cilcain to an unnamed lady, of broadly similar style and technique, is more likely to have been made towards the beginning of the fifteenth century.[64]

Low-relief slabs are also found in south Wales, a particularly fine example being that to an unnamed priest in mass vestments, perhaps dating from the thirteenth century, at St Davids, Pembrokeshire; here the head is in high relief and the remainder of the figure in flat relief. Another slab at St Davids again shows the head in high relief and had the remainder of the figure incised, though only traces of the drapery of the chasuble dripping over on to the chamfered edge have escaped obliteration. An incised inscription on the chamfer identifies the priest as John, Archdeacon of Brecon, *ob* 1274. At Llandyfodwg, Glamorganshire, is a naïvely drawn low-relief figure of a pilgrim, probably dating from the mid-fourteenth century, and there is a series of late thirteenth-century slabs of distinctive design combining full relief, low relief and incising at Llanfihangel Abercowyn, Carmarthenshire.

Finally, there are a number of slabs in the English tradition in south Wales.[65] A late thirteenth-century example at St Dogmael's Abbey, Pembrokeshire, which may now be lost, showed a saint, presumably St Dogmael, and may have been a votive offering.[66] At West Walton, Pembrokeshire, a fragment built into an interior wall shows the head of a lady of *c* 1300. At Christchurch, Monmouthshire, John Colmer, *ob* 1376, and his wife are depicted standing on either side of a cross. Fragments of two effigial slabs are preserved at Ewenny Priory, Glamorganshire. One is tiny, showing only a part of a Latin inscription in Lombardic lettering and a few drapery lines. The other, which commemorates Hawise de Londres, who died in 1274, comprises the bottom half of a coffin-shaped slab with a lady standing on a clump of foliage and a French inscription in incised Lombardic letters. The most unusual of the incised slabs of this region is a slab to a lady named Elizabeth, possibly of the le Fleming family, at Flemingston, Glamorganshire. Most of the figure is incised, but a scar reveals that the head was originally inlaid as a separate piece of stone, with the features probably carved in relief. It may be compared with a slab to William and Ismay de Naunton at Penally, Pembrokeshire. Here two limestone relief heads are set into a sandstone slab which was incised with a cross and an inscription in Lombardic lettering.

This brief survey of effigial incised slab production before 1400 shows that the London marblers clearly dominated the market in the south east, but not further afield. There is considerable variety in regionally made incised slabs, but very little evidence for large-scale regional production of effigial slabs in England and Wales, with the exception of the north Wales school, which produced both very low-relief and carved effigial, cross and heraldic slabs, and possibly the Hereford and Lincoln schools. This contrasts with the position for brasses. Early regional workshops of some significance appear to have operated in Newcastle, York, Lincoln and Shrewsbury; nonetheless, the vast majority of pre-Black Death brasses and indents were probably products of the London marblers.

Chapter 4

THE PURBECK MARBLE INDUSTRY

The incised slabs that are the focus of this volume are all made of Purbeck marble, a distinctive and highly prized material. Virtually all the brasses to which we compare them are set in slabs of the same stone. Although there is evidence that some Purbeck slabs were sent from the quarries ready-dressed to have brasses set in by independent craftsmen, in the pre-Black Death period the stone was usually worked only by specialist masons, termed marblers.[1] The common material used both for setting London-made brasses and for London-made incised slabs in itself suggests that the same craftsmen were involved in their manufacture. It is desirable, therefore, briefly to survey the Purbeck marble industry in the pre-Black Death period, its products (particularly monuments), its centres of production and the known marblers working in London at the time these slabs were made.

Purbeck marble is a polishable freshwater limestone, characterized by a distinctive pattern of massed, tiny round fossil shells of the freshwater snail *Viviparus carnifer,* up to 5mm in diameter.[2] These freshwater snails are the most reliable diagnostic feature of Purbeck marble, and are noticeably smaller in size than the *Viviparus fluviorum* found in the otherwise similar Petworth and Bethersden marbles. Petworth marble from Sussex was also used for monuments, though hardly ever before the sixteenth century.[3] From that date it appears to have been used quite extensively by the London marblers based at Southwark for slabs in which to set brasses. Bethersden marble from Kent was exploited earlier than its Sussex counterpart, but its use has yet to be systematically evaluated. Purbeck marble has been mistakenly identified as Sussex marble on occasion; the surface patterning is similar, but the fossil size is not. Purbeck marble comes in a variety of hues, including green, blue-grey, reddish-brown and fawn. Some of the beds have a scattering of shells of the freshwater mussel *Unio valdensis* among the *Viviparus* shells; these show as white horse-shoe-shaped streaks some 20mm to 30mm long. Purbeck marble is found only in the Upper Purbeck beds of Dorset, which run from Peveril Point westwards to Worbarrow Tout, approximately halfway down the northern slope of the southern Purbeck Hills. There are at least two beds of marble along the outcrop and several more along the eastern part of it. The most extensive evidence for quarrying is around Wilkeswood and Downshay, near the village of Corfe. There is evidence that carving was carried out mainly at the quarry workshops but possibly also in Corfe itself.[4]

Purbeck marble has been exploited since Roman times[5] and some architectural components appear to date from the early twelfth century, but systematic production probably began in the mid-twelfth century, encouraged by such influential patrons as Bishop Henry of Blois.[6] Architectural components and fittings, such as column bases, shafting, capitals, string courses and fonts, as well as mortars, were produced in considerable numbers, but monumental usage accounted for the largest element of the Purbeck marble trade. The majority of the 4,000 or so known brasses and indents dating to before 1500 are set in Purbeck marble and many thousands more have doubtless been destroyed. Over 550 Purbeck marble coffin lids, most carved with crosses, dating from the mid-twelfth to the mid-fourteenth centuries, have been recorded; many times that number must have been destroyed, suggesting a total possible output of over 10,000 in 200 years. When effigies, tomb chests and incised slabs are also taken into account, the total production of Purbeck marble for monumental purposes can be seen to have been enormous.

Cross slabs and low-relief effigies were produced in the Isle of Purbeck from the second half of the twelfth century. The effigies are generally well known and have been extensively studied, but the cross slabs have attracted little attention. Examples dating to the twelfth and the early thirteenth centuries are usually of very high quality, particularly outstanding examples being at Rochester Cathedral, Kent, Bindon Abbey, Dorset, Temple Church, London, Cobham, Kent, and Great Milton, Oxfordshire. Most effigies and cross slabs of this period are devoid of any inscription, perhaps because these were originally painted on the memorials, but there are exceptions. The effigies to Bishop Clement, who died in 1163, at Sherborne Abbey, Dorset, and to Philip the Priest at Tolpuddle, Dorset, both have incised inscriptions.[7] On the former, the inscription is incised round the canopy, though on the latter it is on the single straight chamfer. A few early high-quality Purbeck marble relief cross slabs at Pamber Priory (also known as Monk Sherborne), Hampshire,[8] Durford Abbey, Sussex,[9] and slabs excavated from the site of Lesnes Abbey, Kent,[10] also have incised inscriptions. The Durford Abbey slab is thought to have commemorated the founder, Henry de Hoese, or his son Henry, and to date from *c* 1200. The two Lesnes Abbey slabs commemorate Fulc, the second abbot of Lesnes, who died *c* 1200, and Avelina, daughter of Richard de Lucy and wife of Gilbert de Montfichet, who is also thought to have died *c* 1200. The inscriptions on these twelfth-century monuments are in an essentially Roman alphabet, though the letter forms vary from slab to slab. The inscriptions are in Latin, often with contractions. Additionally, the Sherborne, Tolpuddle and Pamber slabs show one letter incised within another.

Most thirteenth-century Purbeck effigies were carved in greater relief than the earlier ones. Those with incised inscriptions, notably the effigies at Britford, Wiltshire, and Faulkbourne, Essex, and the low-relief heart slab to Maud, Countess of Sussex, *ob* 1236, taken from Lewes Priory to Chichester Cathedral, both in Sussex,[11] display the Lombardic alphabet. Cross slabs and other coffin-shaped slabs were produced in increasingly great numbers, particularly in the second half of the century. A few incorporate incised Lombardic inscriptions, notably those to William de Witemerse at Stoke Poges, Buckinghamshire, William ...ari at Bray, Berkshire, John de Sharstede, *ob* 1271, at Wingham, Kent, John 'vicarius' at Sturminster Marshall, Dorset, and an unknown person at St Martin, Canterbury, Kent.[12] However, the letter shapes on these monuments are all different and do not display the particular Lombardic letter forms characteristic of any of the London series of slabs which are the main subject of this monograph. The Stoke Poges and Wingham slabs include Roman forms of F, M, N and T, possibly indicating an earlier date than the other examples, which are in purely Lombardic scripts. However, a coffin-shaped slab at Christchurch, Hampshire, to Baldwin, son of William Redvers, Count of Devon, *ob* 1216, has an inscription in a purely Lombardic script.

Both tombs and other products of the Purbeck marble industry in the thirteenth century had a widespread distribution, facilitated by Corfe's near-coastal location. They are commonly found in high-status churches, even those far distant from Corfe, but the extent to which Purbeck cross slabs, for example, are found in parish churches appears to depend both on the proximity to water transport and on the availability of good local stone which could be quarried in large slabs. Thus they are relatively rare in Somerset, Devon and Cornwall despite the relative proximity to Corfe, probably because of the dominance of stones such as Ham, Beer, blue lias and the oolitic limestones of the Bath and Bristol areas. Purbeck cross slabs are virtually unknown on the west coast, but are found in large numbers on the coastal fringes of southern England and East Anglia, with particularly high concentrations in Hampshire, Kent and Norfolk. Where they penetrate further inland, it is generally along navigable river courses. Further north, where they came into competition with locally produced quarry products, such as Barnack and Ancaster, the numbers diminish considerably. Overall, however, Purbeck marble products can be found over a very wide area. There is ample evidence for the shipment of architectural components to, for example, Durham, Bishop Auckland in Co. Durham, London, Vale Royal in Cheshire and Mont St Michel in France;[13] of effigies to Carlisle, York, St Davids in Wales (Pembrokeshire), Welton in Yorkshire,[14] Dublin in Ireland[15] and Lisieux in France;[16] and of slabs to Bayeux and Coutances in France,[17] and Trim and Dublin in Ireland.[18]

The closing years of the thirteenth century saw the beginning of a period in which there were marked changes in the Purbeck marble industry. The most significant shift was in the type of wares produced, notably the fall from popularity of the carved Purbeck marble effigy, which Firman has speculated may possibly have been due to a difficulty in supplying Purbeck marble of sufficient thickness to produce fully rounded, life-size effigies.[19] Examples dating from the fourteenth century are rare, though some may well have been produced as late as the 1340s, notably the knight at Dodford, Northamptonshire, attributed to Sir William de Keynes, who died in 1344.[20] Firman has pointed out, however, that the decline in the effigy trade would not necessarily have proved economically disastrous to the Purbeck marblers, given the steady and considerable demand for Purbeck marble architectural features and its rapidly growing use as slabs for brasses and incised slabs, for which thinner material would suffice.[21]

The other great change was in the organization of the industry. John Blair has shown that by the closing years of the thirteenth century the Purbeck marblers had begun to settle in London.[22] Factors influencing the move were the marblers' involvement in the royal works and the growing volume of minor works commissioned by the gentry and burgess classes. The evidence for the establishment of a London centre is twofold. First, the distribution of Purbeck fonts, coffin-shaped cross slabs and minor architectural features in parish churches suggests two centres of supply: one around Dorset and the other, presumably emanating from London, concentrated in Hertfordshire, Buckinghamshire, Bedfordshire, Cambridgeshire, Northamptonshire, Essex, East Anglia, Kent and the Thames Valley.[23] Secondly, from about 1280, men with the occupational name 'the Marbler' suddenly appeared in the London records. Many of them were from established families of Corfe marblers and for the first fifty years or so the London marblers had strong and continuing links with the Corfe marblers, often working in association with them.

These early London marblers, some of whom may have made incised slabs, included John the Marbler, Godfrey the Marbler, Walter the Marbler[24] and Ralph of Chichester.[25] Little is known about the first two. Walter the Marbler was active from the 1280s and died some time between 1327 and 1331. Harvey has suggested that he may have been identical with Walter of Canterbury, who was the King's Master Mason from 1323, if not earlier.[26] Although there is no documentary evidence, apart from his name, linking him with the production of brasses, incised slabs or other Purbeck marble products, he certainly had connections with the trade. In 1293–4 he stood surety for the fulfilment of a contract by a known Corfe marbler, Master John Doget.[27]

Interestingly, Doget may also have worked with another of the London marblers listed above. In 1287, Doget and Ralph of Chichester undertook to supply marble columns, capitals, bases and cornice moulding for the works of Vale Royal Abbey, Cheshire.[28] Between the years 1291 and 1294 Master Ralph also supplied cross-shafts and various marble details ready worked for the Eleanor Crosses at Charing, Dunstable, St Albans, Stony Stratford and Woburn.[29] As explained in Chapter 14, he was also involved in the monumental trade.

In the early fourteenth century the Purbeck trade in London seems to have been dominated by a fifth craftsman, Adam the Marbler, also known as Adam of Corfe or Adam Laurenz.[30] Active between *c* 1305 and his death in 1331, he had shops on the north side of St Paul's Churchyard and may well have been responsible for the brasses from the main London workshops termed the 'Camoys' and 'Septvans' series (discussed in Chapters 7 and 8). As the bequest in his will of two tenements in Corfe shows, he maintained local interests throughout his working life. After his death, his London and Corfe properties were divided between his heirs, Hugh le Marberer, Hugh's son Adam, Adam the Marbler's niece Joan Bonville, a member of another prominent family of Corfe marblers, and his nephew, William. His main property, the tenement in Paternoster Row in St Paul's Churchyard, with houses and two adjoining shops, was inherited by Hugh le Marberer, but though Hugh kept the family name, he did not practise the craft, trading instead as a cloth merchant. Thus Adam's business was probably sold or subcontracted.

Thereafter the London trade seems to have functioned independently of Corfe, with no more than one or two businesses active at any one time. Five other known London marblers may have been connected with the production of brasses and incised slabs in the fourteenth century. Richard de Sonyngdon is known only from his will, made in 1346, but this is quite informative. He described himself as a 'Marberer' of London and amongst his bequests are, to Brother John of St Albans, 'a great marble tombstone seven foot in length' and to 'Sir' John Munden, canon of St Bartholomew's, London, another marble tombstone.[31] Possibly these were from his own workshop. Various Purbeck marble incised slabs from St Bartholomew the Great, London, are discussed in Part 2 of this monograph, but none, unfortunately, can be connected with John de Munden's tombstone.

More is known of John Ramsey III, sometimes called Marbler, who operated from the 1340s to his death in 1371; though he cannot be linked specifically with the production of monuments, he may well have been responsible for the earliest London A brasses.[32] Richard and Henry Lakenham's names occur from the mid-1350s until Henry's death in 1387.[33] Henry operated, like Adam the Marbler before him, from St Paul's Churchyard. A contract of 1376 survives in which Henry Lakenham agreed to make a tomb of marble and freestone with brass inlays;[34] John Blair and Emmerson have both argued that he was responsible for the London B series of brasses, which began in the 1350s.[35] His father, Richard Lakenham, and the King's Master Mason, Henry Yevele, were almost certainly involved alongside him in the operation of this workshop in the second half of the fourteenth century.

CHAPTER 5

THE DATING OF PRE-BLACK DEATH LONDON BRASSES

The earliest known securely dated English brasses are the 1241 consecration plate at Ashbourne, Derbyshire, which is commemorative rather than monumental, and the group of indents with lettering of a type termed Westminster Abbey style,[1] in some of which a few brass letters survive. The latter includes the inscription dated 1268 of separately inlaid brass Lombardic letters in the Cosmati mosaic pavement in the presbytery of Westminster Abbey, which again is not strictly monumental,[2] and the associated cross brasses to Margaret and John de Valence, who died in 1276 and 1277.[3] However, none of these non-effigial brasses has received much attention, particularly in contrast with the quest for the earliest English figure brass.

For many years it was universally believed that the brass at Stoke d'Abernon, Surrey, to Sir John d'Abernon (Figure 5.1) dated from 1277 and was thus the oldest surviving figure brass, with the remaining early military brasses being dated to the following thirty years. This traditional dating of the early military brasses, established by the 1850s, was based not on certain knowledge of identity but rather on the confident, but erroneous, assignment of their equipment and armour to the late thirteenth rather than the fourteenth century, and a strong romantic association with the Crusades of both the mail armour and the cross-legged pose of three of the figures.[4] This dating was not effectively questioned until the late 1960s, when a convincing case for significant redating of the Acton knight was made by Ward[5] and of the Trumpington knight by Spittle.[6] A period of intense reappraisal followed, culminating in the publication of research by Rogers, Binski and John Blair, which proposed a radical and wide-ranging redating of the early English brasses.[7] It seems apposite at this point to summarize the findings of these writers, which provide the framework for our analysis of the fourteenth-century London-made Purbeck marble incised slabs.

Although full-length figures are generally thought of as typifying brasses of this period, Blair has shown that they constitute less than one-fifth of all known pre-1350 English brasses, with simple inscription and cross brasses accounting for two-thirds of known brasses and indents.[8] The vast majority of these brasses have individual inlay inscriptions in the style of Lombardic alphabet termed Main Group.[9] These letters are thought to have been cast centrally,

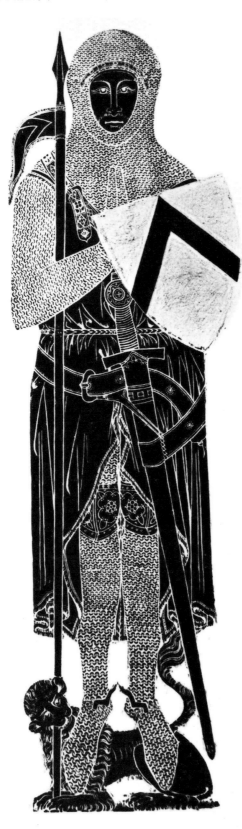

5.1 *Stoke d'Abernon, Surrey: Sir John d'Abernon II, ob 1327. Camoys-style brass. Rubbing by M W Norris.*

in a brazier's workshop possibly based in London, and supplied to brass-engraving workshops both in London and in the provinces. The earliest known use of this alphabet is the inscription set in a slab of oolitic limestone, probably from the Ancaster quarries, at Easton-on-the-Hill, Northamptonshire, to Sir Richard de Lindone and his wife.[10] It may have been laid down some time after his death in 1254, but as the manor was in royal hands by 1290, the slab was certainly made before then.[11] The earliest datable examples of Main Group lettering set in Purbeck marble are the slabs to Isabel de Pleci, who died between 1272 and 1278, at Hook Norton, Oxfordshire,[12] and to Sir Nicholas Villiers, who died in 1284, at Down Ampney, Gloucestershire. None of these slabs had any other brass inlay. The dates of death of many of those commemorated by early indents are, as yet, unknown and we consider that the dated indents mentioned here may not necessarily be isolated examples. The Main Group alphabet continued in use until the 1360s.

Blair regarded the main London series as having begun in the 1290s, though he did not consider the products to have become fully established and standardized until *c* 1305. His analysis of inscription and cross brasses showed two main periods of development.[13] In the first, *c* 1305 to *c* 1335, crossheads with ivy-leaved terminals were employed, sometimes with a bust; inscriptions usually began with an initial cross in the centre of the upper end of the slab and had pairs of round stops separating the words, and often had strips of brass fillet bordering them; joining bars, but no rivets, were used in the construction. From *c* 1335, rivets were introduced, an open octofoil crosshead replaced the ivy-leaved type, sometimes enclosing a minuscule full-length figure, fillet inscriptions became more common, and designs became more varied and complex.

Binski's complementary analysis of early London-made figure brasses also identified *c* 1305 and *c* 1335 as significant stylistic breaks, but postulated a more complex series of six styles.[14] Only four examples are dated before 1305. A further four examples, termed Camoys-style prototypes, are dated from the years 1305 to 1310. After that, the designs fused into the fully developed Camoys style, named after the brass to Margaret de Camoys at Trotton, Sussex. Binski's analysis led to the conclusion that in the years between 1305 and 1335 all figure brasses were in this style, except four. These were, wholly or in part, of the Septvans style, named after the brass to a knight of the Septvans family at Chartham, Kent. The Septvans-style brasses overlapped in small but significant details with those of the Camoys style, indicating a common workshop origin. In contrast, Binski's fifth series, spanning the period *c* 1333 to *c* 1350 and termed the Seymour style after the brass to Lawrence Seymour at Higham Ferrers, Northamptonshire, is radically different from the earlier brasses, suggesting little or no continuity in workshop operation. Finally, the 1340s saw the brief-lived Hastings style, only four examples of which are known, typified by the magnificent brass to Sir Hugh Hastings at Elsing,

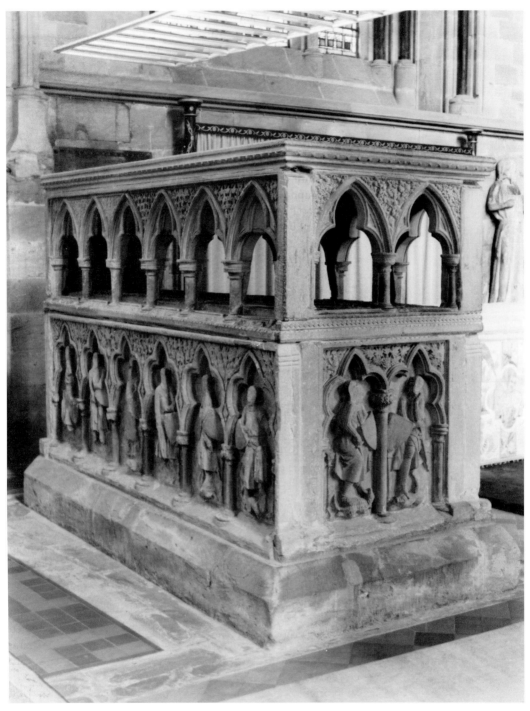

5.2 *Hereford Cathedral:*
Thomas de Cantilupe,
c 1287. Tomb chest.
Photograph by
P S Mitchell.

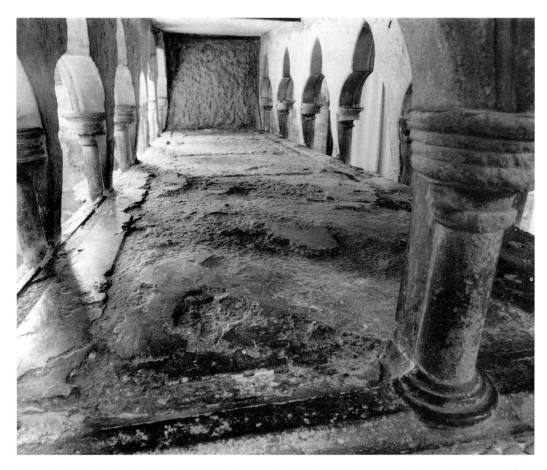

5.3 (above) Hereford Cathedral: Thomas de Cantilupe, c 1287. Slab on top of lower element, showing indent of lost Ashford series brass. Photograph by P S Mitchell.

5.4 (opposite) Hereford Cathedral: Thomas de Cantilupe, c 1287. Ashford series brass. Detail of figure of St Ethelbert. Photograph by P S Mitchell.

Norfolk. (Appendix B lists the brasses and indents that we attribute to these pattern series.) Not all the extant pre-Black Death figure brasses fall within these six series. Binski considered that eight brasses of priests, traditionally dated c 1320 to c 1355 and of varying competence of execution, defied classification, though most can now be attributed to London Series A in its earliest years.

It is now accepted that the earliest full-length English figure brass of which something is known is probably that to Thomas de Cantilupe in Hereford Cathedral (Figures 5.2 and 5.3). Cantilupe died in 1282 at Montefiascone, Italy, after having been excommunicated by John Pecham, Archbishop of Canterbury.[15] He was buried at Orvieto, but his heart and some bones were sent back to Hereford. Pecham tried unsuccessfully to have Christian burial refused. The cult of Thomas de Cantilupe grew rapidly and his relics were translated in 1287. Documentary evidence shows that the brass was in place by then: sworn evidence to a papal commission by John Tregoz, who kept vigil by the tomb on 28 November 1287, describes a vision of the spirit of the bishop coming out 'from underneath the brass image which was set on top of the tomb of the man of God'.[16] Sadly, only one tiny fragment of the brass inlay, a seated figure of St Ethelbert, survives (Figure 5.4).

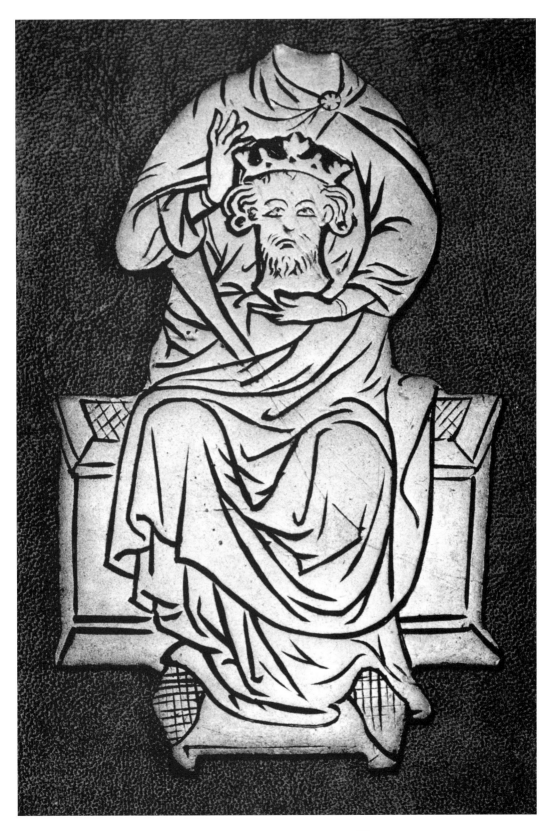

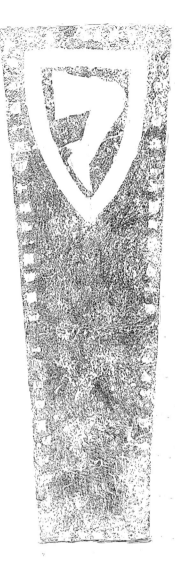

Binski's analysis led him to the conclusion that the earliest brass with figure inlay surviving was that to Margaret de Camoys at Trotton, Sussex, which he dated to *c* 1310. This, and other identified early Camoys series brasses, are of the highest standard, both artistically, in terms of their design, and technically, in terms of the competence and assurance with which they were engraved. Few later brasses are their equal. As such, the early Camoys brasses give the impression that they are the products of craftsmen who had perfected their technique. They cannot be said to present themselves as the work of a craftsman experimenting with a newly introduced medium or technique. It might be expected that the very earliest brasses would have crudities or flaws, which these do not. This alone suggests to us that brasses might have been engraved for some time before the Trotton brass was made.

There is evidence for the production of brasses in London from the 1270s. The small group of monuments with a distinctive style of individually inlaid brass letters in the Westminster Abbey style, virtually all of which are in London and some of which have already been discussed, date from this period. The group's earliest dated product may be the inscription at North Stoke, Oxfordshire, to Robert de Esthall, who died in 1274. Some monuments in this group had other brass components. The 1276 and 1277 slabs to Margaret and John de Valence in Westminster Abbey incorporated brass crosses. The lost indent to Bernat de Jambe, which fortunately was rubbed by Greenhill before Christchurch Greyfriars, London, was bombed in the Second World War, had a huge brass-inlaid shield (Figure 5.5). Although no known Westminster Abbey series brass included effigial representation, it is hard to believe that the earliest figure brasses were not produced either contemporaneously or hard on the heels of this earliest brass-inlaying workshop. (We will return to the subject of the earliest surviving figure brass in Chapter 14.)

5.5 *Christchurch Greyfriars, London: Bernat de Jambe, c 1270–90. Lost Westminster Abbey series indent. Rubbing by F A Greenhill, Society of Antiquaries collection.*

Chapter 6

EVIDENCE LINKING LONDON BRASSES AND INCISED SLABS

The thesis that early brasses and incised slabs were produced in the same London workshops is supported by four strands of evidence. First, there is a similarity of composition and layout, even of relatively unusual types. John Blair, in discussing the derivation of the type of cross brass with a bust above the crosshead, commented that while this combination was popular by the 1320s for freestone slabs carved in relief, it may well have been the marblers who invented it. We know of no relief heads with crosses on Purbeck marble slabs, but there are examples of figures associated with crosses on incised Purbeck memorials. Blair cited the example of the 1295 incised slab in Winchester Cathedral, Hampshire (discussed in detail in Chapter 12), concluding that it 'may provide a link between the relief cross-slabs made in the Purbeck quarries by marblers, and cross-brasses made in London by the same marblers' sons and grandsons'.[1]

Second, both incising and brass inlay were employed on the same slab. Individual-inlay brass Lombardic lettering of the type termed Main Group was combined with incised detail features on Purbeck slabs discussed below at Christ Church Cathedral, Oxford, Pyrton, Oxfordshire, Tilsworth, Bedfordshire, Clothall, Hertfordshire, West Wickham, Kent, Sawbridgeworth, Hertfordshire, Chichester Cathedral, Sussex, and Elsing, Norfolk, and on slabs formerly at Strood and Snodland, both in Kent. This type of lettering is found on all the London brasses with individual-inlay lettering included in Binski's analysis, but is in itself insufficient to prove that the incised slabs originated in a London brass-engraving workshop. As explained above, the letters are thought to have been cast centrally and supplied to workshops both in London and in the provinces. However, Binski included in his analysis the composite slab at Westwell, Kent (discussed in detail in Chapter 9), in which the inscription, canopy and bust were inlaid in brass, the remainder of the figure being incised.[2] This is much stronger evidence for the related incised slabs and brasses having come from a common workshop.

Third, there is evidence of a patron commissioning both incised and brass-inlaid Purbeck memorials, almost certainly from a single workshop. In White Waltham, Berkshire, there is an indent to Gilbert Saddoc, with a perimeter inscription in Main Group lettering and a

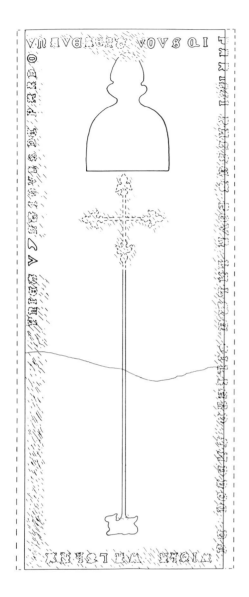

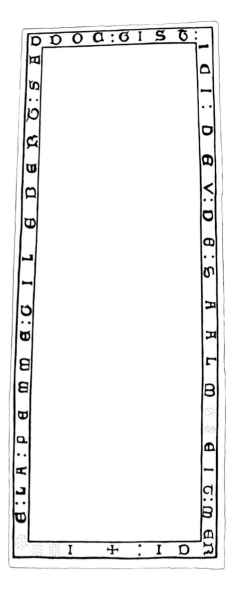

6.1 (above) White Waltham, Berkshire: Gilbert Saddoc, ob after 1297. Possible Ashford-style brass. Drawing by W J Blair.

6.2 (above, right) White Waltham, Berkshire: Joan Saddoc, c 1280–1300. Ashford-style incised slab. Tracing of rubbing by S F Badham.

bust above a cross with ivy-leaved terminals (Figure 6.1). A Purbeck slab with an incised Lombardic inscription to Gilbert's wife Joan is in the same church (Figure 6.2). The slab has no traces of an incised figure, but it is not inconceivable that there was once one, now worn out. The lettering style on this slab links it stylistically with many other Ashford-style monuments (discussed in detail in Chapters 13 and 14), the distribution of which favours a London origin (see Figures 1.1 and 1.2). The marblers appear to have operated a virtual monopoly on the production of Purbeck artefacts in London. Few marblers were active at any one time. Evidence set out in Part 2 of this monograph indicates that there were always two workshops in operation at any one time during the period c 1280 to c 1340, but the Ashford workshop and the

Camoys workshop successively dominated their smaller rivals. Although the type of memorials to Gilbert and Joan Saddoc differ, it is therefore likely that they were commissioned from the same workshop. Other examples of closely related members of a family being commemorated by different types of monument made by the London marblers include William and Elizabeth de Say of Sawbridgeworth, Hertfordshire, and Richard and Alice Duraunt of Dunstable, Bedfordshire. (These monuments are all discussed in detail in Part 2.)

Finally, stylistic analysis of extant and recorded Purbeck marble incised slabs confirms that many of the incised slabs were made in the London workshops responsible for the pre-Black Death brasses. (This evidence is set out in detail in Part 2.)

Within the sixty-six slabs with incised detail which we attribute to London manufacture, there is a wide variety of types, ranging from simple inscriptions, cross and crosier slabs to slabs with full-length figures under architectural canopies. Forty of the slabs have the whole of the design incised and one is associated with a carved free-stone effigy, but the remaining twenty-five incorporate relief crosses or originally had some element inlaid in brass or composition. This use of mixed media, which undoubtedly added an impression of richness to the slab, appears to be an early development, which largely fell out of favour on Purbeck marble monuments early in the fourteenth century. Sixteen of the twenty-five mixed-media slabs belong to the two earliest pattern series, mainly produced in the late thirteenth century. The latest surviving reliably dated slab that incorporates both incising and substantial brass inlay is the 1309 composite slab to John de la More at Westwell, Kent (Figure 6.3). Occasionally, slabs combining an incised figure with brass lettering are found later in the fourteenth century, such as the lost monument at Snodland, Kent, to John de Dennyntone, who died in 1338 (Figure 6.4). Blair sees the use of mixed media as a direct link between figure brasses and incised slabs, suggesting that 'economies could be achieved by combining brass inlay with detail incised on the slab . . . Such compositions may have been more common than appears today: it is impossible to say how many worn slabs, classified as simple separate-inlay inscriptions, may have had incised decoration.'[3]

It is evident that the London workshops produced a spectrum of monumental types to suit a range of pockets. Leaving aside the cost of transport, the more brass in the composition, the more expensive the composition would have been. Incised slabs would have been at the bottom end of the range of effigial monuments. In London in the fourteenth century a blank Purbeck marble slab would have cost between £1 10s 0d and £3.[4] It is difficult to guess how much would have been added to this for the cost of incising, but it may well have been no more than the cost of the slab. No contracts for early incised slabs have so far come to light in England, nor is there useful evidence in wills for the fourteenth

37

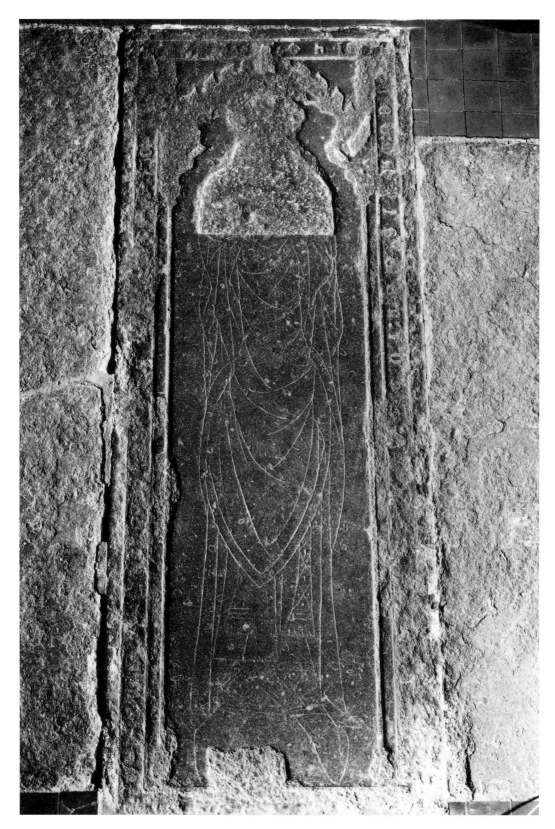

century. Such evidence was available for thirteenth- and fourteenth-century Tournai products, but since the price is quoted either in *livres tournois* or *livres parisis*, both apparently monies of account rather than actual currency, comparisons are difficult.[5] However, in the sixteenth century, by which time the currency was worth somewhat less, there is evidence of incised slabs costing between £1 10s 0d and £10.[6] In contrast, the inlays of an elaborate brass would have cost substantially more than the Purbeck marble slab itself. John Blair has used such evidence as is available for the early fourteenth century to suggest a rough scale of prices.[7] This ranges from £3 for a brass separate-letter inscription only, through £8 for a full-length figure without a canopy, to as much as £20 for an exceptionally large and elaborate brass with complex canopy work and weepers. This was a substantial sum, equivalent to the yearly rent of a manorial demesne or the cost of a timber-framed house.[8]

It is probably no coincidence that all but a very few of the Purbeck marble incised memorials which remain commemorate civilians or parish priests, whose means were almost certainly more limited than their contemporaries, who were commemorated by brasses. The close comparisons that can be traced between certain of these incised slabs and brasses highlight that in general the incised slabs were simplified versions of the brass designs and that the slabs seem less accomplished. The main explanation of this may be that the slabs were cheaper products on which the workmen spent less time. However, it should also be remembered that Purbeck marble is difficult to work and the simplified designs may have been developed the better to suit the medium.

Although the wide range of types which we group together may at first sight cast doubt on whether they had a common origin, there is evidence elsewhere of workshops producing an apparently disparate range of monumental types. In the second half of the fourteenth century, documentary evidence links Robert de Patryngton of York to the production of a wide range of brasses,[9] and stylistic evidence shows that a workshop probably centred at Boston, Lincolnshire, in the early fifteenth century was responsible for designs ranging from simple incised cross slabs to large and elaborate brasses.[10]

In assigning dates to the incised slabs that we consider to have originated from the London marblers' workshops, we have worked on the assumption that, unless there is strong evidence to the contrary, the latest date of manufacture is likely to be a year or two after the date of death. There is good evidence to prove that a significant number of monuments were prepared during the lifetime of the person commemorated. However, in recent years, too much may have been made of the verses used, for example, on a brass at Kelshall, Hertfordshire, and on another formerly at St Edmund, Lombard Street, London, that 'Wydowes be sloful, and chyldren beth unkynd, Executors be covetos, and kep al that they fynd',[11] and Margaret Paston's complaints in 1471 to her eldest son

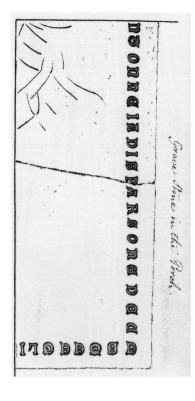

6.3 *(opposite) Westwell, Kent: John de la More, ob 1309. Seymour-style 'composite' slab, with brass inlay lost. Photograph by A C Cooper Ltd.*

6.4 *(above) Snodland, Kent: John de Dennyntone, ob 1338. Lost Camoys-style incised slab with indents for brass letters. Drawing for R Gough, Bodleian Library, Oxford, MS Gough Kent 36, interleaved between folios 192–3. Photograph by Bodleian Library.*

that 'It is a shame and a thing that is much spoken of in this country that your father's gravestone is not made.'[12] To extrapolate from this evidence an argument that many monuments may have been made some considerable time after death cannot be justified. The full context of the Lombard Street inscription suggests that the appropriation of the 'poor man's goods' was the author's concern. In the case of Margaret Paston's letter, it could equally be argued that no scandal would have arisen had it been common for the setting-up of tombs to be delayed. Whatever the truth of these cases, we believe that there is stronger evidence, notably Greenwood's analysis of the evidence from Norwich wills, to suggest that the majority of monuments in England were set up by the first anniversary of death.[13]

Not all the slabs that we discuss below can be dated, but those that are datable span a period wider than that suggested for brass production in Binski's article in *The Earliest English Brasses*. (The sixty-six slabs which we classify as London are discussed in detail in Part 2.) We begin this close examination of individual monuments with those incised slabs that relate to the pattern series first identified in *The Earliest English Brasses*. Of the thirty-two slabs which clearly date from the fourteenth century, sixteen can conclusively be linked by stylistic analysis with the pattern series of brasses identified by Binski.[14] To facilitate comparison with them, they are discussed in the separate chapters in Part 2 within the Camoys, Septvans and Seymour workshop groupings set out by Binski. For the main part, our findings reinforce the conclusions reached by Binski. The Camoys slabs are the most straightforward and fit easily into the framework provided by his analysis of the brasses. Binski regarded the Septvans style as overlapping with the Camoys style and as having been produced in the same workshop; certainly, incised slabs with Septvans features also have some Camoys features. It is with the Seymour slabs that our findings raise questions about the dates assigned to this series. Two of the Seymour incised slabs are firmly dated over twenty years before the first extant brasses assigned to this series, suggesting that the series may have covered a much longer period than previously thought, with any early Seymour brasses having been destroyed. Most importantly, our findings suggest that the Camoys/Septvans styles and the Seymour style overlapped, and that consequently more than one London marbler's workshop producing memorials may have been in operation in the period *c* 1309 to *c* 1335.

There are fifteen other slabs of evident London design which probably also date from the fourteenth century. Thirteen of them appear to be from the first half of the century, but cannot be closely linked with the Camoys, Septvans or Seymour pattern series. There is good evidence to suggest that the remaining three date from after the end of the Seymour and Hastings series. The latest of these is dated 1362 and we have been able to find no other London-made Purbeck marble incised slabs after this.

Having dealt with the slabs dating from the period when the fourteenth-century pattern series identified in *The Earliest English Brasses* were produced, we turn in the later chapters of Part 2 to the earlier workshops, which are identified for the first time in this monograph. The two new pattern series, operating concurrently, pre-date the Camoys series, and merit very detailed examination. We have followed the convention initiated by Binski in naming these series after the earliest surviving figure brass or slab in each of them. The thirteen slabs in the late thirteenth-century Basyng style have only uncertain links with brasses, but the Ashford style, having twenty-one slabs from the late thirteenth century and the very early years of the fourteenth, has clear design links with other Purbeck monuments, including early London brasses, suggesting that thirteenth-century production was on a larger scale than has hitherto been suggested.

From the evidence of the slabs we have identified, a pattern emerges of the balance of production between brasses and Purbeck marble incised slabs over the period *c* 1270 to *c* 1360. It must be stated that we cannot be certain whether the brasses and incised slabs that remain or are known through antiquarian evidence survive in numbers broadly proportionate to those originally laid down. As explained in Chapter 3, a substantial majority of the brasses and incised slabs made in the pre-Black Death period have almost certainly been destroyed, though the absolute numbers are impossible to calculate. Nonetheless, some general, if tentative, conclusions about the relative numbers of brasses and incised slabs made by the London marblers may be proposed. In the period up to *c* 1310, incised slabs are at least as numerous as brasses from the same workshops. Thereafter, brasses outnumber Purbeck marble incised slabs, particularly if non-effigial brasses, hardly any of which can, as yet, be assigned to specific pattern series, are taken into account and the number of Purbeck marble incised slabs produced seems steadily to have declined. This suggests that while brasses were a relatively new form of memorial, the Purbeck marblers were able to sell substantial numbers of cross and effigial incised slabs, despite competition from provincially based work-shops, which, particularly if transport costs were taken into account, could probably produce cheaper, if less prestigious, monu-ments. Thereafter, most customers may effectively have made the choice between London-made brasses and locally made cross and effigial incised slabs, thus reducing the demand for Purbeck marble incised slabs. Finally, in the 1360s, the London marblers may have ceased to offer incised memorials. Those customers whose prefer-ence was for an incised memorial and who could afford a monu-ment superior to the run-of-the-mill products of small regionally based workshops may instead have turned increasingly to the alabaster workshops of the Midlands, which eventually established a marketing zone for incised slabs which was even larger than that of the fourteenth-century London marblers.

PART 2

THE MONUMENTS

CHAPTER 7

THE CAMOYS STYLE

INTRODUCTION

The first of the early London pattern series identified by Binski is termed the Camoys series. He attributed twenty-six figure brasses and indents to this workshop, excluding the Camoys-style proto-types. We agree with his classification in all but two cases. First, we think there is insufficient evidence to justify firm attribution of the knight at Stoke-by-Nayland, Suffolk, which is known only from antiquarian sources, to the Camoys pattern series. Second (as discussed in Chapter 12), we think that the priest at Chinnor, Oxfordshire, is more probably a product of the Basyng workshop. In addition, we have assigned six more brasses and indents to the series. Four are indents discussed in *The Earliest English Brasses*. The two at Walgrave, Northamptonshire,[1] and Hanslope, Bucking-hamshire,[2] were only discovered in time to form an addendum to that volume. The third, an indent found on the seabed at Dunwich, Suffolk,[3] was discounted by Binski on the basis of its non-standard capitals, but in our view seems otherwise to be a standard Camoys product. The lost indent from Wells Cathedral, Somerset, attributed to King Ina, was regarded by Binski as a Camoys-style prototype, but we consider that aspects of the design, notably the powdering of the slab with devices, are more akin to mainstream Camoys-style prod-ucts.[4] A palimpsest fragment of a lady at Stanton St John, Oxfordshire, was not previously recognized as dating from this period. The last addition is a strip of fillet inscription excavated at Bury St Edmunds, Suffolk (Figure 7.1), the lettering on which is very close in style to the fine brass of *c* 1331–8 to Sir William FitzRalph at Pebmarsh, Essex (Figure 7.2).[5] (The full list of brasses and indents we attribute to the Camoys workshop, not all of which are discussed in detail below, is given in Appendix B. In addition, we have identified eleven fragments of incised slabs of Camoys style, listed in Appendix A.)

7.1 Bury St Edmunds, Suffolk: unknown c 1320–40. Fragment of Camoys-style fillet inscription. Rubbing by J F A Bertram.

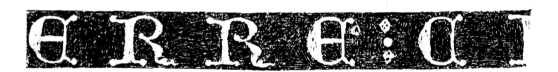

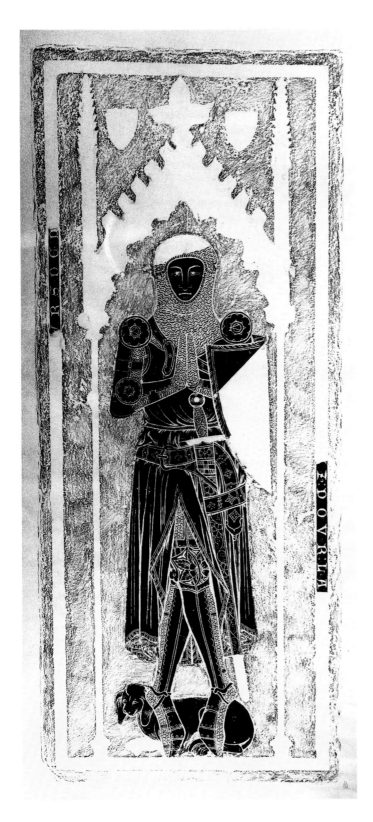

7.2 *Pebmarsh, Essex:*
Sir William FitzRalph,
ob c 1331–8. Camoys-style
brass. Rubbing by
M W Norris.

CAMOYS-STYLE BRASSES

The workshop producing the Camoys-style monuments is believed to have been in operation from *c* 1305 to the mid-1330s and to have been under the direction of Adam the Marbler, alias Adam Laurenz (brief biographical details of whom are set out in Chapter 4). Amongst the earliest surviving brasses Binski attributed to this workshop are those to Margaret de Camoys, née de Braose, at Trotton, Sussex (Figures 7.3 and 7.4), and Joan de Cobham at Cobham, Kent (Figure 7.5), the dates for which require further examination. The former is usually dated *c* 1310, but more recent work suggests that she may have been alive as late as 1318.[6] There are close similarities of the overall composition with the firmly dated brasses once at Saltwood, Kent, to William Archer, who died in 1310,[7] and at Old St Paul's Cathedral, London, to Ralph de Hengham, who died in 1311 (Figure 7.6). All three figures stand under crocketed and subcusped arches; all have a perimeter inscription of separately inlaid Lombardic letters which starts at the top centre of the slab and which is bordered by a pair of brass fillets; and all the slabs are powdered by small devices. These similarities confirm that the Trotton brass was most likely to have been engraved in the second decade of the fourteenth century.

The date of the Cobham brass is less certain. Joan de Cobham died before 1298[8] and her husband, John, who was commemorated

7.3 Trotton, Sussex: Margaret de Camoys, ob before 1319. Camoys-style brass. Photograph by S F Badham of upper portion of slab showing lost inlay of canopy and devices powdering the slab.

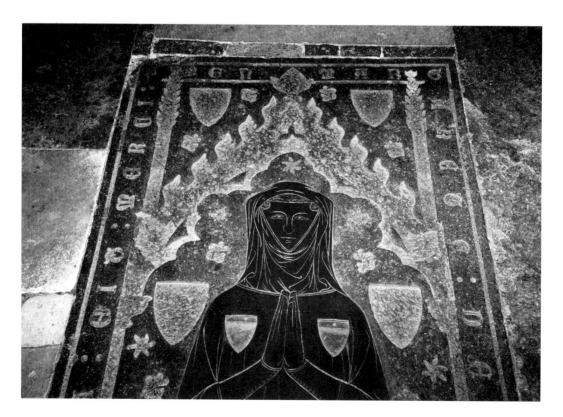

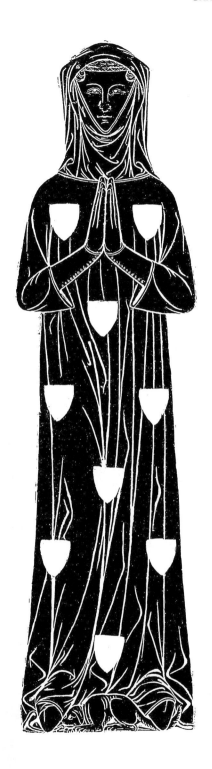

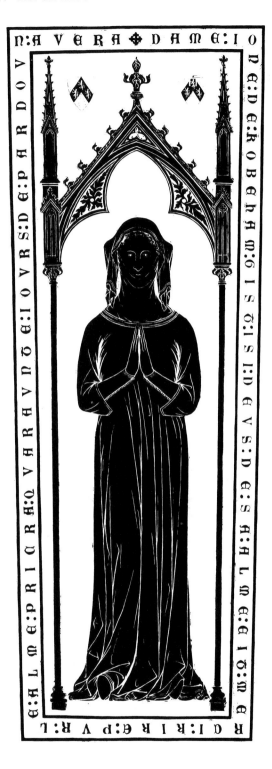

7.4 *Trotton, Sussex: Margaret de Camoys,*
     ob *before 1319. Camoys-style brass.*
     Detail of figure. Rubbing by K Train.

7.5 *Cobham, Kent: Joan de Cobham,*
     ob *1298. Camoys-style brass. Photograph by*
     A C Cooper Ltd of rubbing by D Chivers.

separately, died in 1300. Her figure is similar to that of Margaret de Camoys, but not exactly alike: the facial features are slightly different, the nostrils being drawn in a single line; the wimple forms a curved line rather than a V-shape round the chin; the chest is virtually bare of drapery lines, giving a bulkier impression; the elbow drapery is slightly different, the Trotton lady having lines forming a distinctive oval shape; and, most significantly, the canopy is of an earlier type, a simple trefoil shape without subcusping. It is clearly derived from, and, in our view, probably broadly contemporary with, the type of canopy over the tomb of Aveline de Forz, with modifications from Eleanor de Castile's tomb, both of which are in Westminster Abbey, London, and were erected in the early 1290s. Binski argued that it would have taken time for these architectural innovations to have permeated from court circles in Westminster to the marblers' workshops in the City of London, thus indicating a date of *c* 1310.[9]

We cannot agree with this. It seems to us that for the marblers to have taken twenty years to catch up stretches credibility. After all, the marblers' workshops are known to have been located in St Paul's Churchyard, adjacent to a major metropolitan cathedral which was at the forefront of innovative architectural ideas.[10] A monument at Little Shelford, Cambridgeshire, discussed below, combines an incised inscription from the Camoys workshop with a carved effigy apparently of the court style, indicating close collaboration between the two groups of workmen. And if the marblers had only just incorporated the straight-sided gable into their design *c* 1310, why a second leap directly afterwards to produce the more advanced canopies on the Trotton, Old St Paul's and Saltwood brasses? Moreover, it seems odd that the patrons who had opted for such a modish form of monument as a brass would have been content with such an outdated canopy if they were commissioning it as late as *c* 1310. Indeed, it would have been curious for the preparation of Joan de Cobham's monument to have been delayed by a dozen or more years. Though a woman, she was not an insignificant figure. Her marriage allied her to the Cobhams, a minor baronial family of some consequence. Moreover, as a daughter and co-heiress of Sir Robert de Septvans, whom we suggest in Chapter 8 was himself commemorated on his death in 1306 by the fine early brass at Chartham, Kent, Joan de Cobham was a person of wealth and importance in her own right. Finally, although her figure is related to early Camoys types, in terms of overall design her brass also has as much in common with the indents in Ely Cathedral, Cambridgeshire, to William de Luda, who died in 1298, and in Waltham Abbey, Essex, to Robert de Elenton, who died in 1302,[11] as with the more elaborate, powdered slabs of the Trotton group of Camoys series brasses. Indeed, the canopy on the de Luda indent is more elaborate than that at Cobham. We suggest in Chapter 14 that the Ely and Waltham Abbey indents are products of the Ashford workshop,

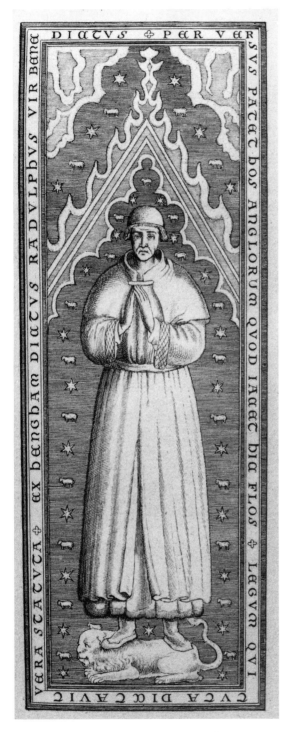

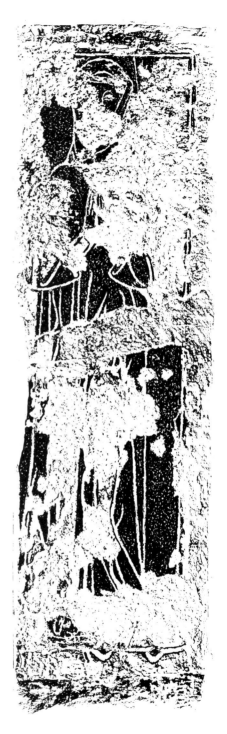

7.6 *Old St Paul's Cathedral, London: Ralph de Hengham, ob 1311. Lost Camoys-style brass. Drawing from Sir W Dugdale,* History of St Paul's Cathedral *(London, 1818 edn), 68.*

7.7 *Sawbridgeworth, Hertfordshire II: Elizabeth de Say, ob after 1299. Camoys-style incised slab. Rubbing by F A Greenhill, Society of Antiquaries collection, photograph by A C Cooper Ltd.*

which we regard as the precursor of the Camoys style. This suggests that Joan de Cobham's brass may be one of the very earliest products of the Camoys series and that a date of *c* 1300–5 may be more appropriate for it.

CAMOYS-STYLE INCISED SLABS

The incised slabs that we assign to the Camoys series fall into two groups. Six slabs have incised effigies which compare very closely to Camoys-style brasses. The other five slabs are more unusual. The parallels between these and the Camoys-style brasses are not as close as with the first group of slabs, but we consider that there is sufficient evidence, most particularly concerning the style of the incised lettering on these memorials, to merit attributing them to the Camoys series.

SAWBRIDGEWORTH, HERTFORDSHIRE II

At Sawbridgeworth, Hertfordshire, is a once magnificent incised slab with a full-length figure of a lady, now hidden under a permanently fixed carpet. The only adequate record of this slab was made by Greenhill. Unfortunately, much of the top surface had by then broken up, leaving only fragmentary remains. Round the perimeter of the slab ran an inscription of individual-inlay Lombardic letters, bordered by fillets, and with double round stops between the letters; only stray letters could be discerned on Greenhill's rubbing, though a close examination of the stone might well reveal more. Similarly, only parts of the incised figure remained, but there was sufficient to show both the overall composition and the style (Figure 7.7). She wears a loose surcoat with demi-sleeves over a close-fitting kirtle, her head is covered by a veil, and a wimple envelops her neck and the lower portion of her face. A delightful dog, with his head turned back, rests at her feet. She is an evident Camoys product, with the incising of the drapery linking her firmly with the Trotton brass. The drapery at her elbow forms the distinctive oval shape already noted on Margaret de Camoys's brass. The drapery of her surcoat also mirrors that at Trotton, though the pattern has been used in reverse, so that on the Trotton lady the drapery moulds itself round her bent right leg, while on the Sawbridgeworth lady it is the left leg that is bent. The sharp angling of the wimple around the chin suggests a closer parallel to Trotton than to Cobham and a date of *c* 1310 to *c* 1320 is thus suggested.

In the absence of information from the inscription, we can only speculate as to whom this slab might commemorate. Also in Sawbridgeworth church is an Ashford series relief cross slab with an incised inscription (discussed in Chapter 13), which we suggest commemorates William de Say, who died in 1295. The de Says held the manor of Sawbridgeworth[12] and were a minor baronial family, comparable in standing with the Cobhams.[13] A female of this family would therefore be a prime candidate for such a splendid slab as the one under discussion. William de Say's widow, Elizabeth, survived him.[14] She is last recorded in 1299.[15] Their son, Geoffrey, was only sixteen at his father's death and died himself in 1322;[16] he was survived by his wife, Idonea de Leyburne, who was still living as late as 1332, when she received the grant of a manor for life from her son, Geoffrey.[17] The likelihood, therefore, is that the incised slab commemorates Elizabeth de Say.

ST BARTHOLOMEW THE GREAT, LONDON III

Another early fourteenth-century incised slab to a lady was at St Bartholomew the Great, London, but no longer survives. In 1930 Greenhill found, loose in the cloister, a fragment of a slab with the left-hand side of a demi-effigy of a lady extending from just below her shoulder and showing the lower part of her hands (Figure 7.8). The sleeve drapery closely parallels Camoys-style brasses, though the well-defined oval formed by two lines at the elbow is much more like the Trotton brass than the earlier Cobham brass, again suggesting a date of *c* 1310–20.

LESNES ABBEY, KENT

The next incised slab of Camoys style was discovered in excavations of the north transept of Lesnes Abbey, Kent, in 1939 and was then nearly complete. A photograph taken shortly after its discovery was fortunately published by Elliston-Erwood in 1947[18] (Figure 7.9), for weathering and wilful damage were already taking their toll.[19] In 1948 it was recorded by Greenhill as lying in three pieces in a storage hut outside and just to the north of the range of the ruined buildings, though the upper part of the slab was missing. Much of the surface had gone, but sufficient remained to make it worthwhile for Greenhill to take a rubbing (Figure 7.10). Both this and Elliston-Erwood's photograph are illustrated here, as the photograph has evidently been touched up, not entirely accurately, and the rubbing shows that the slab was of greater artistic merit than the photograph suggests. The photograph is more useful for consideration of the overall composition and the rubbing for detailed stylistic analysis. If fragments of this slab survive, their location is unknown.

The slab bore the figure, with the head missing, of a man in civil dress, consisting of a cote-hardi with the hood thrown back, worn over an undertunic with buttoned sleeves. The left hand holds a closed book and the right hand is raised. There is no footrest. Elliston-Erwood suggested that the person commemorated was probably a civil employee of the convent, but we consider that it is more likely that it commemorated a benefactor. Whoever he was, no clues to his identity remain. The absence of the face and the unusual position of the hands limit the comparisons that can be

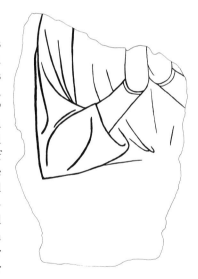

7.8 *St Bartholomew the Great, London III: unknown lady c 1310–20. Lost Camoys-style incised slab. Tracing of rubbing by F A Greenhill, Society of Antiquaries collection.*

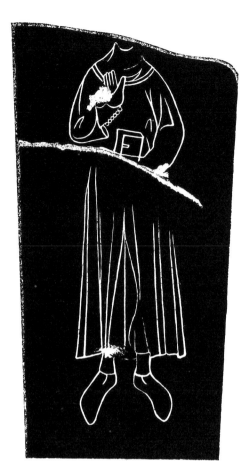

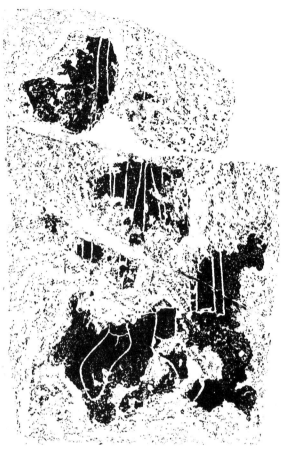

7.9 (above) Lesnes Abbey, Kent: unknown civilian, c 1310–20. Lost Camoys-style incised slab. 1939 photograph by F C Elliston-Erwood.

7.10 (above, right) Lesnes Abbey, Kent: unknown civilian c 1310–20. Lost Camoys-style incised slab. 1948 rubbing by F A Greenhill, Society of Antiquaries collection, photograph by A C Cooper Ltd.

made with brasses in the group. However, the drapery on the left sleeve of the cote-hardi, notably the lines forming an oval at the elbow, follow the distinctive Camoys pattern, and the shape of the end of the sleeve closely parallels the brass at Trotton, Sussex, and the Camoys-style lady at Pitstone, Buckinghamshire.[20] Even bearing in mind the constraints of costume, we consider that there is no doubting the similarity of the skirt and hem drapery to that of the 1311 Hengham brass from Old St Paul's (see Figure 7.6), even though the latter is unfortunately known only from a drawing. Overall, a date of *c* 1310 to *c* 1320 is again suggested.

STOKE, KENT

The Camoys-style incised slab at Stoke, Kent, to an unnamed priest, shown in mass vestments, has only the lower half remaining (Figure 7.11). The folds of the chasuble, particularly the way in which it folds forwards at the sides, are reminiscent of the lost brass from Oulton, Suffolk, to Adam de Bacon, who died after 1327[21] (Figure 7.12). The foot drapery on the slab is simpler, lacking the

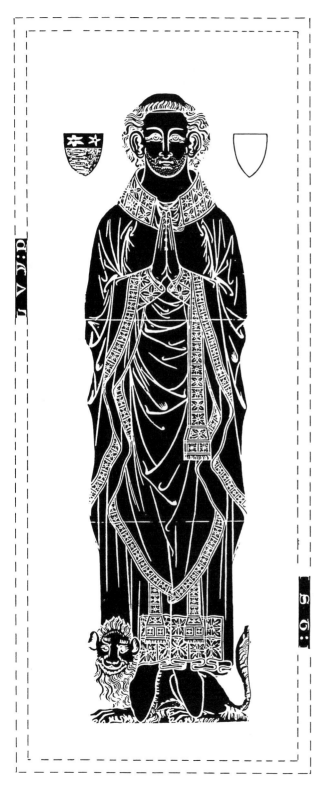

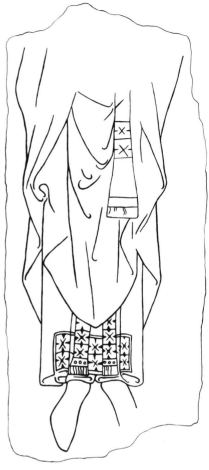

7.11 (above) Stoke, Kent: possibly to John Vaudie, ob 1330. Camoys-style incised slab. Tracing of rubbing by S F Badham.

7.12 (left) Oulton, Suffolk: Adam de Bacon, ob after 1327. Lost Camoys-style brass. Reconstruction by W J Blair from antiquarian rubbings.

serpentine lower edge of the alb, but the skirt of the alb drops vertically like that on the Oulton brass, instead of spreading slightly outwards, as on some other brasses. The feet on the Stoke priest point sharply downwards, in contrast to the incised slab from Lesnes Abbey discussed earlier, but also like the Bacon brass at Oulton. Although it is not known when after 1327 Adam de Bacon died, Binski groups this brass with five other Camoys priests, one of whom died in 1322 and another after 1326. For two of this group, the indents to Abbot Richard de Maners at Bindon and Abbot Walter de Sydelinge at Milton Abbas, both in Dorset, he gave no date of death, only a suggested date of engraving of *c* 1320 to *c* 1330. In fact, Maners died in 1309 and Sydelinge in 1315,[22] indicating that this group of Camoys priests may have had a wider date range than previously suggested. These comparisons suggest a date range of *c* 1310 to *c* 1330 for the Stoke slab. The list of incumbents for Stoke is incomplete, with a gap between Adam de Hakele, who was instituted in 1244, and John Vaudie, who was instituted in 1323. The latter was followed in 1330 by Hamo de Broke and in 1346 by William Symking. The likely date of incising suggests that the slab is most probably to John Vaudie, but his unknown predecessor must also remain a possibility.

SNODLAND, KENT

Interleaved in R Gough's extra-illustrated copy of E Hasted's *History and Topographical Survey of the County of Kent* in the Bodleian Library, Oxford, is a drawing of a fragment of a slab, formerly in the porch at Snodland, Kent (see Figure 6.4).[23] It shows traces of an incised figure of a priest in mass vestments, with the indents of a perimeter inscription in individually inlaid Lombardic lettering of the Main Group type which reads: '...NTONNE IADIS PARSONE DE C / ESTE ECOLI... '. The letters were probably worn by then since the last two words appear to have been incorrectly recorded, a more likely reading being: 'C / EST ECCLI... '. The slab commemorated John de Dennyntone, rector of Snodland, who died in 1338. The last brass in the Camoys series is that to Sir William FitzRalph at Pebmarsh, Essex, dated by Binski *c* 1331–8. The Seymour series (discussed in Chapter 9) was also in operation at this time, but the acute angling of the arms on the Snodland slab is a Camoys, not a Seymour, feature.

BARKING ABBEY, ESSEX

The well-preserved Camoys-style incised slab, formerly in Barking Abbey, excavated in 1912 from the Nun's Cemetery and now a mural in Barking church, Essex, has a firm attribution and date. It features a demi-effigy of a priest in mass vestments, with an inscription '+ MARTINVS: VICARIVS' in incised Lombardic letters above the figure, with the two words separated by a triple

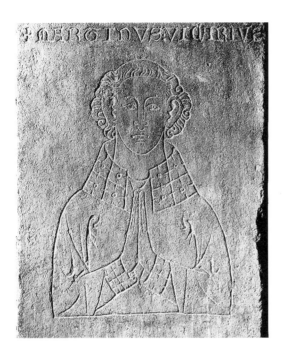
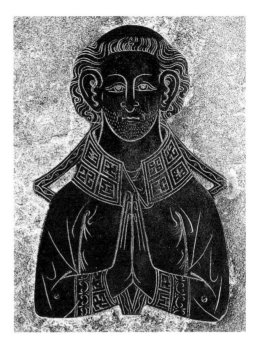

stop (Figure 7.13). Greenhill recorded yellow colouring matter in the incised lines. This brief inscription is not well set out, the individual letters of the second word being more cramped than those of the first. It is also worth noting in passing that two Main Group letters, I and L, were excavated from the site of Barking Abbey about 1884, indicating that other products of the London workshops were also in the Abbey.[24]

Martin was vicar of Barking from 1315 to 1328 and comparison with Camoys brasses suggests that a date of incising of *c* 1328 is credible. The closest parallels are with the 1322 brass to Richard de Hakebourne in Merton College Chapel, Oxford (Figure 7.14), and the lost brass at Oulton, Suffolk. The comparison with the former is indeed quite stunning. The abnormally large ears are identical, as are the three-lobed nose, the eyes, the mouth, the column-like neck and the drawing of the hair. Other points of similarity are the position of the amice, the angle of the arms, the position and drawing of the hands, and the identical folds on the chasuble and the sleeves, including the distinctively finicky folds at the armpits and the pattern of folds at the elbow, which has developed beyond the distinctive oval of the elbow drapery at Trotton. There is no doubt that the Merton College brass and the Barking slab were produced from the same pattern.

COMPOSITE SLABS

Two effigial slabs in Hampshire, at Titchfield and Beaulieu, both unusual and probably special commissions, are less closely tied to the effigial style of the Camoys series but, together with related

7.13 (above, left) Barking, Essex: Martin, vicar, ob 1328. Camoys-style incised slab. Photograph by A C Cooper Ltd.

7.14 (above, right) Merton College, Oxford: Richard de Hakebourne, ob 1322. Camoys-style brass. Photograph by L W Hutchins.

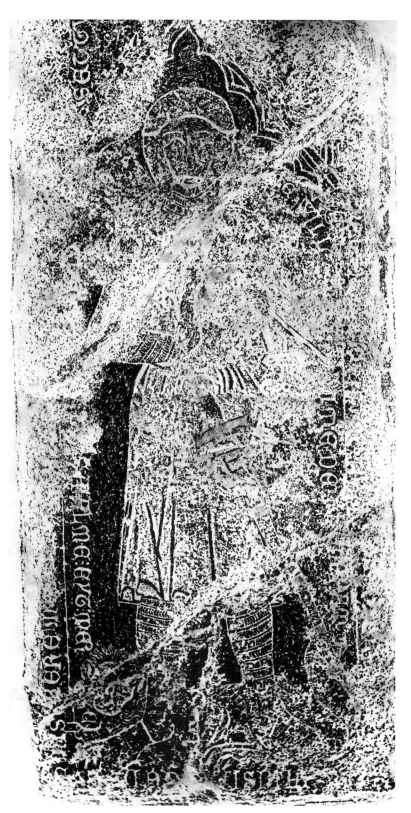

7.15 Titchfield, Hampshire: Sir William de Pageham, ob 1305. Camoys-style incised slab with taille d'épargne *detail. Rubbing by F A Greenhill, Society of Antiquaries collection.*

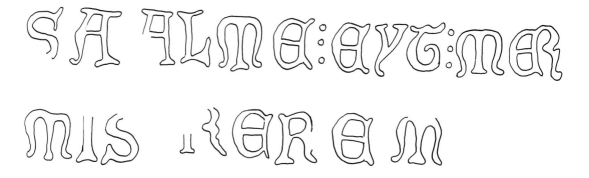

cross slabs from Winchester Cathedral, Hampshire, and the Hospital of St Thomas Acon, London, and an inscription slab from Little Shelford, Cambridgeshire, are attributed to the Camoys series on the basis of their inscriptions, which are incised in the same script as was used for the Barking slab. The two effigial slabs are most unusual in that they display inlay techniques more commonly associated with Flemish and French composite slabs, and hardly ever otherwise found in England, other than on imports from Tournai, such as the fine fragment of a civilian of the 1320s or 1330s, excavated from the site of the Newcastle Blackfriars in 1983.[25] The Newcastle slab has some of the design incised, though brass inlays were used for the inscription, the canopy, the man's tunic and, possibly, the lions at his feet. However, the drapery lines of his overtunic and his cloak are shown as raised incised stone lines, with the surface on either side cut away, a technique known as *taille d'épargne*. The cutaway sections of his cloak were almost certainly filled with composition, which might well have been stamped with designs like those found on the gesso covering of stone effigies, adding to the overall impression of richness.

TITCHFIELD, HAMPSHIRE

Taille d'épargne was used extensively on the rectangular Purbeck marble slab of a knight set in the south chapel of the parish church at Titchfield, Hampshire (Figures 7.15 and 7.16). Greenhill's unpublished notes record that this slab came to light in 1950, but it is not known whether it was found at the parish church or on the site of the nearby Abbey Church at Titchfield. The knight's face, gown, sword, belt and shield and the lion's face are all in this technique, the remainder of the figure having been incised. The small size of the areas between the raised lines and the absence of backing plates suggest that the inlay was entirely white or coloured composition and that none of it was of brass. Parts of the design, particularly the inscription, are hard to decipher because the surface is in poor condition.

7.16 Titchfield, Hampshire: Sir William de Pageham, ob 1305. Camoys-style incised slab with taille d'épargne *detail. Tracing of letters from rubbing by F A Greenhill, Society of Antiquaries collection.*

The knight stands with his feet apart, a feature which itself cannot be paralleled on contemporary brasses. The only pre-Black Death military brass which does not show crossed legs is the 1327 Camoys-style brass at Stoke d'Abernon, Surrey (see Figure 5.1), though there the legs are straight, rather than splayed, as at Titchfield. Like the knights on Camoys series brasses, the Titchfield figure holds his hands in prayer, has a lion at his feet and has a shield on his left arm. His shield appears not to curve round his body, as shown on the cross-legged Camoys knights, such as that at Pebmarsh, Essex (see Figure 7.2), but rather is heater-shaped, like that shown on the Stoke d'Abernon brass (see Figure 7.23). The shield is charged with *a fleur-de-lis and over all a bend*. Few details of the armour are sufficiently clear to provide indicators of the likely date of this slab. The figure wears a long gown over his mail, with no split visible in front, thus hiding the form of his poleyns. The area around his elbow is so badly damaged that it is impossible to detect whether couters were shown. Nor is the method by which the sword was attached to the belt clear.

Though the type of spurs shown cannot now be determined with any certainty, Greenhill thought that they were probably of the prick type. However, the head is rather better preserved and it is clear that he wears a skull-cap under his mail hood. The dating of the form of skull-cap with an arched lower edge has recently been investigated by Claude Blair, who concluded from an examination of effigies and brasses that it probably started to come into use around *c* 1310.[26] The skull-cap shown on the Titchfield effigy is an intermediate form between the type with a straight-line edge and the fully developed shaped form,[27] suggesting a date slightly earlier than *c* 1310.

The canopy was incised and, for the most part, is of a form very similar to the early Camoys series prototypes, showing a straight-sided arch with cusping and crocketing, supported by plain, slim shafts and having crocketed pinnacles. The closest parallels on brasses are the 1298 de Luda indent at Ely Cathedral, Cambridgeshire, and the 1308 de Haselshaw indent at Wells, Somerset, both late Ashford series products. However, the Titchfield canopy has a very slight ogee at the apex. Unusually, the side shafts are incised with parts of a Latin inscription in Lombardic letters. The inscription begins near the top on the dexter side, continuing along the top of the slab, then down the sinister canopy shaft, along the bottom of the slab and finally up the dexter side of the slab. Much is now illegible but what survives reads: 'SET TV / DOMI....... / .... / ..ARIS D..CE DEVS / MISERE ME[I]......... '. Additionally, there is a second inscription, in Norman-French, that appears to begin just within and parallel with the sinister pinnacle, proceeding from there under the sinister side of the canopy arch, then vertically down the sinister side of the slab parallel to and inside the sinister shaft of the canopy, then finally parallel to and within the dexter shaft, again reading from top to bottom. These last two sections of the French inscription are interrupted, on the sinister side by the shield and on the dexter side by the lion's head. This inscription reads: '[P]RIET P[O]VR / LALME: WILL [gap for shield] AME: DE: .....AM: ?KY / GIS[T] ..... [DI]EV: D[E]: SA: ALME: EYT: MER [gap for lion's head] CI:'. Where stops can be seen between words, they are triple stops.

Various suggestions have been made as to the identity of the person commemorated by this slab. Greenhill suggested that he was a member of the Aguillon family, whose arms were *azure, a fleur-de-lis argent*. Three factors argue against this attribution. First, the name Aguillon does not fit the traces of the lettering that survive. These indicate that the surname was about seven letters long, began with a letter that may have been a 'P' and definitely ended with the letters 'AM'. Second, the Aguillons were a Hampshire family, but held land in Greatham in Alton Hundred, a considerable distance away from Titchfield.[28] Finally, their arms did not include a bend, traces of which survive on the Titchfield slab. A more plausible candidate is Sir William de Pageham, whose name fits the surviving letter indents on the slab. His career can be traced from 1282.[29] He was assessor of subsidy for Sussex in 1294, justice of gaol delivery for Chichester, Guildford and Arundel at various times from 1294, and Sheriff of Sussex in 1294. As a knight of the Rape of Chichester, he was enrolled for the defence of the coast in 1296 and was summoned from Sussex to serve against the Scots in 1298. He is recorded as having witnessed documents in 1297 and *c* 1300.[30] In 1300 and 1301 he was assessed as having lands valued at £40 in Hampshire. He died in 1305, leaving to his son John, then aged sixteen and a half, manors at Merston, on the Isle of Wight, and at Funtley, which is only about a mile from Titchfield Abbey.[31] Sir William also passed on lands at Titchfield which had come into the possession of the de Pageham family on the marriage of his father, also named William de Pageham, to Joan de St Martin.[32] Unfortunately, we have been unable to establish the Pageham family arms, which would have provided the best proof of whether or not our attribution to Sir William de Pageham is correct.[33]

CAMOYS-STYLE LETTERING

Three other slabs, at Winchester Cathedral, Hampshire, Little Shelford, Cambridgeshire, and the Hospital of St Thomas Acon, London, may be attributed to the Camoys series on the basis of the lettering style, examples of which have already been seen at Barking (see Figure 7.13) and Titchfield (see Figure 7.16). Letter forms from the Camoys series slabs are shown in Figure 7.17. Some letters, notably the variants of the A, L, M and R shown on the right of each pair in Figure 7.17, are close in form to the shape of the letters used on the largely thirteenth-century Ashford series slabs (discussed in Chapter 13). This provides more evidence to suggest that the Camoys style developed out of the Ashford style. Other variants of the letters A, L, M and R are more developed types;

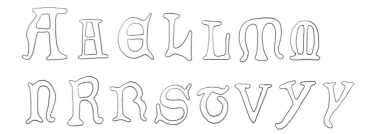

7.17 Letter forms on Camoys-style slabs.

these are shown on the left of the pairs in Figure 7.17. The wedge-shaped L and the M with its outward-curling downstrokes are particularly distinctive. Some letters, particularly the S, V and Y, are more individual in type.

WINCHESTER CATHEDRAL, HAMPSHIRE V

The Camoys style of incised lettering can be found on two continuous fragments of an incised cross slab, formerly in Winchester Cathedral, Hampshire, which is known only from a rubbing by Greenhill (Figure 7.18). This slab has a clustered crosshead of unusual design, across the top of which are two lines of an inscription reading: '... HIDE: .OCSTON: M... / ET: HAYLIN[G] ... '. The words are separated by triple stops. Whilst it could otherwise be argued that the use of *taille d'épargne* on the Titchfield slab might be the product of a French or Flemish craftsman working in England using the native Purbeck marble, there can be no doubt that the Winchester fragment is an essentially English product.

LITTLE SHELFORD, CAMBRIDGESHIRE

7.18 Winchester Cathedral, Hampshire V: unknown, c 1305–20. Lost Camoys-style incised slab. Tracing of a rubbing by F A Greenhill, Society of Antiquaries collection.

Lettering of the same distinctive script, though with double rather than triple stops separating the words, is used for an inscription on a rectangular Purbeck marble slab bordered by a raised moulding

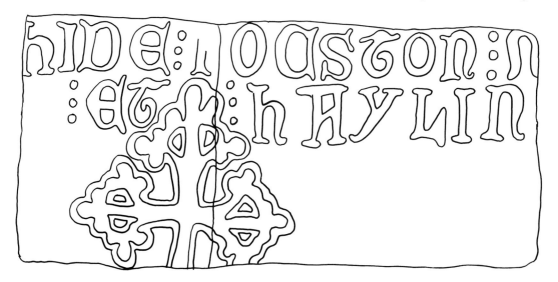

set in the back of a tomb-recess at Little Shelford, Cambridgeshire (Figure 7.19).[34] The inscription is set out in four lines reading: 'ICI: GIST: SIRE: IOHAN: DE: FRIV / ILE: KE: FVST: SEIGNIOVR: DE: CES: / TE: VILE: VOVS: KE: PAR: ICI: PASSE / T: PAR: CHARITE: PVR: LALME: PRIET:'. On a plain tomb chest in the recess is a freestone effigy of a knight, identified by the inscription as Sir John de Frevile. He served both Edward I and Edward II on the Borders and in Scotland, was knighted in 1305, attended Edward II's coronation and died in 1312.[35] The figure is of high quality and has been linked by Claude Blair with the court workshop which produced, amongst others, the effigies of Edmund, Earl of Lancaster, in Westminster Abbey, London, made between 1296 and 1300, Aymer de Valence, Earl of Pembroke, in Westminster Abbey, carved after 1324, and John de Hastings, *ob* 1325, in Abergavenny, Monmouthshire.[36] This provides important evidence of close collaboration between the masons of the court workshop and Adam the Marbler's workshop in St Paul's Churchyard.

HOSPITAL OF ST THOMAS ACON, LONDON

Another example of the Camoys-style script appears on the portion of a coffin lid found during excavations by the Museum of London Archaeology Service in September 1997 in a lift pit at 10–18 London Bridge Street.[37] Historically, the site was part of the Hospital of St Thomas Acon, founded on the site in 1215, and it is likely that the slab was originally from the chapel there. It was clearly discarded and reused as building material as little as a hundred years after it was laid down, for the fragment was found as part of the construction fabric of a cesspit and cellar of fourteenth- to

7.19 Little Shelford, Cambridgeshire: Sir John de Frevile, ob 1312. Camoys-style incised inscription associated with a freestone effigy attributed to the court workshop. Tracing of rubbing by S F Badham.

7.20 Hospital of St Thomas Acon, London: unknown 1305–35. Camoys-style relief cross slab with incised inscription. Tracing of letters from rubbing by S F Badham.

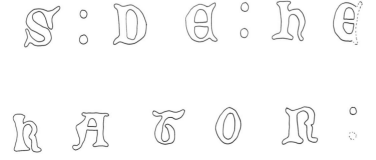

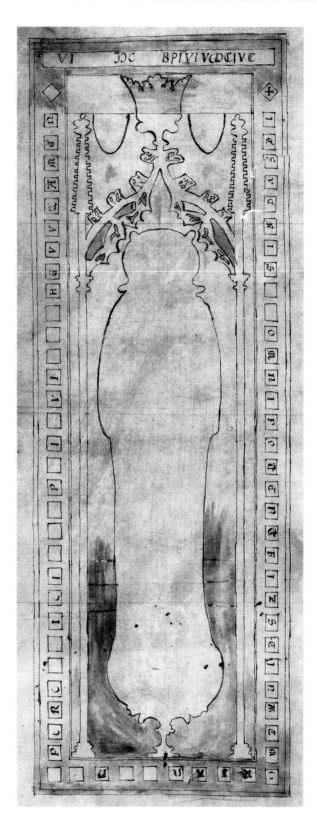

7.21 Beaulieu Abbey,
  Hampshire: Princess
  Eleanor, ob 1311.
  Camoys-style incised slab
  with composition inlays.
  Late eighteenth-century
  drawing made for
  R Gough, Bodleian Library,
  Oxford, Gough Maps 225,
  fol 103. Photograph by
  Bodleian Library.

fifteenth-century date. The surviving portion is from the middle of the coffin lid. On the upper surface is the stem of a relief cross. The sides have a double hollow-moulded chamfer on the inner order of which is an incised inscription (Figure 7.20). The text is in Norman-French, probably indicating that it commemorated a member of the laity. It ran in an anti-clockwise direction, the words being separated by double round stops. The two surviving portions read: 'S: DE: HE', probably part of the commemorated's name, and 'KATOR:', which probably formed part of an indulgence text offering fourteen days or years of pardon to those offering prayers for the deceased.

BEAULIEU ABBEY, HAMPSHIRE

The Titchfield and Winchester Abbey slabs can also be linked with a Purbeck marble slab, found in a field near Lord Montagu's house on the site of Beaulieu Abbey, Hampshire.[38] It now stands upright in the museum, formerly the Lay Brothers' Frater. The overall design is best appreciated from a drawing made for Gough in the closing years of the eighteenth century (Figure 7.21), though Greenhill's rubbing of 1936 shows useful detail of the inlays (Figure 7.22). At that time the slab was on the floor of the Lay Brothers' Frater, a position which permitted much closer examination than is possible now that the top of the slab is some 3 metres off the ground. It bore a female effigy, placed on a low bracket, under a canopy. The 1308 Haselshaw indent at Wells, a late Ashford series product, also shows a figure on a similar low bracket. Like the Titchfield slab, the canopy on the Beaulieu slab is cusped, but not subcusped, has crocketed finials and is supported by plain, slim shafts. However, it is otherwise of a more advanced design than the Haselshaw slab, since it has a marked ogival curve. The large central finial is surmounted by a crown. There are two shields between this finial and the pinnacles, and a marginal inscription runs round the edge of the slab.

Greenhill carried out a detailed inspection of this slab to determine the nature of the inlays, which he recorded in his unpublished notes. He concluded that the inlays were of white composition, so brittle that where it has survived it has cracked into tiny pieces. The matrices, which are about 5mm deep and have a roughened surface, presumably to aid adhesion, have been smeared with pitch, some traces of which survive in the canopy, bracket and inscription. The composition inlays were then inset in sections held together with a whitish cement. The inscription, apart from a line at the top of the slab, which is a fillet, is inlaid in small squares, with a single letter incised on each one. In total there are some seventy squares, plus two diamond-shaped foliage stops which mark the beginning and end of the individually inlaid inscription, some forty-nine squares of which survived in whole or in part when Greenhill examined it. Most are badly damaged, all that now remains of the inscription reading: 'IESV: CRI[ST]: OMNIPOTENT: FI. ....E ... '. More traces of letters survived when the slab was drawn for Gough, but the

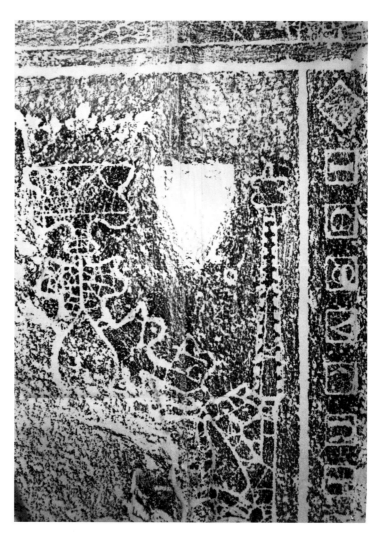

7.22 Beaulieu Abbey, Hampshire: Princess Eleanor, ob 1311. Camoys-style incised slab with composition inlays. Detail of upper part of slab from rubbing by F A Greenhill, Society of Antiquaries collection.

artist appears to have had difficulty deciphering what remained and little sense can be gleaned from his drawing, other than that the inscription continued with the words 'FIZ: SAINTE: M / ARIA' and ended with 'AMEN'. The style of such letters as survive is consistent with the lettering on the Titchfield, Winchester, Little Shelford, St Thomas Acon and Barking slabs, indicating a common workshop origin. The inlay of the figure, none of which remains, would undoubtedly also have been incised, like the series of inlaid slabs thought to have been produced in Hereford at the end of the fourteenth century.[39] The matrices of the crown and the two shields are differently treated; they are very shallow and much smoother. Greenhill conjectured that they might have been inlaid with very thin brass or, more likely, enamelled copper. Inlays of enamel are known to have been employed by the London marblers at this time, a notable example being the shield on the 1327 Camoys-style brass at Stoke d'Abernon, Surrey (Figure 7.23), already noted as resembling in some respects the Titchfield slab.

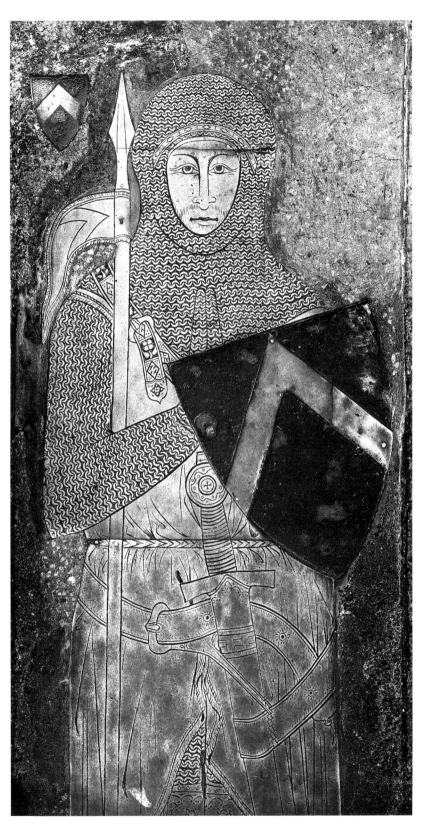

7.23 Stoke d'Abernon,
Surrey: Sir John
d'Abernon II,
ob 1327. Camoys-
style brass. Detail
of upper part of
figure showing
enamelled shield.
Photograph by
K & S Commercial
Photographs Ltd.

Gough recorded that the Beaulieu slab was believed in his day to have commemorated Princess Isabel, first wife of Richard, King of the Romans, and thus would be dated to *c* 1240, though he himself appeared dubious about this attribution. The crown on the top of the canopy indicates that the slab commemorates royalty, but design parallels clearly demonstrate that it cannot be as early as 1240 and is indeed most unlikely to date from earlier than the fourteenth century. Fowler suggested that the slab formerly marked the grave of Eleanor, daughter of Edward I and his second wife, Margaret.[40] Eleanor died at Amesbury in 1311, at the age of five, while in the care of her half-sister, Mary, who had taken the veil.[41] Her remains were taken to the Cistercian abbey at Beaulieu and preparations made for her burial at the expense of Edward II.[42] Although the effigy on the Beaulieu slab is not obviously a diminutive figure, it is placed on a bracket or pedestal, a device often used to indicate the commemoration of a child. The likelihood of a second, unrecorded, royal burial of a child at Beaulieu at the same time is remote; we therefore consider the attribution to Princess Eleanor to be almost certainly correct. A date of 1311 for the Beaulieu slab fits well with the attribution of the Titchfield slab to Sir William de Pageham, *ob* 1305. This was not the first royal monument of Purbeck marble; indeed, Purbeck was used in the construction of nearly all the royal tombs of the Plantagenets. The effigy to King John at Worcester, made in 1240, some twenty-four years after his death, is of Purbeck marble; Henry III's tomb chest of 1272 at Westminster Abbey is of Purbeck marble inlaid with mosaic; Eleanor of Castile's latton effigy at Westminster Abbey rests on a Purbeck marble slab; Edward I had a plain Purbeck marble altar tomb at Westminster Abbey; and Edward II, who paid for Princess Eleanor's burial, had a tomb chest of Purbeck marble to support his alabaster effigy at St Peter's Abbey, Gloucester, now the Cathedral. Moreover, in 1254 a Purbeck marble effigy of a queen was provided for the tomb at Tarrant Monkton, Dorset, to Joan, wife of Alexander II of Scotland and sister of Henry II of England.[43]

The use of inlays of incised composition is a technique mainly associated with the *ateliers* of Tournai and Paris. A few examples are known of domestically produced slabs in England employing this technique, but the Beaulieu slab is the only known example in Purbeck marble. The use of Franco-Flemish techniques on a Purbeck marble slab links it with the Titchfield slab, with its extensive use of *taille d'épargne*, not otherwise known to have been employed by English craftsmen. Although these slabs are geographically close to Corfe, they are more likely to have originated in London, where the marblers would undoubtedly have been familiar with the products of their prestigious foreign competitors. In their original condition, the Titchfield and Beaulieu slabs would have been ostentatiously magnificent examples of the tombmaker's art. They are certainly London quality in terms of the techniques displayed. The design of these slabs, for example in the use of the ogee arch, was in the forefront of contemporary design. This should not be surprising considering that Sir William de Pageham and John de Frevile were men of affluence and the Beaulieu slab was almost certainly a royal commission. The related Winchester fragment, in view of its location, may also be assumed to have had an important patron. There can be little doubt that these slabs were made by the London marblers and were probably amongst the earliest recorded products of the Camoys series.

SUMMARY

Thus we have records of eleven fragments of incised slabs (which are listed in Appendix A). For most, the comparisons with the Camoys-style brasses are clear and very compelling. Though the figures on no two Camoys brasses or slabs superimpose exactly, ruling out the use of templates, most are clearly drawn from the same set of patterns. There can be no doubt that they were made either in one workshop or by the same group of marblers working to common patterns, presumably under the direction of Adam the Marbler, alias Adam Laurenz. The five incised slabs which are firmly dated, at Titchfield, Beaulieu, Little Shelford, Barking and Snodland, fit well with the dates given to contemporary Camoys-style brasses in Binski's analysis and it is possible to date the remaining slabs by reference to the Camoys brasses with a fair degree of confidence. Thus, the broad framework provided in *The Earliest English Brasses* is fully confirmed as far as the Camoys style is concerned, although we have questioned Binski's dating of a handful of individual brasses within the series.

Chapter 8

The Septvans style

INTRODUCTION

The next style of London brasses is the Septvans series, a small group with features which overlap with those of the Camoys style and which are thought to have been produced in the same workshop. Binski identified five brasses of this style, to which we propose to add another three brasses and two incised slabs.

SEPTVANS-STYLE BRASSES

The dating of this series presents problems. Of the five brasses Binski assigned to this group, only the indent at Letheringham, Suffolk, is reliably attributed, on the basis of an antiquarian drawing by Craven Ord, to Sir William Bovile, who died in 1320.[1] Two Septvans products, at Cople, Bedfordshire, and All Hallows Barking, London, are palimpsest and have no attribution or date. The attribution of the so-called 'ghost' of a lost brass at Canterbury Cathedral, Kent, is highly speculative and must also be discounted. The question of whom is commemorated by the fine knight at Chartham, Kent (Figure 8.1), is also problematic. The inscription is badly decayed and all that can be established with certainty is that it commemorates a son of Sir Robert de Septvans and, given that the arms are undifferenced, should represent a head of the family. The only two possible candidates are Sir Robert de Septvans, who died in 1306, and Sir William de Septvans, who died in 1322. In 1980 Binski argued persuasively that the Septvans brass was produced in the same artistic environment as the De Lisle Psalter and was stylistically similar to mainstream court products of the opening years of the fourteenth century; also that there was a strong association between the art of Westminster and that of the Canterbury region at that time; and that the brass probably commemorated Sir Robert de Septvans, and should be dated to 1306.[2]

A range of arguments has subsequently been deployed to support the 1322 date,[3] but, in our view, none carries the same degree of conviction as Binski's original thesis. It has been argued that the other Septvans-style brasses date from the 1320s, but only one is so dated, providing neither a *terminus ante quem* nor a *terminus post quem*. Similarly, the argument that knightly brasses

8.1 (opposite) Chartham, Kent: Sir Robert de Septvans, ob 1306. Septvans-style brass. Photograph by K & S Commercial Photographs Ltd.

68

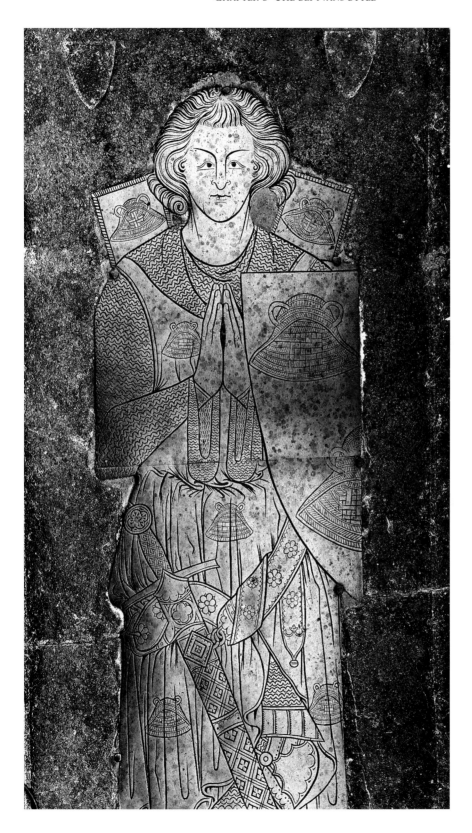

were only produced from the 1320s because no other known and reliably dated brass to a knight can be dated before then does not hold water. With so many brasses having been lost, what remains cannot be regarded as a representative sample. If brasses to priests and ladies could be produced as far back as the thirteenth century, why not also to knights? Moreover, Rogers, in his recent authoritative re-examination of the art-historical context of this brass, also concluded that it was designed earlier than the 1320s.[4] A more weighty argument for the later date of 1322 is perhaps that, unlike the other early knights, the Chartham brass shows the scabbard attached to the sword belt by means of interlocking rings. When this method was first depicted is highly controversial; however, it is now accepted that it was not a development of the diagonal-thong method, but was, more or less, a contemporary type.[5] Ring lockets are known in Italy from the first decade of the fourteenth century; the earliest firmly and uncontroversially dated example is their representation on the figure of St George carved on the tomb in the old cathedral at Brescia to Bishop Berardo Maggi, who died in 1308, though they are also shown on the figure of Temperanza in Giotto's frescoes in the Scrovegni Chapel, Padua, which probably dates from 1305.[6] The date of their introduction in England is less certain, though it could have been broadly contemporary. Fully developed ring-locket attachments appear in Westminster Abbey, London, on the royal effigy to Aymer de Valence, which cannot date from before June 1324.[7] It is to be expected that royal effigies would have been at the forefront of design innovation, but it has to be pointed out that this was the first royal military effigy to survive since that commemorating Edmund Crouchback, made *c* 1296–1300, a notable lacuna. Thus, all the Valence effigy tells us is that fully developed ring-locket attachments were in use by 1324, not that they necessarily made their first appearance then. However, a transitional form of ring lockets is shown on all carved military effigies from Yorkshire Series B, which Brian and Moira Gittos have convincingly demonstrated to have been carved between *c* 1300 and *c* 1317.[8] Moreover, the Chartham brass also shows the scabbard attachment in a transitional form, albeit not identical to the form on the Yorkshire Series B effigies, with the longer section of the belt attached by a locket and ring and the shorter section, which carries the buckle, still attached by a thong, suggesting a very early use of this type of scabbard attachment. In our view, the balance of all these arguments weighs more heavily in favour of the brass having been made shortly after Sir Robert de Septvans's death in 1306, though the possibility of it dating from 1322 cannot be entirely dismissed.

None of the additional brasses we consider to be products of the Septvans workshop provides any useful evidence about the dating of this series, since all three are palimpsest reverses and we do not know whom any of them commemorates. One, which is most likely to have come from Bury St Edmunds Abbey, Suffolk, is on the reverse of the *c* 1470 Norwich-made brass at Ingham, Norfolk.[9] The others are sections of two magnificent pontifically vested figures on the reverse of Robert Rugge's brass at St John Maddermarket, Norwich.[10] Though these fragments were not included in Binski's analysis, in our view the sinuous drapery folds of the chasuble leave no doubt about the Septvans origin of these three palimpsest brasses.

WEST WICKHAM, KENT I

In the Society of Antiquaries' main collection of rubbings and dabbings of incised slabs is a dabbing by Waller, probably made in 1837, of an otherwise unknown fragment of an incised slab formerly at West Wickham, Kent, showing the middle section of a priest in mass vestments (Figure 8.2). It was probably once the finest of the three London incised slabs to priests in this church. Waller's dabbing shows the folds of the chasuble, with the alb revealed beneath. It is unfortunate that insufficient remains of this slab to make it certain whether it was of Camoys or Septvans style, though the latter is more likely.

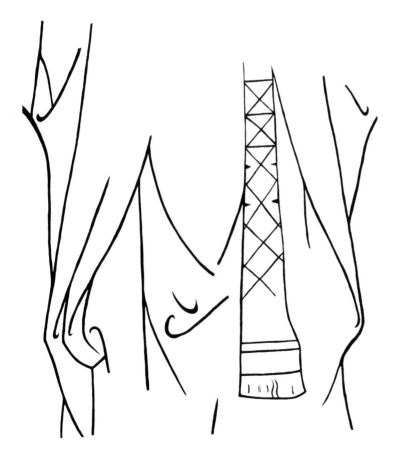

8.2 *West Wickham, Kent I: possibly for Nicholas Louseby, ob 1324, or his successor, Peter de St John. Lost Septvans-style incised slab. Tracing of 1847 rubbing by J Waller, Society of Antiquaries collection.*

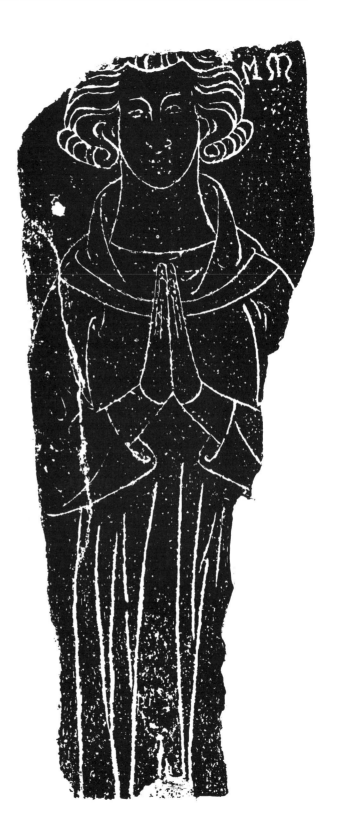

8.3 *Victoria and Albert Museum, London, from destroyed church of St Christopher-le-Stocks, London: unknown civilian, c 1305–25. Septvans-style incised slab. Rubbing by F A Greenhill, Society of Antiquaries collection, photograph by A C Cooper Ltd.*

Four brasses bear close comparison with this slab at West Wickham. The first is the lost Camoys-style brass from Oulton, Suffolk (see Figure 7.12), and the others are the Septvans-style palimpsest fragments at Ingham and Norwich, both in Norfolk. The West Wickham slab does not show the sinuous folds on the Ingham and Norwich fragments, but otherwise compares well: the folds of the drapery are similarly full and luxurious. The fringed maniple, with its quatrefoil decoration and asymmetrical end, hangs down on the sinister side of the figure and is positioned fairly well towards the centre. All these features can be mirrored both on the Oulton brass and on the Norwich fragments. Whether the slab forms part of the Camoys series or the Septvans series, these stylistic comparisons suggest a date around the 1320s. The early fourteenth-century rectors of West Wickham were Nicholas Louseby (1293–1324), Peter de St John (1324–7) and Walter de Cestreford (1327–44). The last named was commemorated by another slab at West Wickham, so this must be for either Louseby or St John.

VICTORIA AND ALBERT MUSEUM, LONDON

The slab to an unknown civilian discovered during reconstruction of the Bank of England, London, and probably originally from the church of St Christopher-le-Stocks, destroyed in 1780, is now preserved in the Victoria and Albert Museum (Figure 8.3). It has been cut down at top and bottom with much of the sinister side broken away, though the top surface is well preserved. The surviving portion of the slab shows a bare-headed civilian from about mid-thigh level to the top of his head. The crudely incised Lombardic letters 'AM', perhaps the end of his surname, appear at the top sinister corner of the slab. Williamson has twice discussed the slab and compared it to brasses. In 1987 he made a totally inappropriate comparison with the mid-fourteenth-century civilian at Taplow, Berkshire, and dated the slab to the second quarter of the fourteenth century.[11] A year later he revised this assessment, instead linking the slab more aptly with brasses from the London workshops of the first quarter of the fourteenth century, specifically the Chartham brass.[12]

Detailed analysis of the figure shows many Septvans features, but also some more readily associated with the Camoys style. The hair is identical to that on the Chartham brass and the absence of ears accords more with Septvans than Camoys styling, large jug-ears being a very apparent feature of bare-headed Camoys men. The flaring eyebrows and the eyes with a straight lower lid are also of Septvans style. The nose, with its three equal-size lobes, however, is of the Camoys style, as are the shape of the face and the heavy neck, devoid of cording. There are no Septvans brasses with sleeve drapery to compare with this slab, but there is a close similarity to the sleeve drapery of the Camoys-style brasses at Trotton, Sussex, and Merton College, Oxford (discussed in Chapter 7). This analysis again suggests a mix of Septvans and Camoys features. In view of the problems in dating this style discussed at the beginning of this chapter, this slab cannot be closely dated, but is probably in the span *c* 1305 to *c* 1325.

SUMMARY

The two incised slabs discussed in this chapter both display a mix of Septvans- and Camoys-style features. This is entirely consistent with Binski's analysis of the brasses, which also show a mix of features. It is consonant with them being an 'off-shoot' group of the Camoys workshop, possibly representing the work of one workman or subcontracting marbler. The dating of this style is clearly problematic and we have been able to add little evidence to help resolve the difficulties discussed at the beginning of this chapter. Although we have doubled the number of known products of this pattern type, there are still only ten. Only the date of the Letheringham indent is undisputed. This highlights the problem of dealing with pattern series of which most examples have undoubtedly been lost and reinforces the need for caution when attempting to reach conclusions on the basis of limited evidence.

CHAPTER 9

THE SEYMOUR STYLE

INTRODUCTION

The third style identified by Binski is the Seymour style, which he regarded as forming part of the third generation of brasses, produced after the death of Adam the Marbler. The finest surviving Seymour brass is the one from which the series is named, Lawrence Seymour's brass of 1337 at Higham Ferrers, Northamptonshire (Figure 9.1). Binski assigned eight brasses to this series. We agree with this classification for all but one brass. In addition, we assign one new brass, one indent and three incised slabs to the series.

SEYMOUR-STYLE BRASSES

Of the brasses Binski regarded as belonging to the Seymour pattern series, one, the palimpsest reverse at Norbury, Derbyshire, of parts of the brass to Matilda de Verdun, who died between 1302 and 1312, seems to us to be of a different style, and is almost certainly French in origin, as was first suggested by Norris in 1977.[1] The arrangement and detail closely resemble the incised slab to Michel le Bourgeois of Neauphil-le-Château at the Abbey of Vaux-de-Cernay.[2] The drapery of the lady's surcoat bears a superficial resemblance to Seymour brasses, but the drawing shows considerably more assurance and gives a better impression of volume, making even the splendid Seymour-style brass at Westley Waterless, Cambridgeshire (Figure 9.2), seem somewhat flat in comparison. The pattern of drapery folds shown on the Norbury palimpsest can be paralleled on lost French slabs and brasses drawn for Gaignières, for example at the Abbey of Ourscamp to Pierre de Candoire, who died in 1296, and his wife Agnes,[3] and at the Abbey d'Ardenne to Lucie de Vierville, who died in 1315.[4] The sideshafts inhabited by weepers with the inscription adjoining, engraved on a separate piece of metal from the figure, but believed to have come from the same brass, is another feature of French slabs and is again shown on Lucie de Vierville's incised slab. Binski argued that the semi-naked figure of Christ in judgement in the gable is not a standard element of French tomb iconography. However, the Gaignières drawings show that on lost monuments such figures, both semi-naked and clothed, were found in canopies between the late twelfth and the late fourteenth centuries.[5] Thus, all the elements of the Norbury palimpsest fit comfortably in the French tradition.

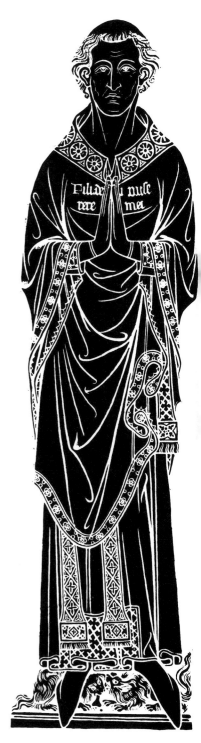

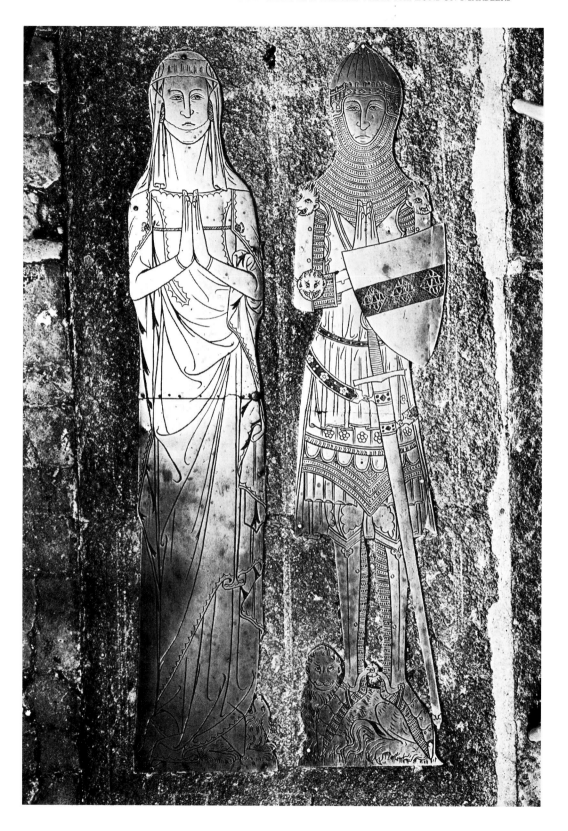

The people commemorated by four of the remaining Seymour-style brasses, at Durham Cathedral, St Albans Abbey, Hertfordshire, Higham Ferrers, Northamptonshire, and Bowers Giffard, Essex, have dates of death spanning the period 1333 to 1348. Sir John d'Abernon II, whose Seymour-style brass is at Stoke d'Abernon, Surrey, died some time between 1339 and 1350.[6] The dates of death of those commemorated by the brasses at Westley Waterless and Great Brington, Northamptonshire, are not known. The commemorative plate from Bisham Abbey, preserved as a palimpsest at Denchworth, Berkshire, dates from *c* 1333; the black-letter inscription is identical in style to the lettering on the Higham Ferrers brass. The indent we have added to the series, on the basis of the outline of the figure, is that at Westleton, Suffolk, and commemorates an unknown priest.[7]

Binski considered the earliest product of the Seymour series to be the large and spectacular indent to Bishop Beaumont in Durham Cathedral.[8] He stated categorically that these brasses were produced in all probability in London by a workshop whose activity cannot be traced before *c* 1333,[9] but this dating is not substantiated by the evidence. Beaumont is known to have prepared his brass in his own lifetime,[10] which puts its date anywhere between 1317 and 1333. Of the three incised slabs we attribute to this series, only the date of that at West Wickham, Kent, fits comfortably within the span of 1333 to 1348 proposed by Binski. The other two, at Westwell, Kent, and Rothwell, Northamptonshire, appear to have been produced over twenty years before this.

WESTWELL, KENT

At Westwell, Kent, is a composite slab to a priest with the inscription, the canopy and the upper part of the figure formerly inlaid in brass and the lower part of the figure incised (Figure 9.3). He wears mass vestments, though, as on the Camoys series slab at Stoke (discussed in Chapter 7), no maniple is shown. The indents for the inscription in Main Group brass letters are now worn, but are more clearly shown on a nineteenth-century rubbing in the main incised slab collection at the Society of Antiquaries. It reads: '+ HIC:/[IA]CET: MA[G]ISTER: IOH.....: MO............./........./ ..........A...................E...../... '. Binski discussed this slab in his analysis of the Seymour brasses, drawing attention to its problematic nature.[11] Though he regarded the canopy and lettering as linking with the second generation of brasses largely produced in the Camoys workshop, the style of the incised figure, with its slender frame and criss-cross drapery folds, seemed to him more closely allied to the Seymour style. The bust is slightly asymmetrical, a feature found on brasses of a wide date, including both Camoys and later products. Overall, he concluded that a date in the 1330s was most likely. We agree with most of the details of the stylistic analysis, but not the date. Although the Westwell canopy has the same hanging tracery and subcusping as on the Higham Ferrers

9.1 *(page 75) Higham Ferrers, Northamptonshire: Lawrence Seymour, ob 1337. Seymour-style brass. Rubbing by M W Norris.*

9.2 *(opposite) Westley Waterless, Cambridgeshire: Sir John and Lady Alyne de Creke, c 1340–5. Seymour-style brass. Photograph by K & S Commercial Photographs Ltd.*

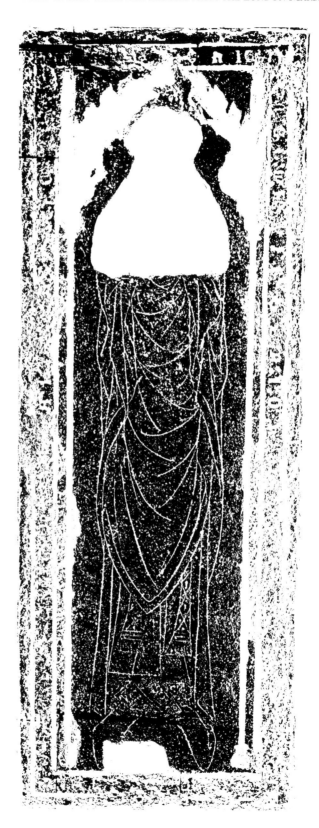

9.3 Westwell, Kent: John de la More, ob 1309. Seymour-style 'composite' slab with lost brass inlay. Rubbing by F A Greenhill, Society of Antiquaries collection, photograph by A C Cooper Ltd.

brass, it has not even the hint of an ogee. We consider the steep and straight-sided arch to the canopy as being indicative of a date rather earlier in the fourteenth century than that of the Higham Ferrers brass.

Hitherto, no attribution has been given for this slab, though it is not difficult to identify. We know from the inscription that the man's Christian name was John. The list of rectors and vicars of Westwell includes in the fourteenth century only two with the name John: John de la More (1305–9) and John Barnet (1349–55).[12] In fact, John Barnet can be ruled out. He exchanged the living of Westwell in 1355 and went on to become Bishop of Ely in 1367 and Treasurer of the Exchequer from 1262 to 1269.[13] He died at Hatfield, Hertfordshire, on 7 June 1373 and was buried at Ely on the south side of the altar, where the grey marble base of his tomb remains.[14] This leaves John de la More. The remaining letters recorded in the key section of the inscription on the rubbing in the Society of Antiquaries are 'IOH.....: MO.. '. This fits perfectly with the name 'IOHANNIS: MORE' and there can be no doubt that the slab commemorates him. We do not know for certain that More's vacation of the living in 1309 was through death, though this is the more likely explanation. No record of him has been found elsewhere and if he had exchanged the living after only five years at Westwell, it is difficult to understand why he would have chosen to be buried there. A priest, who would of necessity have been without direct descendants, is most unlikely to have been commemorated by a tomb made very many years after his death. Thus the date of 1309 for this slab is suggested with some confidence.

ROTHWELL, NORTHAMPTONSHIRE

The second Seymour-style incised slab can also be dated to *c* 1309. It is at Rothwell, Northamptonshire, mounted on the wall in the locked south porch, and commemorates William de Williamstorpe. Only a fragment of it remains, showing a priest from eye to waist level, dressed in mass vestments (Figure 9.4). It is well preserved except for the details immediately next to the broken upper edge, though a small piece at the lower sinister corner has disappeared since Greenhill rubbed it in 1937 (Figure 9.5). It was probably originally coffin-shaped. The only part of the original edge surviving is on the dexter and there is an inscription in two lines on the double hollow-moulded chamfer. This is a feature commonly found on Basyng-style slabs (discussed in Chapter 12), though the lettering on the Rothwell slab is unlike the Basyng script. Moreover, unlike some other fourteenth-century slabs, the lettering does not imitate Main Group letters. The inscription reads: '[ORATE: P]RO: ANIMA: WILI: DE: W[ILLIAMSTORPE:]........ / .... ROWELLE: CUIUS: C... '. Williamstorpe was instituted on 11 February 1271 and his successor on 17 February 1310.[15]

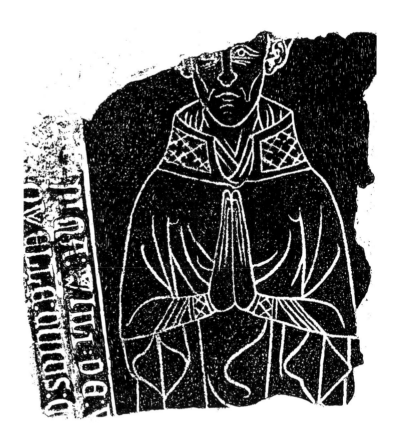

9.4 *Rothwell, Northamp-*
tonshire: William de
Williamstorpe, ob 1309.
Seymour-style incised slab.
Rubbing by F A Greenhill,
Society of Antiquaries
collection, photograph by
A C Cooper Ltd.

Analysis of individual features reveals many parallels with Seymour-style brasses, though some features seem closer to the Camoys type. The face is thinner than those on contemporary brasses, but seems nearer the Seymour type than any other. Similarly, the mouth is of the short downwards-turned Seymour type, and the lined cheeks and the drawing of the ears can best be paralleled on the Higham Ferrers brass itself, but the nose has three equal-sized lobes, more akin to Camoys brasses. Little of the neck is exposed, but some neck cording can be seen; it is most like the Seymour-style priest at Great Brington, Northamptonshire (Figure 9.6), but without the Adam's apple. The amice sits far higher on the shoulders than on Seymour-style brasses; in this respect a better comparison can be made with the Camoys-style brass at Merton College, Oxford, but the central folds follow the Seymour, rather than the Camoys, pattern. The chest drapery of the chasuble is close to that of the Higham Ferrers brass and the upper arm folds are not dissimilar, but something has gone badly wrong with the drapery on the forearms, for which there are no good parallels on brasses. The hands have no gap between them, but the palm of the right hand is fatter than the left; this is also seen on the Seymour-style brass at Westley Waterless. Again, a purely stylistic comparison with brasses suggests a likely Seymour origin, which Binski regards as generally indicating a date not earlier than the mid-1330s.

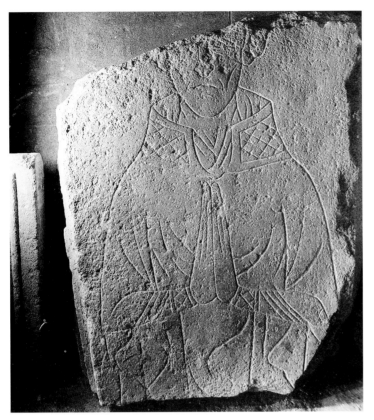

9.5 *Rothwell, Northamp-*
tonshire: William de
Williamstorpe, ob 1309.
Seymour-style incised slab.
Photograph of slab,
showing present condition,
by S F Badham.

However, as with the Westwell composite and for the same reasons, it is difficult to believe that the memorial could have been delayed so long after Williamstorpe's probable death in 1309.

WEST WICKHAM, KENT II

The final Seymour-style incised slab does not raise such difficulties for the previously accepted dating of Seymour-style brasses. Most of what we know of the slab at West Wickham, Kent, to Walter de Cestreford, who died in 1344, is gleaned from antiquarian sources. Waller's notebook in the Society of Antiquaries, with notes dated 1837, refers to 'A figure of a priest engraved in stone. All is worn away but a few lines of the vestments. Inscription around in Lombardic characters. The lower end of the slab is concealed under the raised steps of the Communion.'[16] This may not have been its original location. Waller also gave the following inscription, recorded by Weales on 7 August 1775, when fragments were in the tower: '...ORD: QVO: RECTOR: HVIVS: ECCLES: .Q.I: OBIIT: SEXTO: DIE: M... '. A dabbing by Waller also survives in the main collection of rubbings of incised slabs in the Society of Antiquaries; it shows the middle portion of the slab with fragmentary remains of incising of a priest in mass vestments, with indents of a marginal inscription in Main Group size I brass letters between incised fillet

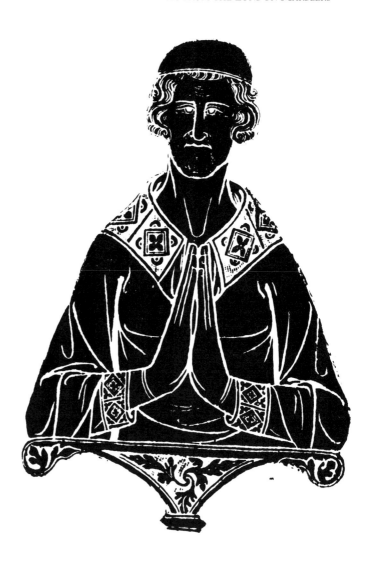

9.6 *Great Brington,*
    Northamptonshire:
    unknown priest,
    c 1310–40. Seymour-style
    brass. Rubbing by
    M W Norris.

strips. The inscription read: 'FORD: QVO .... OBIIT: SEXTO: DIE: M... '.

All that now remains of this slab are two fragments of Purbeck marble outside the south porch of the church. No trace of incising survives but both have worn indents of individual-inlay Lombardic lettering. The traces of lettering that survive fit with the inscription recorded by Weales and thus these fragments clearly form the bottom section of the slab that was concealed in 1837. The larger fragment was from the lower left-hand corner of the slab; the lettering reads: 'S: EC... /........IIT: .... / ... '. The second fragment is now too worn for the lettering to be deciphered. The fragments have been in this position since at least the 1940s, according to d'Elboux[17] and Greenhill. They both interpreted the second fragment as reading 'VIV'; it evidently formed the lower right-hand corner of the slab and the letters were part of the word 'HVIVS'. Greenhill's rubbing shows

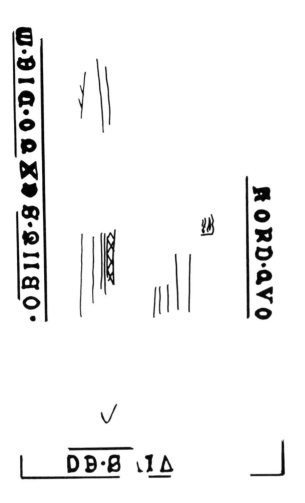

9.7 *West Wickham, Kent II:*
Walter de Cestreford,
ob 1344. Lost Seymour-
style incised slab. Tracing
from 1847 dabbing by
J Waller and 1947 rubbing
by F A Greenhill, both in
the Society of Antiquaries
collection, which show
different portions of the
slab.

that the larger fragment retained incising of part of a shoe with a
pointed toe. Waller's and Greenhill's rubbings can be pieced together
to show the bottom half of the slab (Figure 9.7).

The traces of incising on the Waller dabbing show the fringe of a
maniple on the extreme sinister side of the figure and, below what
would have been a relatively short chasuble, the diamond-patterned
dexter side of a long stole and the vertical drapery lines of the alb.
Such a representation is found on the Seymour-style priest of 1337 at
Higham Ferrers and the 1353 priest at Sparsholt, Berkshire,[18] which
is of London A style. The pointed toe is also consistent with Seymour
styling. Camoys priests, in contrast, have the maniple positioned
more to the centre, a longer chasuble that hid far more of the stole,
and rather more rounded shoes. The little surviving detail is therefore nonetheless sufficient to indicate a likely Seymour workshop
origin at a time consistent with the 1344 date of death.

SUMMARY

The three incised slabs discussed in this chapter all display characteristics of the Seymour style, but the parallels between the slabs and
the brasses are not as close as those discussed in previous chapters
on the Camoys and Septvans styles. There is also a greater disparity
in quality. The brasses, particularly those at Higham Ferrers and
Westley Waterless, are of a very high standard, to which the incised
slabs just do not match up. Indeed, some aspects of the draughts-
manship on the Rothwell slab verge on the incompetent. It is
difficult to explain why this might be so. Possibly, the more inexperienced marblers were given the cheaper commissions and the best
craftsmen concentrated on the more prestigious monuments.
Alternatively, it may be that the less competent brasses of the
Seymour style happen not to have survived. Or possibly the brasses
and incised slabs were made by different workmen operating in
separate businesses, but basing their products on the same
patterns.[19] Here, we can only speculate.

Our findings certainly suggest that the Seymour style may have
spanned a much longer period than previously thought. Since there
appear to have been incised slabs produced to these patterns as far
back as *c* 1309, why not brasses also? If this were so, it would
suggest that production overlapped with the Camoys/Septvans
workshop for some decades. After the Black Death there were
always two, and sometimes, three, brass-engraving workshops
operating in London at any one time.[20] We demonstrate in
Chapters 12 to 14 that there were two workshops working concurrently at the end of the thirteenth century and producing Purbeck
marble incised slabs and other monuments. John Blair has
suggested, on the basis of surviving documentary evidence, that in
the first half of the fourteenth century, Adam the Marbler, alias
Adam Laurenz, probably operated a virtual monopoly on the
Purbeck marble trade in London.[21] The dating of the Seymour-
style incised slabs, limited though the evidence is, casts some doubt
on this. Perhaps there was competition in the Purbeck tomb trade
in London in the first half of the fourteenth century also, with
another workshop or group of workshops producing brasses and
incised slabs to Seymour patterns from the first decade of the
century, though probably with a much smaller output than the
dominant Camoys/Septvans series workshop. Even after the
Camoys/Septvans workshop ceased production towards the end of
the 1330s, the Seymour workshop would not have held a monopoly
position for long, if it did at all, for the Hastings workshop
(discussed briefly in Chapter 5) was almost certainly operational in
the 1340s. We do not know for certain who headed the Seymour
firm, but it may be no coincidence that the Seymour series ended
shortly after the death of Richard de Sonyngdon, a known London
marbler, who (as we have already seen in Chapter 4) made two
bequests of marble gravestones in his will.

Chapter 10

Post-Seymour-style Brasses and Incised Slabs

INTRODUCTION

Binski's analysis of London figure brasses ended in the late 1340s with the cessation of the Seymour and Hastings styles. It has generally been thought that brass engraving suffered a hiatus during the Black Death and that large-scale workshop production did not begin again until the establishment in the mid-1350s of Kent's London Series A and a few years later with Series B.[1] However, current research suggests that Series A in fact began in the mid-1330s and Series B in the 1350s, though their main production until *c* 1360 was of minor compositions, notably demi-effigies, cross brasses and simple plate inscriptions.[2] Three Purbeck marble incised slabs date from this period, two of which are effigial and bear similarities to London Series A brasses, thus suggesting that they might have originated in the same workshop.

NEWNHAM, HAMPSHIRE

The first, at Newnham, Hampshire, is a portion of a whitewashed Purbeck marble slab, now positioned high on the north wall of the sanctuary, showing the bust of a priest in mass vestments under a simple canopy and with traces of a perimeter inscription within a fillet (Figure 10.1). It is remarkably like the London A brass to Henry de Grofhurst at Horsmonden, Kent, undated but probably *c* 1340 (Figure 10.2). The hair, eyes, 'double eyebrows', chin, shape of neck and odd outline of the Newnham priest are all exactly replicated on the Horsmonden brass. The amice, however, does not compare well with Horsmonden; the latter has it positioned much higher on the shoulders and the central drapery is very different. More satisfactory parallels for this feature are with the London A brasses to Richard de Beltoun at Corringham, Essex (Figure 10.3), and to Thomas de Hop, who died in 1346, at Kemsing in Kent (Figure 10.4), particularly the former, which has an identical drapery pattern. The Y-shaped orphrey, however, which appears on the Newnham slab, is shown on brasses only at Horsmonden, where the decoration is also identical. A date around 1340 is most probable for this slab, but as only one of the brasses is securely dated, a margin of ten years either way should be allowed.

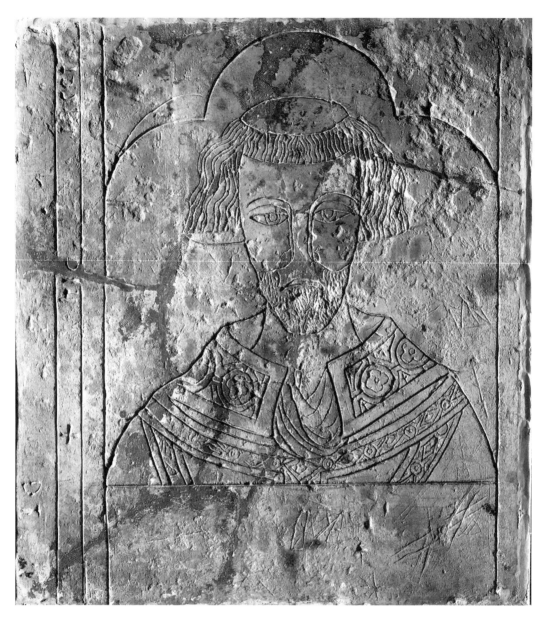

10.1 Newnham, Hampshire:
    unknown priest c 1340.
    London A incised slab.
    Photograph by
    A C Cooper Ltd.

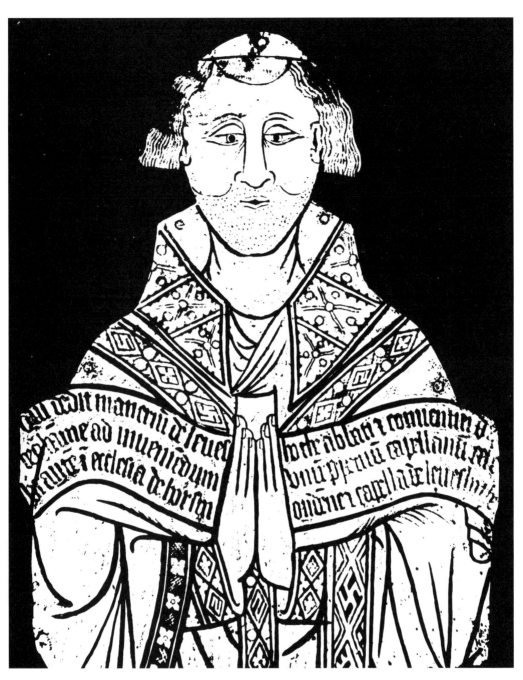

10.2 Horsmonden, Kent: Henry
de Grofhurst, c 1340.
London A brass. Detail of
rubbing by L A Smith.

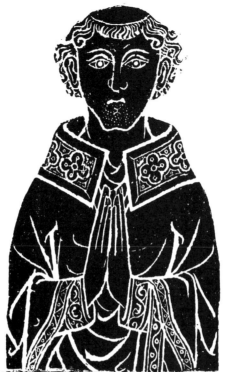

10.3 Corringham, Essex:
Richard de Beltoun,
c 1338–50. London A brass.
Rubbing by M W Norris.

WEST WICKHAM, KENT III

The third slab from the group at West Wickham, Kent, commemorates John de Huntingfeld, who was vicar there from 1361 to 1362. Situated under the carpet in the Leonard chapel on the north side of the church, it has been broken into fragments and repaired. The surface is very badly damaged and much of the incising is lost. Parts of a priest in mass vestments can be seen, but there is no trace of any inscription. A dabbing in the main collection of incised slab rubbings in the Society of Antiquaries of London, made by Waller in 1837, shows far more of the detail (see Figure 1.4) and a drawing by Fisher shows it in even better condition, with more of the inscription remaining (see Figure 1.3).[3] The slab had the incised demi-effigy of a priest in mass vestments with the maniple hanging 245mm below the bottom of the half effigy. The inscription was of incised majuscule letters comparable in size and style to Main Group size III type, a late use of this lettering, but not the only example from the 1360s. The inscription recorded in the drawing reads: 'H[IC]:] / [I]ACE[T: MAGISTER:] / [JOHN]: DE: / H[VN]TIGFELD: [R]ECT / O[R]'.

88

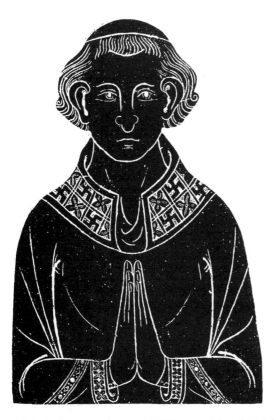

The parallels in brass are less straightforward for this slab than for the Newnham slab. Overall, the design of the figure is most like the Corringham brass, but similarities can also be drawn with Kemsing and other contemporary brasses. There are also lingering traces of Seymour influence. Huntingfeld's head has a wide jaw and a chisel-shaped chin, most strongly reminiscent of Corringham, though the neck cording is similar to that of the Seymour-style brasses and William de Herleston's London A brass of 1353 at Sparsholt, Berkshire, and related diminutive figures in crosses. The shape of the mouth and the half-moon beneath indicating the chin are again like Kemsing. Only part of one ear remains, but it best compares with the Corringham and Kemsing brasses. The traces of hair are very distinctive: it is very short, finishing above the level of the earlobe; there is a springy curl above the ear and straightish strands standing out from the ear, similar to the styling of the hair at Corringham. The shape of the amice most closely resembles Kemsing, but the decoration is of small quatrefoils; the central folds no longer remain clear. The hands are held in prayer and end halfway up the amice, as at Corringham and Higham Ferrers. The loop of drapery across the

10.4 Kemsing, Kent: Thomas de Hop, ob 1346. London A brass. Rubbing by H M Stuchfield.

breast, the shape of the arms and the arm drapery are all closest to the treatment of the Corringham brass.

SOUTHWARK CATHEDRAL, SURREY II

Finally, in the retrochoir of Southwark Cathedral, Surrey, is the upper half of a Purbeck marble coffin-shaped slab with an incised perimeter inscription in Lombardic letters (Figure 10.5). The perimeter inscription reads: '+ [ALEI] / [N] FERTHI[N]G GIS[T] .... / ..... / .... EIT MERC[I A] / [M]EN'. Unlike the other slabs discussed in this monograph, the words are not separated by stops. The lettering bears a resemblance to Main Group brass lettering, but can be readily distinguished from it. The slab was brought to Southwark Cathedral from the site of St Margaret, Southwark, in 1833.[4] Alein Ferthing lived in Southwark,[5] was six times an MP and is thought to have died in the Black Death in 1349.[6]

10.5 Southwark Cathedral, Surrey II: Alein Ferthing, ob 1349. Incised slab. Tracing of rubbing by S F Badham.

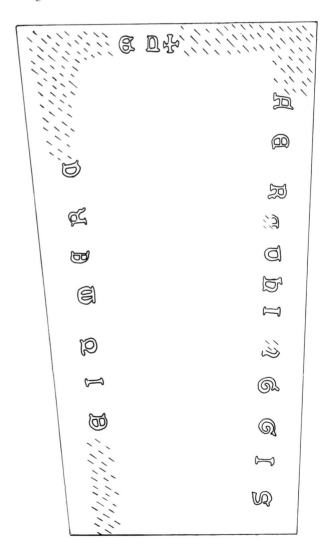

CHAPTER 11

UNCLASSIFIED FOURTEENTH-CENTURY PURBECK MARBLE INCISED SLABS

INTRODUCTION

In addition to the incised slabs discussed in the previous four chapters, there are fourteen slabs of likely fourteenth-century date which may be from the London workshops, but cannot be assigned specifically to one of the established pattern series. Five include effigies and the other eight have incised inscriptions.

STROOD, KENT

The fine incised slab to Mariote and John Creye once at Strood, Kent, was almost certainly destroyed when the church was rebuilt in 1812.[1] Fortunately drawings of it survive in the Fisher[2] and Gough[3] collections (Figures 11.1 and 11.2). These show the full-length incised figure of a lady under a simple gable arch, above which are two large cinquefoils, possibly indicating foreign influence on the design. Mariote Creye is dressed in a kirtle and surcoat with a cloak, the folds of which are caught up in the crook of her right arm. Her head is covered by a veil and a wimple envelops her neck. She rests her head on a cushion, placed crosswise and decorated with a pattern of quatrefoils. Round the perimeter of the slab is an inscription that was formerly inlaid in brass letters, which appear to have been of Main Group type, bordered by a pair of fillets which may also have been of brass. The inscription reads: '+ KI: PV / R: LALME: MARIOTE: E: IOHAN: / CREYE: PRIER: / A: CIS: VINT: IVRS: DE: PAR: DVN / AVERA'.

A number of features suggest that this slab probably came from the London brass-engraving workshops, though the evidence is not sufficiently conclusive to enable us to assign the slab to any identified group. The inscription was probably of brass Main Group letters, but these were supplied to workshops both in London and in the provinces. The use of Norman-French for the inscription is more usual at an early date and the format of the

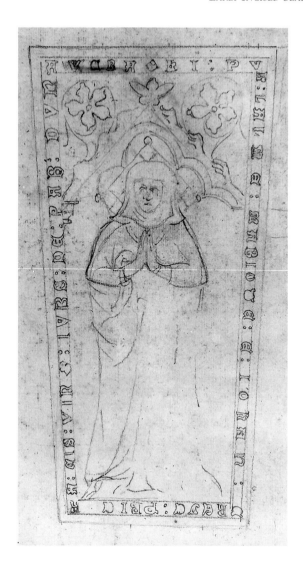

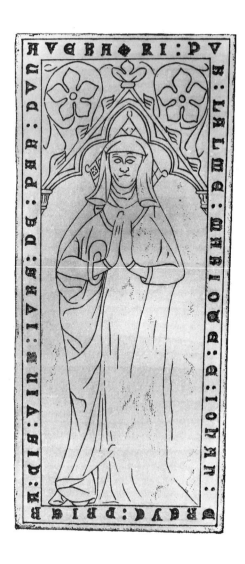

11.1 (above) Strood, Kent: Mariote and John Creye, c 1320–35. Lost incised slab with indents for brass letters. Drawing for R Gough, Bodleian Library, Oxford, Gough Maps 226, fol 240v. Photograph Bodleian Library.

11.2 (above, right) Strood, Kent: Mariote and John Creye, c 1320–35. Lost incised slab with indents for brass letters. Drawing by T Fisher, Society of Antiquaries, 'Kent Illustrations: Prints and Drawings' collection, 3, fol 42.

initial cross, double stops and bordering fillets is common on Camoys- and Septvans-style brasses. The gable arch is not unlike that on the brass to Joan de Cobham, though it lacks the pinnacles at the sides. The use of a cushion to support the head cannot be paralleled on any early London brass or indent, although a pair of cushions is shown on the Ashford series incised slab at Tilsworth, Bedfordshire (discussed in Chapter 13). Although a Camoys origin cannot be ruled out, this slab may equally have come from another London workshop.

HARROW, MIDDLESEX

Part of another Purbeck marble incised slab of possible London origin forms the doorstep to the parvise at Harrow, Middlesex.

92

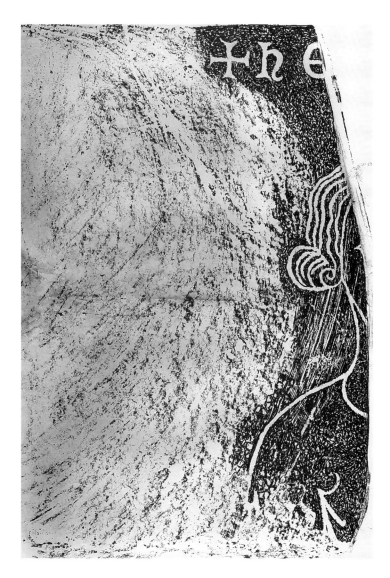

11.3 Harrow, Middlesex: unknown civilian c 1340. Incised slab. Rubbing by F A Greenhill, Society of Antiquaries collection, photograph by A C Cooper Ltd.

Some of this slab is now obscured by pipework, though fortunately Greenhill rubbed it before this was installed (Figure 11.3). His rubbing shows part of the head and right shoulder of a man in civil dress. He wears his hair long; it waves gently as it falls and ends with a large roll on the shoulders. The slab once had a perimeter inscription in incised Lombardic lettering. All that remains is 'HE', possibly the beginning of Henricus. What remains of this slab seems rather different in style from any surviving brasses, suggesting a separate workshop origin.

WIMBORNE MINSTER, DORSET

However, the Harrow slab appears to be related to a Purbeck marble slab at Wimborne Minster, Dorset, now on the floor in the

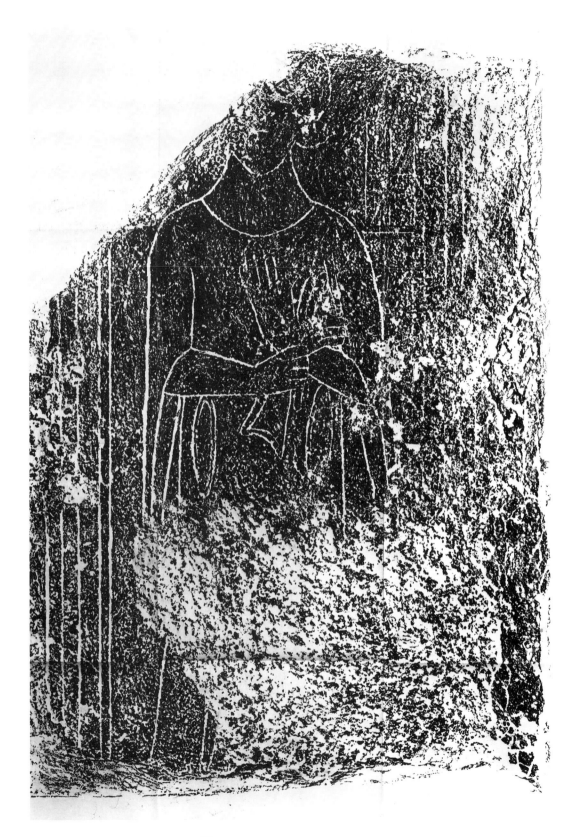

south-west corner of the west tower.[4] Only the middle section now survives and that has lost much of its top surface (Figure 11.4), though virtually the entire slab remained in the late eighteenth century, when drawings of it were made for Gough and Hutchins (Figure 11.5).[5] It depicted a man in a long robe with hanging sleeves, holding a pair of gloves. The pose suggests French influence, being reminiscent of slabs such as that to Conte Chase-Conée, *ob* 1303, at Arpajon, Essone, France.[6] The drawing of the hair, chin, neck and neckline are the same on both the Wimborne slab and that at Harrow. The Wimborne figure stands under a canopy of singular design, with fleur-de-lis on the pinnacles and at the apex. There were heraldic banners on either side of the figure and two shields above the canopy. The arms on the dexter side are *a cross between four crosslets*, and on the sinister side *1 and 4 fretty, 2 and 3 per bend sinister* with the tinctures unknown. Hutchins ascribed the latter coat to Despenser, though, if he is correct in this, the craftsman must have inadvertently reversed the arms, since the fret should be 2 and 3 for Despenser. The arms on the dexter banner are unknown, but might have been intended to represent Jerusalem.[7]

There is no inscription on the slab and the identity of the person commemorated is unknown. One suggestion that has been made is that as the slab originally lay in the part of the south transept known as the Bembre Chantry, it commemorates Dean Thomas de Bembre, who died in 1361. Hutchins pointed out that the arms of Bembre are very different from either coat shown on the slab and suggested instead that it was for Dean John de Berwick, who died in 1312, but this too can be discounted. A civilian, not a cleric, is clearly represented and the dress suggests a later date. The hanging sleeves are not often encountered before the 1340s, though the loose cut of the robe points to a slightly earlier date.

SALISBURY CATHEDRAL, WILTSHIRE

At the west end of the nave of Salisbury Cathedral, Wiltshire, is a virtually effaced Purbeck marble incised slab to a priest in mass vestments under a canopy.[8] Round the perimeter of the slab is an inscription in incised Lombardic lettering. The letters 'HIC IAC' remained when Greenhill saw it earlier this century, but only the slightest traces of individual letters now remain. Insufficient detail survives for stylistic comparison, but the composition suggests a London origin.

ELSING, NORFOLK

Beneath the altar table in the sanctuary at Elsing, Norfolk, is a slab with indents of two shields and, between a pair of fillets, a perimeter inscription formerly inlaid in brass Lombardic letters,

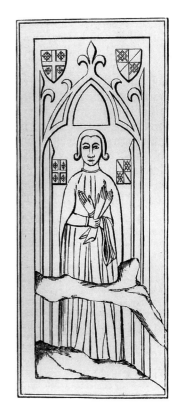

11.4 (opposite) Wimborne Minster, Dorset: unknown civilian c 1330–40. Incised slab. Rubbing by F A Greenhill, Society of Antiquaries collection, photograph by A C Cooper Ltd.

11.5 (above) Wimborne Minster, Dorset: unknown civilian c 1330–40. Incised slab. Drawing from J Hutchins, The History and Antiquities of the County of Dorset (1796–1815, 2nd edn) 3, 205.

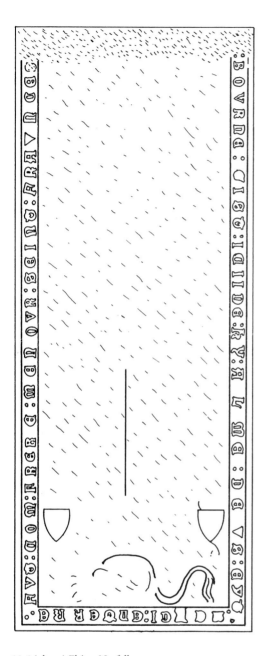 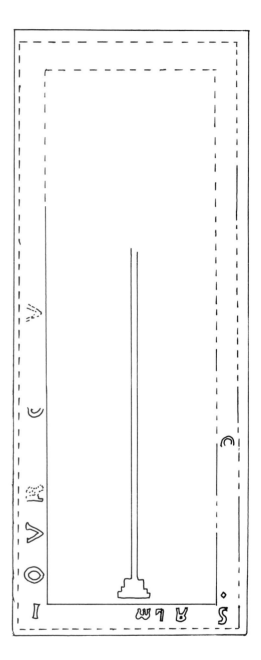

11.6 (above) Elsing, Norfolk: ... bourne, c 1310–50. Incised slab with indents for brass letters. Reconstruction by W J Blair.

11.7 (above, right) Christ Church Cathedral, Oxford: Edmund de Ludlow, ob after 1327. Incised slab with indents for brass letters. Drawing by J F A Bertram.

mostly of Main Group size II, but intermixed with some size I and size III letters. The letters are irregularly spaced and some are poorly aligned. The inscription reads: '.... / ..: BOVRNE: GIST: ICII DE: KY: ALME: DEUS: EYT / : MERCI: ENTERRE: / FVT: COM: FRERE: MENOVR: SEINT: FRAVNCES.. / ...... '. Although no traces of incising now remain, an 1864 woodcut shows the remains of an incised beast, probably a lion, at the foot of the slab and a long vertical line above it (Figure 11.6).[9] The latter has been interpreted variously as being the stem of a cross or the drapery lines of a figure; in view of the cramped spacing of the shields, a figure is perhaps more probable. This slab may have come from the main London workshop, but the mixture of letter sizes and the uneven setting-out of the inscription suggest that a minor workshop origin may be more likely.

CHRIST CHURCH CATHEDRAL, OXFORD

The remaining five unclassified Purbeck marble slabs are simpler compositions. In the Lady Chapel of Christ Church Cathedral, Oxford, is a rectangular slab of Purbeck marble with very worn traces of the indents of a perimeter inscription in irregularly spaced Main Group brass letters, bordered by a pair of incised lines (Figure 11.7). In the centre is a stem and stepped calvary of an incised cross. Research by Bertram, based on the church notes of Antony Wood, has shown that this slab commemorates Edmund de Ludlow, whom Wood describes as having been Rector of Beckley in the time of Edward III.[10] He was presented as Rector in 1318, but it is not known when he vacated the living, though it was vacant in 1351.[11]

ST BARTHOLOMEW THE GREAT, LONDON, IV AND V

Next to be considered are three fragments with inscriptions which are virtually indistinguishable in shape and size from indents for Main Group brass letters. The main difference between indents and these incised letters is the profile; indents have straight sides and wide flat bottoms, whereas the incisions forming incised letters approximate more closely to a V-shape. Additionally, some of the letter shapes differ. These incised inscriptions contrast sharply with the more usual type of incised inscription with thin, rather spindly letters, such as those of the Basyng and Ashford series (discussed in Chapters 12 and 13).

Greenhill recorded two fragments of incised lettering loose in the cloisters of St Bartholomew the Great, London. Neither now survives. They are similar, except that the lettering on them is of different sizes, showing that they are probably not part of one monument. The first, with letters which are virtually indistin-guishable from Main Group size I lettering, and with double stops separating the words, read: '[M]INHELE: SA: FE[ME]' (Figure 11.8). It is possible that this might have formed part of the Camoys series incised slab with the demi-effigy of a lady (discussed in Chapter 7), but the difference between the lettering on this fragment and that on other Camoys-style incised slabs with inscriptions makes this unlikely. The second fragment at St Bartholomew the Great has lettering similar to Main Group size II lettering, with the words again separated by double stops (Figure 11.9). It read: 'T: GISVC'.

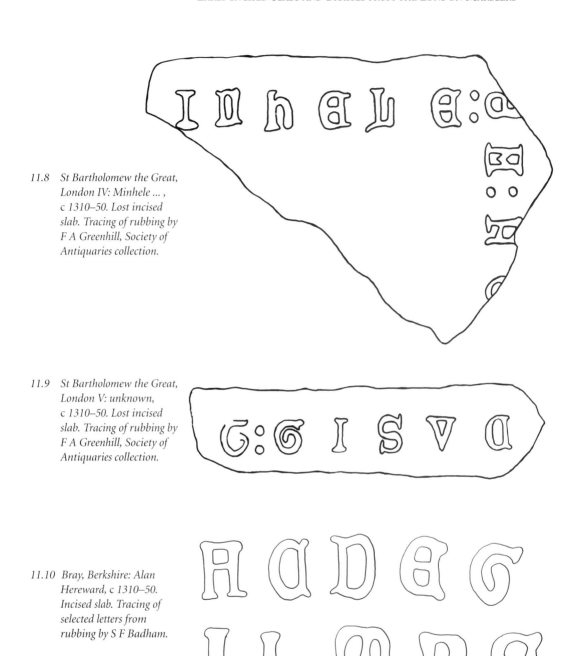

11.8   St Bartholomew the Great,
       London IV: Minhele ... ,
       c 1310–50. Lost incised
       slab. Tracing of rubbing by
       F A Greenhill, Society of
       Antiquaries collection.

11.9   St Bartholomew the Great,
       London V: unknown,
       c 1310–50. Lost incised
       slab. Tracing of rubbing by
       F A Greenhill, Society of
       Antiquaries collection.

11.10 Bray, Berkshire: Alan
       Hereward, c 1310–50.
       Incised slab. Tracing of
       selected letters from
       rubbing by S F Badham.

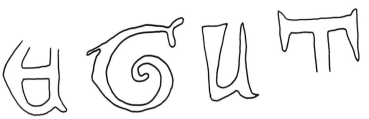

11.11 Great Bookham, Surrey I: possibly for John de Pollesdene, ob before 1335. Incised slab. Tracing of selected letters from rubbing by W J Blair.

BRAY, BERKSHIRE

At the west end of the south aisle at Bray, Berkshire, is a worn rectangular slab with traces of a perimeter inscription in Lombardic lettering, the words separated by single stops (Figure 11.10). This slab has previously been classified as an indent with letters of the Main Group script,[12] but close inspection reveals that it is an incised slab. The surviving traces read: '+ [A]LA / N˙ HE[R]EWARD˙ GIST˙ I / CI˙ D[I]EV˙ DE / ˙ [SA˙] ALME .... ˙ A / MEN'. Nothing can be traced of Alan Hereward.

GREAT BOOKHAM I AND SOUTHWARK CATHEDRAL I, SURREY

Built horizontally into the northern buttress supporting the west wall of the tower at Great Bookham, Surrey, is a rectangular slab of Purbeck marble. Only two edges, with their double hollow-moulded chamfers, of which no other example on a rectangular Purbeck marble slab is known to us, can now be seen. However, the outer margins of the upper surface were excavated by John Blair in 1970 to reveal an incised perimeter inscription in Lombardic lettering (Figure 11.11).[13] The portion of lettering that could be uncovered read: ''DE˙ P[OL]LESDENE˙ / GIST /'. The words were separated by only single stops and the letters themselves were of a type only paralleled on a fragment recently recorded in the roof at Southwark Cathedral. The centre of the Bookham slab could not be examined; there appeared not to be room for a figure, though there might have been a cross. The monument is difficult to date, though the use of a rectangular slab most usually suggests a fourteenth-century date. It is uncertain which member of the de Pollesdene family was commemorated, though Blair suggested as the most likely candidate John de Pollesdene, who died before 1335.

EGHAM AND GREAT BOOKHAM II, SURREY

Finally, at Great Bookham and Egham,[14] both in Surrey, are two incised inscriptions, executed in the same distinctive lettering style and both of outstanding quality (Figures 11.12 and 11.13). Neither is strictly monumental; they both commemorate the building of a

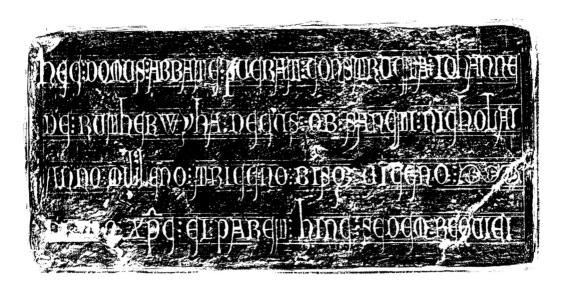

11.12 (above, top) Great Bookham, Surrey II: commemoration of building of chancel by Abbot Rutherwyke in 1341. Incised slab. Rubbing by F A Greenhill, Society of Antiquaries collection, photograph by A C Cooper Ltd.

11.13 (above, bottom) Egham, Surrey: commemoration of building of chancel by Abbot Rutherwyke in 1327. Incised slab. Photograph by N E Saul.

chancel by Abbot Rutherwyke of Chertsey. The Egham slab is dated 1327 and the Great Bookham slab 1341. Though they may have been made by the Chertsey masons, rather than the London marblers, they are of sufficient interest to merit a mention here.[15]

CHAPTER 12

BASYNG-STYLE INCISED SLABS

INTRODUCTION

Having discussed the London-made Purbeck marble incised slabs from the fourteenth century, the period examined in detail in *The Earliest English Brasses*, we turn to the newly identified pattern series produced in the period when the marblers first operated in London. Blair's and Binski's research suggested that though brasses began to be made in London from the 1290s, few indents and no extant brasses can be dated to the thirteenth century. However, we have identified two series of London-made Purbeck marble incised slabs that appear to date from the thirteenth century, with a total of thirty-four slabs belonging to these pattern series. In addition, we provide new evidence to redate some brasses to the thirteenth century.

The smaller group of thirteenth-century incised slabs, with which we deal in this chapter, we have termed the Basyng series after the slab to Prior Basyng in Winchester Cathedral, Hampshire, the earliest datable effigial slab in this series. There are thirteen slabs in the series, all of them coffin-shaped. Unfortunately, only three are dated; they span the period 1289 to 1295. None of the Basyng series slabs has any brass inlay and stylistic links with brasses are very limited; if there were brasses that came from the same marblers' workshop, with one possible exception we are not aware of their survival. The vast majority of the fourteenth-century incised slabs we have discussed in previous chapters are effigial; consequently, the stylistic features which have been used to identify the pattern series have been mainly facial features, drapery style and the like, with the form of the letters used having relatively little diagnostic significance. In contrast, only two of the slabs in the Basyng series include a representation of part of a figure and it is incised inscriptions which are critical in identifying products belonging to this series and in distinguishing them from the partly coeval Ashford series products (discussed in Chapter 13) and from other slabs of similar appearance. The latter include incised slabs in Bethersden marble, such as the early fourteenth-century inscription slab under the altar table at Bidborough, Kent, which has more elaborate letter forms.

There is a superficial disparity between different examples of Basyng-style inscriptions, but this is because the setting-out of some inscriptions is much less competent than on other examples. Six of the inscriptions are incised on a hollow-moulded chamfer, which must have been technically more difficult than working on

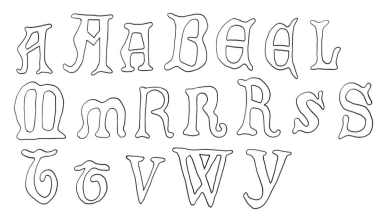

12.1 Letter forms on Basyng-style slabs.

a flat surface. Most of the chamfer inscriptions show notable variation in the size of letters and in their alignment. Particularly where the inscription is a long one, the letters are cramped together, becoming even more so towards the end of the inscription. A further seven examples where the inscription is incised on the upper face of the coffin lid appear much more competent, with letters evenly spaced out and of equal size.

Of more importance diagnostically than the overall appearance of the inscription are the individual letter forms; these provide the link between the different Basyng series products. The most useful letters for analysis are the A, B, E, M and R, all shown in Figure 12.1. The A has a kinked leading leg, ending in a curl, the upper stroke is flat or very slightly curved and the crossbar is usually sharply angled, though sometimes a chevron crossbar is used instead. The B and R are of a 'closed' form, with the curved strokes touching the centre of the downstroke; the R ends in a curl. On the E, the downstroke on the right-hand side of the letter is prominent, standing at least as high as the rest of the letter. Finally, on the M, the three downstrokes all approximate fairly closely to the vertical, with relatively little angling of the outer two strokes. In all these cases, the letter shapes are different from those employed in the Ashford series. Additionally, many inscriptions on Basyng series slabs show two letters joined in a ligature; this is a feature found only rarely on Ashford or Camoys series slabs.

WINCHESTER CATHEDRAL, HAMPSHIRE I

At Winchester Cathedral, Hampshire, is a slab to William de Basyng, Prior of St Swithun's, who died in 1295 (Figure 12.2). It was moved to its present position in the retrochoir from the south transept in the early nineteenth century. The monument consists of a coffin-shaped slab with an inscription in two lines round three of the sides of the double hollow-moulded chamfered edges of the slab. The main feature of the design is an incised open-headed cross botonnée, with curious cinquefoil terminals. The stem is broken by foliations and ends in a stepped calvary. Above the cross is the head

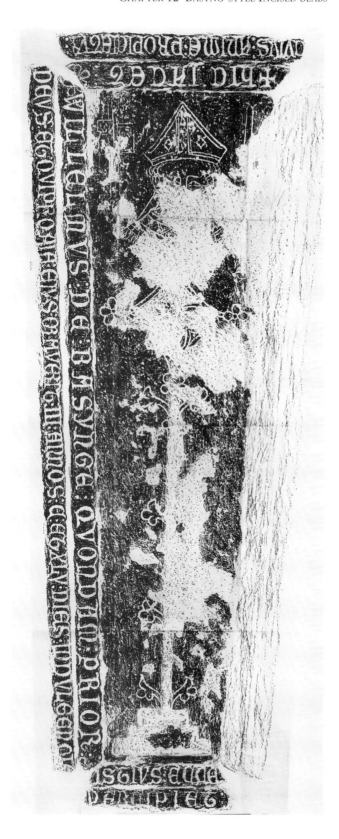

12.2 Winchester Cathedral, Hampshire I: Prior William de Basyng, ob 1295. Basyng-style incised slab. Rubbing by F A Greenhill, Society of Antiquaries collection, photograph by A C Cooper Ltd.

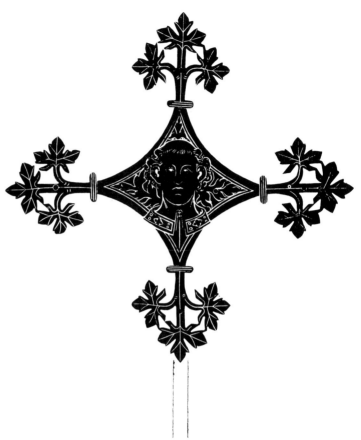

12.3 Chinnor, Oxfordshire: unknown priest c 1290–1300. Possible Basyng-style brass. Rubbing by M W Norris.

of a mitred prior, with a pair of keys to the left and a sword to the right, devices representing St Peter and St Paul, reflecting the main dedication of the Cathedral Priory.

The inscription on the chamfer is incised in Lombardic lettering in the distinctive script of the Basyng series slabs, with the words separated by triple stops. The inscription takes up both chamfers, beginning on the inner order and continuing on the outer. Other Basyng series slabs mirror this arrangement, though it is more common amongst incised slabs generally for perimeter inscriptions in two lines to have the continuation line inside the first line. The letters themselves are boldly cut, but the inscription was not well planned, with insufficient text being placed on the first line; consequently, the letters on the second line are crammed very close together. Since the inscription takes up only three sides of the slab, it clearly once rested with its sinister side against a wall; thus the inscription naturally runs in an anti-clockwise direction. It reads: '+ HIC: IACET: / WILLELMVS: DE: BASYNGE: QVONDAM: PRIOR: / ISTIVS: ECCE / CVIVS: ANIME: PROPICIETVR: / DEVS: ET: QVI PRO: AIA: EIVS: ORAVERIT: III: ANNOS: C: ET: XLV: DIES: INDVLGENCIE: / [P]ERCIPIET:'.

The top surface of this slab is now in very poor condition, with much of the surface detail lost. A dabbing in the main collection of incised slab rubbings in the Society of Antiquaries made by Waller, probably in the second quarter of the nineteenth century, shows slightly more detail than currently survives, but the best indication of its original state is provided by drawings made in 1786 by Carter.[1] Although the facial features are badly defaced, one eye and eyebrow remain clear. The eye is narrow, with the lower eyelid drawn as a long, dead straight line. The lid is depicted by only one line. The angle between the nose and the eyebrow is acute, with the eyebrow appearing to arch upwards and outwards. The curls of hair spring from the temples, with large ears showing beneath. The amice is unusually narrow. In many respects the detailed design of the prior's head appears most closely related to the head of a priest enclosed in a rare survival of a cross brass at Chinnor, Oxfordshire (Figure 12.3). This comparison suggests that the traditional date of *c* 1320 for the Chinnor brass may be up to a quarter of a century too late. This brass appears to have had a fillet inscription, usually regarded as an indicator of relatively late date, but it should be remembered that the Cantilupe brass at Hereford, which (as explained in Chapter 5) cannot be later than 1287, also had this type of inscription. The Chinnor cross appears to belong to the main series of brass-inlay crossheads with clustered ivy-leaf terminals which John Blair suggests first appeared *c* 1305; possibly it was one of the earliest products of this series.

The overall composition of the Winchester slab can be paralleled on only one other Purbeck marble incised slab, also from the Basyng series, though (as mentioned in Chapter 5) a bust above or superimposed upon a crosshead is a combination commonly found on London brasses believed by Blair to date from the period 1305 to 1335. The shape of the crosshead on the Winchester slab is often found on brasses, indents and cross slabs of this period, though the terminals are different. Indeed, if the cinquefoil terminals and the head, key and sword are discounted, this coffin-shaped cross slab with a double hollow-moulded chamfer is a common type, found across much of southern England.

ROMSEY, HAMPSHIRE

Close to the south porch of Romsey Abbey, Hampshire, on the floor of the south aisle, is a coffin-shaped Purbeck marble slab with a double hollow-moulded chamfer and, on the top face, worn traces of incising of letters round the perimeter and a few lines in the centre (Figure 12.4). Although the head end of the slab is rather battered, the presence of the chamfer shows that the full extent of the slab survives, with only a small section of the top surface broken away. An early nineteenth-century sketch from the Broadlands collection, published by Liveing, shows more of the original composition (Figure 12.5).[2] Round the perimeter of the slab was an inscription in incised Lombardic lettering, the words separated by triple stops. It read: '... / .. IOHANNA: HIC: IACET: HVMATA: / IPS / IVS: ANIME: CRISTVS: DET: PREMI.. / .. '. The traces that remain show that the letter shapes are of the Basyng-style script, albeit with fewer curls and flourishes than on the slab to Prior Basyng. The remainder of the incised design is far more unusual. The sketch, which is probably fairly reliable, shows a female figure, possibly with her feet on an animal, with the stem of a cross on top of her. The stem is broken by foliations, of the same design as those of Prior Basyng's slab. The head of the cross is unclear, though the uppermost foliations on the sketch may in fact be the lower half of a small open-headed cross botonnée, which perhaps framed the woman's head.[3]

This combination of a figure with a cross superimposed upon it is very unusual, but not unique. We know of three monuments, none of which are of Purbeck marble or seem in any way directly related to the Basyng series, featuring such a design. The closest is a damaged incised slab at Tullylease, County Cork, Ireland, which shows a figure of uncertain gender with a superimposed cross running from the breast to the feet.[4] Second, at Preston Gubbals, Shropshire, is a slab with a sunk panel which contains, under a crocketed ogival gable arch, the bust of a man with a foliated cross on his breast.[5] His identity is unknown but the ogival arch suggests a date not earlier than the beginning of the fourteenth century. Third, at Penshurst, Kent, there is the upper portion of a coffin-shaped slab of likely late thirteenth-century date, which was excavated in 1854

12.4 (right) Romsey, Hampshire: Johanna ..., c 1290–1300. Basyng-style incised slab. Tracing of rubbing by S F Badham.

12.5 (far right) Romsey, Hampshire: Johanna ..., c 1290–1300. Basyng-style incised slab. Drawing from H Liveing, Records of Romsey Abbey (Winchester, 1906), 120.

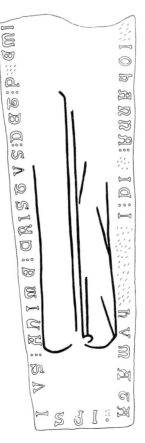

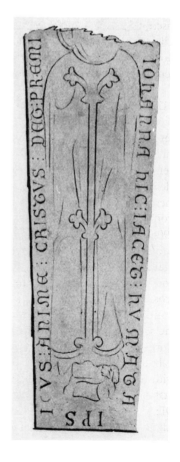

during the rebuilding of the church.[6] It shows in low relief a cross superimposed on the image of a lady in a sideways-turned pose, with her hands uplifted in prayer. Rogers has suggested, very plausibly, that this depiction represents the deceased bursting from her coffin at the moment of the Resurrection and that similar resurrection imagery may be intended on the many other coffin-shaped slabs which show demi-effigies.[7] Possibly such resurrection imagery was also intended in the case of the Winchester and Romsey slabs.

Regrettably, we do not know whom the Romsey slab commemorated. An added inscription, possibly of eighteenth-century date, across the centre of the slab records the slab as commemorating Johanna Icthe, who was Abbess of Romsey from 1333 to 1349. Spence therefore suggested that the inscription originally began '+ ABBESS: IOHANNA: ... '.[8] Why the possibility of the slab commemorating the next abbess, Johanna Gerveys, who died in 1352, is discounted is far from clear. However, we believe neither is a credible candidate for this slab. The use of a style of lettering confined to slabs in the Basyng series suggests that this slab dates from the closing years of the thirteenth century, not the mid-fourteenth century. Moreover, normally in an inscription of this period, the name of the person commemorated is given before his or her position of office, as we have already seen in the case of Prior Basyng's slab at Winchester. We have no alternative suggestion to offer as to the identity of Johanna. At this date a Latin inscription usually indicates the commemoration of a member of a religious community, with the laity having French inscriptions instead. However, the possibility that the Romsey slab commemorates a lay benefactor of Romsey Abbey cannot be ruled out.

DUNSTABLE, BEDFORDSHIRE

Seven more Basyng series slabs combine inscriptions with relief or incised crosses. Although in all cases at least part of the name of the person commemorated survives, in only two cases can a clear identification be made and a date of death provided. The first of these datable slabs is in Dunstable Priory, Bedfordshire. Excavated from the foundations of the south-west buttress of the church in 1906, it was not moved inside the church until 1932 and suffered considerably from weathering in the meantime.[9] It now rests against the wall at the east end of the south aisle and is in a very poor state of preservation. The top was originally decorated with a cross in relief, though all traces of this have long gone. It has a double hollow-moulded chamfer, on both orders of which is incised an inscription in the distinctive Basyng script, with the words separated by double stops. As with the Winchester Cathedral slab, the first line of the inscription was incised on the inner order, with the continuation line on the outer order. When the slab was first excavated the inscription read: '... ALIZ: DVRAVNT: ICI: GIT: DE: LY: EIT: MERCI: K..... / ...IE: WS: PRI: CAR: PATER: NOSTRE: KI: DIRA: Q... ', though all of the first line and some of the second

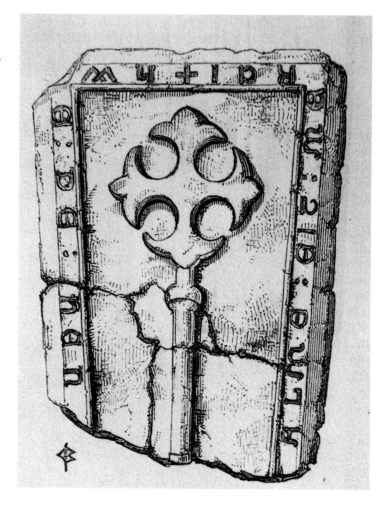

12.6 Dunstable, Bedfordshire I: Alice Duraunt, ob 1289. Basyng-style slab with relief cross and incised letters. Tracing of rubbing by S F Badham of detail showing surviving lettering.

have since been effaced (Figure 12.6). Alice was the wife of John Duraunt, a benefactor of Dunstable Priory. She died in 1289 and was given a lavish funeral by John.[10] One of her sons, Richard, was also buried in Dunstable Priory and was commemorated by an Ashford-style incised slab (discussed in Chapter 13).

ST BARTHOLOMEW THE GREAT, LONDON I

The second datable Basyng-style incised slab was found in 1843 at St Bartholomew the Great, London, and was later in the possession of W Chafters, but has since been lost.[11] Drawings by Boutell and Webb show the upper half of a coffin-shaped slab, which Webb describes as being of Purbeck marble, with a relief cross with fleur-de-lis terminals (Figure 12.7). The inner order of the double

12.7 St Bartholomew the Great, London I: Prior Hugh de Hendon, ob 1295. Lost Basyng-style slab with relief cross and incised letters. Drawing from C Boutell, Christian Monuments in England and Wales (London, 1854), 38.

hollow-moulded chamfer held an incised inscription which, judging from the drawings of it, was probably in the distinctive Basyng script. The words were separated by double stops. Rather unusually, the inscription ran anti-clockwise. It read: '+ HW / E: DE: HEN[DON: GIST: ICI: DIEV: DE: SA:] ALME: EIT: ME / RCI'. It undoubtedly commemorated Hugh de Hendon, Prior of St Bartholomew's, who died in 1295.[12]

ST CROSS, WINCHESTER, HAMPSHIRE

On the north side of the sanctuary in the chapel of St Cross Hospital, Winchester, Hampshire, is a diminutive Basyng series cross slab (Figure 12.8); its small size suggests that it was for a heart burial or marked the grave of a child. The slab is unchamfered and set flush with the floor. Though it has the stem and calvary of a cross in relief, the head has been worn completely flat. The incised Basyng style inscription appears to run down the two long sides of the slab, on either side of the cross. The words are separated by triple stops. The portions that survive read '... [PET]RVNELE: LA: FY / SIRE: IOHAN: DE: [?L] ...' (Figure 12.9). Had a little more of the name survived, it might have proved possible to identify the person commemorated.

SOUTH BENFLEET, ESSEX

The same problem arises with the Basyng-style cross slab at South Benfleet, Essex.[13] Now mural at the west end of the south aisle, it was previously at the east end of the nave.[14] Though it is limewashed, there can be little doubt that the slab is of Purbeck marble. Only the upper portion survives and that is damaged, but the main features are clear. It has a double hollow-moulded chamfer, but all the decoration is on the top face of the slab. This consists of a relief cross botonnée, a standard Purbeck type, with an incised Basyng-style inscription, which starts at the top dexter corner of the slab and runs round the perimeter (Figure 12.10). Where stops are shown, they are of the double variety. Although the lettering is well set out, the overall design is less well planned, for the finials of the cross protrude into the area occupied by the inscription. The top surface of the slab is damaged and part of the inscription is now unclear; however, more of it is preserved in a rubbing now held in the Hollytrees Museum, Colchester.[15] It reads: '+ ICI GI[T] / MARCELIE: PR... '. Unfortunately, this again provides insufficient information for an identification of the person commemorated by the slab.

ST BARTHOLOMEW THE GREAT, LONDON II

In 1930 Greenhill recorded a fragment, now lost, of an incised slab with a trefoil-ended foot of a cross on a low tomb in the cloister of St Bartholomew the Great, London (Figure 12.11). Though there is no record of the type of stone used for this slab, the likelihood is

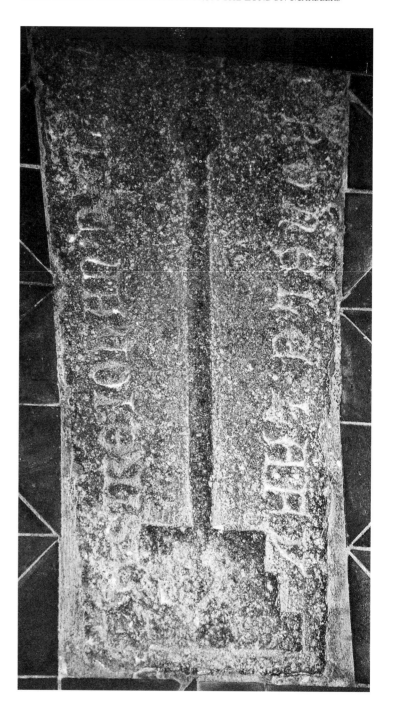

12.8 St Cross, Winchester, Hampshire: Petrunele ..., c 1290–1300. Basyng-style slab with relief cross and incised letters. Photograph by S F Badham.

12.9 St Cross, Winchester, Hampshire: Petrunele ..., c 1290–1300. Basyng-style slab with relief cross and incised letters. Tracing of rubbing by S F Badham of detail showing surviving lettering.

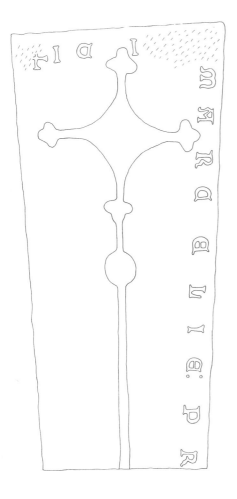

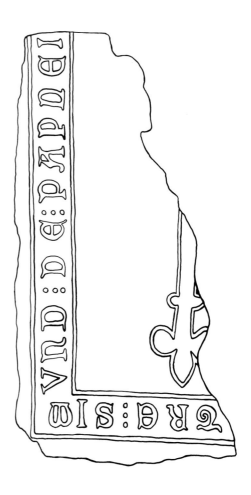

that it was Purbeck marble. Round the perimeter was a very competent incised inscription, the words separated by triple stops. Most of the letters look to be particularly well-executed examples of the Basyng script, though curiously the M is drawn in a manner more usually associated with the Ashford series slabs (discussed in Chapter 13). Unlike all the other examples assigned to the Basyng series, this inscription is bordered by a pair of incised fillets, a feature associated by Binski with fourteenth-century dating.[16] Possibly this was one of the latest examples of the series, but though the name of the person commemorated by this fragment is known, no trace of him has been found in documentary sources. The surviving section of the inscription reads: '...TRE: SIM / VND: DE: PAPNEI'. The first few letters of the inscription were probably part of MESTRE, suggesting that the person commemorated was a graduate of one of the universities, though his name does not appear in either of the biographical dictionaries of graduates of Oxford or Cambridge; nor can he be traced in any document relating to St Bartholomew's.

12.10 (above, left) South Benfleet, Essex: Marcelie Pr..., c 1290–1300. *Basyng-style slab with relief cross and incised letters. Tracing from rubbing by H M Stuchfield.*

12.11 (above, right) St Bartholomew the Great, London II: Simon de Papnei, c 1290–1300. *Basyng-style incised slab. Tracing from rubbing by F A Greenhill, Society of Antiquaries collection.*

WHERWELL, HAMPSHIRE

Loose on a stone bench at the west end of the north aisle at Wherwell, Hampshire, is the battered remains of the lower part of a Purbeck marble coffin-shaped slab with a double hollow-moulded chamfer.[17] The top face of the slab is in very poor condition, though a very small fragment of the stem of a relief cross can just be detected. The chamfer held an incised inscription, which began on the inner order and continued around three sides of the outer order (Figure 12.12). The surviving lettering on the inner order reads: '... [M]VLIERIBVS: ET: BENE / DICTVS: / FRVCTVS: V[ENTRIS] ... '. Little remains of the lettering on the outer order; this reads: '... AM: S .... / ... ERNE: AMEN: /'. The words on the inner order clearly formed part of the Ave, though what remains of the letters on the outer order suggests that the inscription continued with some sort of customized prayer. The lettering is of the Basyng style, with the words separated by triple stops, though a more elaborate form of T is used in 'FRVCTVS' in place of the standard form used elsewhere in what survives of the inscription. The present church dates from 1857 and itself replaced a Tudor building on the site. The slab was moved inside the church in 1939 from its former position in or against the churchyard wall.[18] It undoubtedly came originally from the Benedictine abbey at Wherwell. Whether it commemorates one of the nuns or a lay benefactor is unclear, though the use of Latin for the inscription suggests that the former is more likely. If it commemorates one of the abbesses, Elaine de Percy, who died in 1300, may be the most likely candidate.[19]

12.12 Wherwell, Hampshire: unknown, c 1290–1300. Basyng-style slab with relief cross and incised letters. Tracing of rubbing by S F Badham of detail showing surviving lettering.

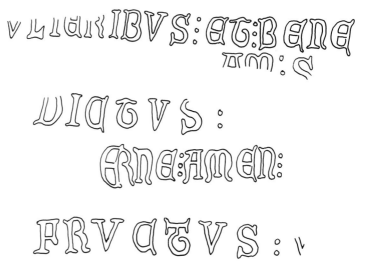

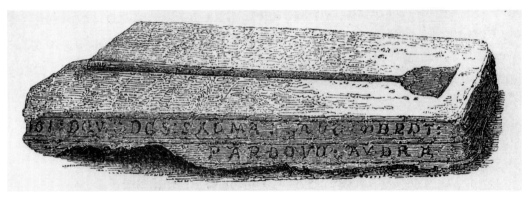

BOREHAM, ESSEX

The last cross slab in this group can be attributed to the Basyng series only tentatively as it is known solely from a nineteenth-century sketch and the type of stone is not recorded. However, the composition is closely paralleled on other Basyng products discussed above. In 1845 Suckling recorded the lower half of a coffin lid at Boreham, Essex, which had been dug up in the churchyard (Figure 12.13),[20] but which had disappeared by 1900.[21] It was coffin-shaped and on the top face was part of a relief cross, ending in a stepped calvary. Round the sides was a double hollow-moulded chamfer, on which was incised an inscription in Lombardic letters, running anti-clockwise and with the words separated by double stops. It read: 'HENRI: LE: MARCHAVNT: GIST: ICI: DEV: DE: SALME: AYT: MARCI: QVI: POVR: LE: PRIERA: GRAVNT: PARDOVN: AVERA'. The lettering is not totally clear from the sketch, but the individual letter shapes appear consistent with Basyng styling.

GUILDFORD MUSEUM, SURREY

Three Basyng series slabs are simple coffin-shaped slabs, adorned only by an incised inscription. The mutilated remains of a slab with a double hollow-moulded chamfer are in the Guildford Museum; it is said to have come from Holy Trinity, Guildford.[22] The incised inscription on the inner chamfer is in Basyng style lettering, with the words separated by triple stops (Figure 12.14). It reads: '[P]AR: ICI: PASSEZ: PVR: I....... DE: PARDOVN: A[MEN]'. The top surface was probably originally blank, but was later appropriated

12.13 Boreham, Essex: Henri le Marchaunt, c 1290–1300. Lost Basyng-style slab with relief cross and incised letters. Drawing from A Suckling, Memorials of the Antiquities and Architecture of Essex *(London, 1845), 32.*

12.14 Guildford Museum, Surrey, from Holy Trinity, Guildford: unknown, c 1290–1300. Basyng-style incised slab. Tracing of surviving lettering from rubbing by W J Blair.

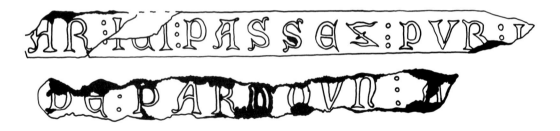

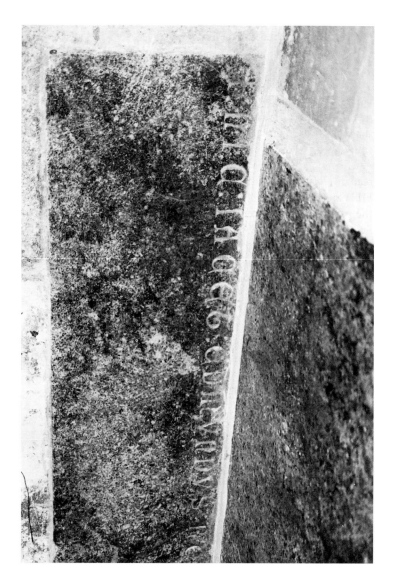

12.15 *Winchester Cathedral, Hampshire II: Prince Edmund, c 1290–1300. Basyng-style incised slab. Photograph by S F Badham of detail of lettering.*

12.16 *Winchester Cathedral, Hampshire III: Prince Richard, c 1290–1300. Basyng-style incised slab. Photograph by S F Badham of detail of lettering.*

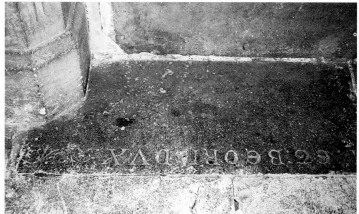

with the addition of two brass shields and an inscription plate. It is not known whom the slab commemorates.

WINCHESTER CATHEDRAL, HAMPSHIRE II AND III

Under Bishop Fox's early sixteenth-century screen on the south side of the choir in Winchester Cathedral, Hampshire, are two coffin-shaped Purbeck marble slabs. Both coffin lids have incised inscriptions on the top face, the words separated by double stops. The first, which commemorates Edmund, the son of King Aethelred, reads: '+ HIC: IACET: EDMVNDVS: REX: EYELDREDIE: REGIS: FILIVS:' (Figure 12.15). It was apparently moved to this position in the early nineteenth century, a rearrangement which must have necessitated temporary removal of part of the screen, and marks the position of a lead coffin said to contain the remains of another Edmund, probably an infant son of King Alfred.[23] The second slab, which was in this position prior to the erection of Fox's screen, has an inscription in two lines reading: '+ HIC: IACET: RICHARDVS: WILLI' / SENIORIS: REGIS: FILI: ET: BEORI DVX' (Figure 12.16). It purports to mark the position of the lead coffin of Richard, the son of William the Conqueror, which also contains the remains of the Danish Duke, Beorn.[24] The style of lettering on these two slabs is the same as on the Basyng series slabs already described. The inscriptions are of late thirteenth-century date and therefore clearly posthumous.

WINCHESTER CATHEDRAL, HAMPSHIRE IV

Finally, Greenhill recorded a small fragment of a slab, loose in the north transept of Winchester Cathedral in 1931, but no longer to be found (Figure 12.17). Though he did not note the type of stone

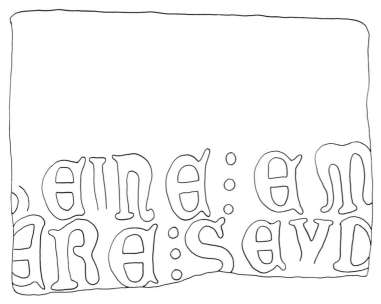

12.17 Winchester Cathedral, Hampshire IV: unknown, c 1290–1300. Basyng-style incised slab. Tracing from rubbing by F A Greenhill, Society of Antiquaries collection.

employed, the inscription appears to be in the Basyng-style script. The inscription was set out in two lines across the slab, with the words separated by triple stops. It read: '...EINE: EM... ...ERE: SEYD ... '.

THE BASYNG WORKSHOP

In conclusion, two general points need to be made about the Basyng series. First, although its products often incorporate a double hollow-moulded chamfer and have a cross as a prominent feature, neither of these features is in itself an indicative Basyng-style characteristic.[25] The incised crosses on the Winchester Cathedral I and Romsey Abbey slabs are a somewhat unusual variant of a standard Purbeck design. It may well be that there are other surviving cross slabs of this type, perhaps made by the same marblers. Identifying them presents a problem, particularly as no thorough surveys of cross slabs have been carried out in the south of England to compare with the invaluable work of Lawrence Butler in the east Midlands[26] and Ryder in the north east.[27] In contrast, the simpler relief cross with fleur-de-lis terminals of Hugh de Hendon's slab at St Bartholomew the Great and the relief cross botonnée on the South Benfleet slab are both common Purbeck types. In these cases, only their incised inscriptions, in the distinctive Basyng style of Lombardic lettering, mark them out from the plethora of chamfered Purbeck marble cross slabs of these types to be found in southern England. Clearly other cross slabs should be attributed to the Basyng series only if they incorporate inscriptions in the lettering style of the thirteen slabs discussed here.

The second general point to be made about the Basyng series is that, unlike the fourteenth-century slabs discussed in the previous chapters, they cannot be indisputably linked to an established series of brasses demonstrably emanating from a London workshop. Indeed, we cannot be absolutely certain that they were distributed from London at all. A substantial proportion of the Basyng series products are to be found in Hampshire, in locations at least as convenient to Corfe, the other known centre of the Purbeck marble industry. However, three factors suggest London as a more likely location than Corfe for the Basyng workshop. First, among the large number of Purbeck marble coffin lids in Dorset, none has Basyng-style features.[28] Second, the location of five Basyng series slabs in London, Essex and Bedfordshire is more consistent with a marketing zone based on London. Third, although Winchester, Romsey and Wherwell are closer to Corfe than to London, the Basyng slabs to be found there were laid down in high-status churches, and were undoubtedly commissioned by patrons who might be expected to have gravitated more naturally to the more eminent London workshops. This last argument is not so strong as it would have been if applied to the fourteenth century when the London marblers were very firmly established, but nonetheless has some force.

One possible, if totally speculative, explanation of the distribution pattern is that the workshop might have been located in Southwark, at the northern end of the Winchester diocese, a place where later engravers of brasses are known to have had their workshops.[29] Such a link with the bishopric of Winchester might explain why such a high proportion of the Basyng series slabs have grants of pardon as part of the inscription. Perhaps the workshop was conveniently situated to obtain the necessary episcopal grants? Might they have offered a package deal?[30] Since the only bishop's register of this date to record indulgences is that of John le Romeyn at York[31] and there are no known Basyng series slabs that far north, there is no way of checking whether there are any grants which tie in with the Basyng series slabs and these suggestions can be made only tentatively.

From the points made above, we conclude that the Basyng workshop was probably a London-based operation, which sold modified versions of standard coffin-lid types. This raises the question of the extent to which the London workshop was a manufacturing operation, as well as a showroom and distribution centre. It is clear that, except in rare and exceptional circumstances, Purbeck marble was exported from Corfe ready worked, rather than in raw blocks.[32] Documentary evidence demonstrates that blank polished slabs could be bought direct from the quarry by individual customers, as well as by independent craftsmen.[33] As explained in Chapter 4, the marblers working in London between the 1280s and the 1330s often had Corfe family origins and continuing contacts with the trade there.

It is thus almost certain that the Basyng workshop would have been sent cut and polished coffin lids from Corfe, for sale to individual customers, either as they were or with further embellishment. It appears probable to us that these blank slabs would have included both vertical-sided slabs and slabs with double or single hollow-moulded chamfers already carved on them. It could well also be the case that some slabs sent from Corfe were already carved with relief crosses in established Purbeck patterns. Examples can be found in many parts of the country of standard quarry products in a range of stone types, including both cross slabs and semi-effigial slabs, which appear to have been bought by retailers who added inscriptions to order,[34] but this is the first time that a series of such slabs in a single style has been identified. The need to adapt a ready-carved coffin lid to incorporate an incised inscription could explain the infelicitous layout of the South Benfleet slab and also why Basyng series inscriptions were so often on the chamfer, despite the added technical difficulties involved. If this were so, then perhaps only the incised detail, which on most Basyng slabs is a minor feature of the entire monument, can be attributed to the London-based marblers. This would suggest that the manufacturing aspect of the Basyng workshop was limited to finishing and customizing the products of the Corfe quarries.

CHAPTER 13

ASHFORD-STYLE INCISED SLABS

INTRODUCTION

We have termed the second series of early incised slabs and brasses from the London marblers the Ashford style, named after the earliest figure brass which we have attributed to this pattern series. The series is in marked contrast to the Basyng series in terms of the range of monumental types produced. We have identified twenty-one incised slabs in this style, including effigial slabs, cross slabs, crosier slabs and slabs with an inscription only. These products (listed in Appendix A) are analysed in this chapter. Additionally, there are firm links between these slabs and other classes of Purbeck marble monument, including early London brasses, providing important new evidence for the development of the brass-engraving industry in the late thirteenth century. (These other products of the Ashford workshop are listed in Appendix B and discussed in Chapter 14.)

One of the more frustrating problems presented by this series is the difficulty we have experienced in establishing firm dates for its products. Though the names of most of those commemorated by the incised slabs in the series are known, and there are dated documentary references to some of them, their dates of death mainly remain a mystery. Such documentary evidence as is available on these people suggests that production of Ashford series slabs spanned the last two decades of the thirteenth century and the very first few years of the fourteenth century. This is reinforced by the evidence of the Ashford series brasses, many of which commemorate important people, whose dates of death are known; ten brasses, attributable to the series with varying degrees of certainty, are to people who died between 1273 and 1308. Thus the series may well have begun before the Basyng series and continued after it finished, suggesting that there were two marblers' workshops in operation for a brief period in the late thirteenth century. Stylistic evidence suggests that the Ashford series was the precursor of the Camoys series (discussed in Chapter 7), which dominated the London market in the first third of the fourteenth century.

As with the Basyng series, the single most important feature of the Ashford series stylistically is the lettering used for the incised

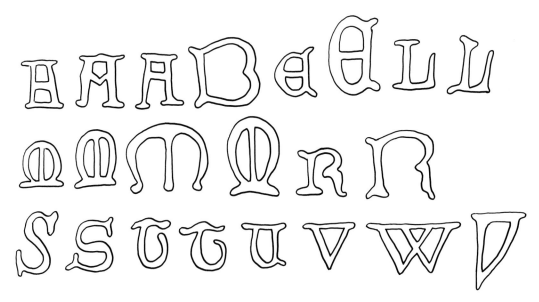

13.1 Letter forms on Ashford
series incised slabs.

inscriptions that appear on thirteen of the slabs. The standard of
production of the Ashford slabs is markedly higher than on those
of the Basyng series and the inscriptions give a tidier first impression. The individual letters on most inscriptions are uniformly
sized and are consistently well set out and evenly spaced. Even on
the London Museum I slab, which has a long inscription difficult to
fit on such a small slab, the letters do not appear unduly squashed
together, as they undoubtedly would have been on a Basyng series
slab.

The outlines of the key individual letters are different from the
forms used in the Basyng script, and in most cases are quite broad
in relation to their height. Again the most useful letters are the A, B,
E, M and R (Figure 13.1). The A has two slightly splayed, straight
downstrokes and a horizontal bar. The B and R are of an 'open'
form. The downstroke of the E, which has small points at the ends,
does not dominate the letter in the way that it does in the Basyng
script. The M has a notably rounded form, with the two outer
downstrokes curving in at the bottom to meet the horizontal stroke
across the bottom of the letter. A final interesting feature of the
Ashford lettering is that many, though not all, of these slabs include
both the U and the V in the inscriptions; this is extremely unusual
in Lombardic inscriptions, which normally utilize the V for both
letters.

Seven of the Ashford slabs include incised figures in their
design, with a wide variety of types of costume, including clerical
and academic dress, as well as male and female civilian dress.
Nevertheless, common stylistic features can be detected in the
drapery style, the facial features and the drawing of the figures.

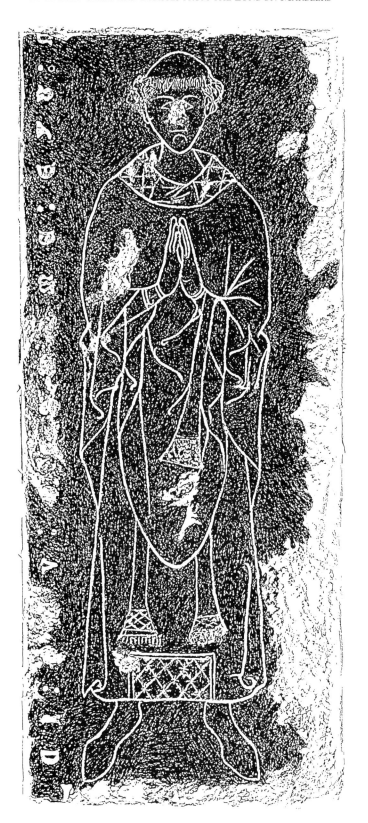

13.2 Pyrton, Oxfordshire:
Richard de Gretton,
ob c 1280–9. Ashford-style
incised slab with indents
for brass letters. Rubbing by
M W Norris.

PYRTON, OXFORDSHIRE

The Ashford-style incised slab to a priest in mass vestments at Pyrton, Oxfordshire, occupies a pivotal position in the series (Figures 13.2 and 13.3). It is in the sanctuary, partly under the altar, and is complete except for a strip at the top, which has been trimmed, perhaps when the church was rebuilt in 1856. Fortunately, this missing section is recorded in a rubbing made in

13.3 Pyrton, Oxfordshire: Richard de Gretton, ob c 1280–9. Ashford-style incised slab with indents for brass letters. Detail showing face. Photograph by Gillman and Soame.

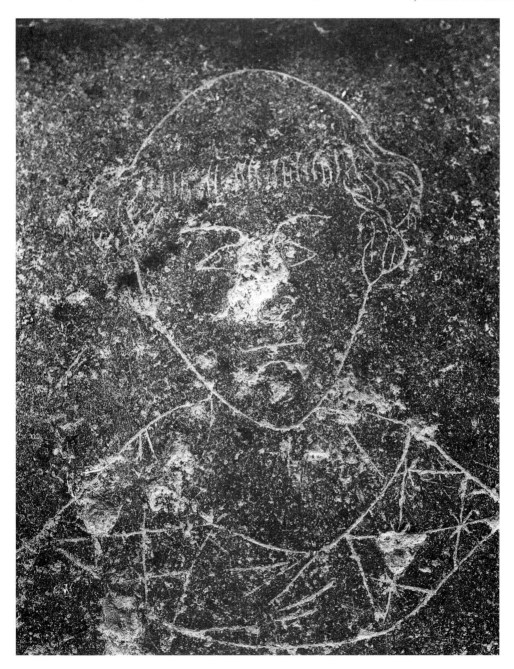

1847 by Franks, now in the main collection of incised slab rubbings in the Society of Antiquaries. Round the perimeter of the slab is an inscription with indents for Main Group brass lettering, of which only two stops remain, though an additional three were present in 1847. The indents are now rather battered, but are shown considerably more clearly on Franks's rubbing, which shows the inscription as reading: '+ DRIES: [P]VR: LAL[ME]: R..E.[D or O][:] / KE: GIST: I / CI: DEV: DE SALME: EYT: MER / C[Y:]'. [1]

The drawing of the figure is much less sophisticated than on the fourteenth-century slabs from the London marblers' workshops (discussed in Chapters 7 to 11). The feet are clumsily placed apart and the drapery, both of the chasuble and of the skirt of the alb, fails to give a realistic impression. A noteworthy feature is the way in which the hem runs straight across most of the figure, but folds forward at the sides. The amice drapes limply around the neck, and looks more like a circle of material than the draped and tied square of linen which it was intended to represent. The neck itself is thick and rather like an inverted funnel or cone. The shape of the head is very distinctive, with a broad brow, from which the sides of the face curve gradually to a pointed chin. The tonsure is very large; a sparse fringe of hair is shown above the forehead and neat curls are placed around the small ears. The facial features are obscured by an area of damage centred on the nose, but the unusual almond-shaped eyes and curving eyebrows joined to the lines outlining the nose, as well as one broad nostril, remain. The mouth is shown as a straight line, with a curve defining a prominent chin below. The shoulders are sloping and the elbows are tucked tightly into the sides, so that the forearms form an inverted V-shape. The palms of the hands are notably fat, producing a distinctive gap between the hands at the base of the fingers. The slab has previously been dated *c* 1330, but parallels discussed below suggest that a date in the late thirteenth century is more likely.

It is frustrating that the only part of the inscription not clearly shown on Franks's rubbing is the name of the person commemorated. Only a relatively small space is left for the name and it is likely that only the Christian name was recorded. This is unusual, but not unprecedented. Another Ashford series slab, at Doddington, Kent (discussed below), gives only the Christian name of the person commemorated and a diminutive Purbeck marble effigy of a civilian at Britford, Wiltshire, holds a scroll, which is now difficult to decipher but is recorded by Leach, on the basis of information from Dru Drury, as reading: 'ORATE: PRO: ANIMA: NICHOLAUS: KI: GIST: ICI'.[2] This practice was more common in the case of ecclesiastics, notable examples being the twelfth-century Purbeck marble effigies to Philip the Priest at Tolpuddle and Abbot Clement at Sherborne, both in Dorset, and Bishop Anselm at St Davids, Pembrokeshire. The gap left for the name on the Pyrton slab appears to be about six characters long. Surviving traces of indents and Franks's rubbing show that the first letter was an R, the fourth an E and the last one was a D or an O.

Unfortunately, antiquarian sources do not throw any further light on this dilemma; thus any attempt to identify the person commemorated by this slab must rely mainly on the surviving evidence of incumbents. Institutions for the vicarage of Pyrton are recorded in the registers for the Bishops of Lincoln. The list is complete for the relevant period, apart from one lacuna spanning the years 1280 to 1289.[3] The name which most readily fits the letters recorded in Franks's rubbing is Roberd, but there are no incumbents with the name Robert recorded for Pyrton. Of the four priests recorded in the period covered by the operation of the Ashford workshop, two can be ruled out. Richard de Burdens was instituted in 1302,[4] but resigned the living only two years later,[5] so is most unlikely to have been buried at Pyrton. His successor, Thomas de Modburgh, is ruled out because his name does not fit the surviving traces of letters. This leaves Richard de Gretton, who was instituted in 1268,[6] and his successor, Roger de Corby, who died in 1302.[7] We cannot be certain when Gretton vacated the living and Corby was instituted, but it is most likely to have been between 1280 and 1289, the only period for which records have not survived. Nor can we be certain that de Gretton vacated the living through death, though this is the most likely explanation. By the 1280s he would have spent fifteen to twenty years at Pyrton and there is no record of him elsewhere.[8]

Of the two candidates for this slab, Richard de Gretton is favoured, for two reasons. First, stylistic evidence suggests that a date towards the beginning of the series is more likely than a date at the end of the series. Second, the surviving fragments of lettering comprising the name fit with 'RICERD'. This is not a spelling of Richard that we have come across elsewhere, casting some doubt on this attribution of the slab, though the form 'RYCARD' appears on the Ashford-style slab at Stoke d'Abernon (discussed below). However, the alternative is more problematic. While some of the letters also fit 'ROGER', this name does not seem long enough for the space and the final letter of the name has a right-facing curve, consistent with a D or an O, but not with an R. Roger de Corby cannot entirely be ruled out as the person commemorated by this slab. It is also possible that it commemorates an unrecorded person with the name Robert who was vicar for a short period in the 1280s. However, an attribution to Richard de Gretton, who probably died in the 1280s, seems more probable.

DUNSTABLE, BEDFORDSHIRE II

The closest parallel with the Pyrton slab is that to Richard Duraunt at Dunstable, Bedfordshire (Figure 13.4).[9] This slab was discovered in 1906, built in as a support under one of the buttresses of the priory church. Damage across the centre of the slab and on the

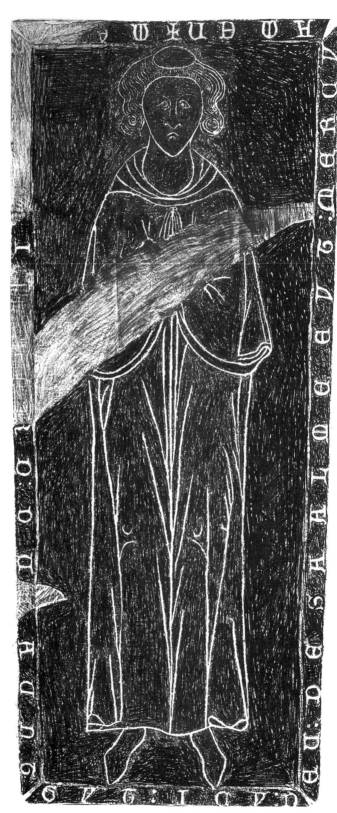

13.4 Dunstable, Bedfordshire II: Richard Duraunt, ob after 1284. Ashford-style incised slab. Rubbing by F A Greenhill, Society of Antiquaries collection, photograph by A C Cooper Ltd.

upper dexter side has been repaired with cement; some lines have been incised into the cement to indicate continuations of lines of the original design of the figure, though missing letters of the inscription have not been restored. It is not known whether any further repairs were carried out; generally the incising looks original, but the corkscrew line used to depict the left eyeball seems very odd and may be suspect. Though the mortar that must have covered the surface of the slab has been cleaned, an obscuring bloom remains and only close examination reveals that the slab is of Purbeck marble.

The slab is dominated by a boldly incised figure in the academical attire of master. The feet are placed apart and the drapery is simple, but unconvincing. The hem drapery has a relatively straight line across the feet, but forward-facing folds at the sides. Duraunt's elbows are tucked closely into his sides, his shoulders are slight and sloping, and his neck is a thick inverted cone. The face is broad at the brow, narrowing to a pointed chin, has almond-shaped eyes, flaring eyebrows and very broad nostrils. The mouth curves downwards, but a semi-circle underneath defines a prominent chin. All these features are the same as those on the Pyrton slab.

The inscription is on the chamfered edge of the slab and reads: '+ ME[S] / [TRE: R]I[CHA]RD: DU[R]AUNT: / GYT: ICY: D / EU: DE SA ALME EYT: MERCY / AMEN'. The inscription runs in an anti-clockwise direction. It is incised in the distinctive Ashford-style script, but nonetheless has some parallels with the inscription on the Pyrton slab, including the use of Norman-French and the way in which the words 'DE SALME' on the Pyrton slab and 'DE SA ALME EYT' on the Dunstable slab have no stops between the words. Where the words are separated by stops, double stops are used.

A little is known of Richard Duraunt. He was one of the sons of John Duraunt, a benefactor of the Priory, by his wife Alice, who was commemorated by a Basyng-style cross slab (discussed in Chapter 12). In 1275 Richard received a grant of one mark from the Priory until such time as a benefice was provided for him.[10] In 1284 he and his brother William were incepted into the arts at Oxford University. Nothing further is known of him. Though the inscription and his depiction in academical attire indicate that he must have lived long enough to have completed his degree, his name does not appear in the list of those admitted as canons of Dunstable Priory; nor is there any record of him being given a benefice.

LONDON MUSEUM I

On display in the London Museum is the Purbeck marble coffin lid of a heart burial, commemorating Joan de St Edmonds (Figure 13.5). It was excavated on the site of St Swithin, Cannon Street, London, in 1961. Her clothes are simple and undecorated. She wears a kirtle, with a loose-fitting surcoat over. Part of the skirt of the latter is tucked into a loop in the crook of her right arm, permitting an unusual amount of the skirt of the kirtle to be revealed. Over her head and neck she wears a veil and wimple. Her hands are held unusually high and clasp a heart. At her feet rests a hound, with his head looking upwards and his long tail looped up above his back.

As the slab is only 650mm square, the figure is much smaller than the Pyrton and Dunstable figures, allowing less scope for fine detail. Nonetheless, some parallels can be seen. Joan's face is longer than either that of Richard Duraunt or the Pyrton priest, but she too has a pointed chin. The facial features are particularly close. Her eyes are almond-shaped, her eyebrows flare upwards, her nose

13.5 London Museum I, from the site of St Swithin, Cannon Street, London: Joan de St Edmonds, ob before 1306. Ashford-style incised slab. Rubbing by F A Greenhill, Society of Antiquaries collection, photograph by A C Cooper Ltd.

has broad nostrils and her mouth is dominated by a straightish central line. Though the hands are shown in a different position, they have the fat palms of the Pyrton slab. The drapery is much more assured than on the other slabs. Round the chamfered edge of the slab is an incised inscription, with the words separated by triple stops. It reads: '+ LEQWER: IONE: KEFU: / LA FEM[ME: DE:] SIRE: FU / LKE: DE: SEINT: E[DMONDS: / GIT]: ICI: PRIEZ: PUR: LALME'. Like the Dunstable slab, the inscription reads in an anti-clockwise direction and the individual letter shapes of the Norman-French inscription on the two slabs are similar, though to squeeze such a long inscription on to such a small slab the marbler had to make the letters unusually long and narrow for this series.

Although no records remain relating to Joan de St Edmonds, more is known of her husband. Sir Fulk was Sheriff of London 1289–90, was active in London in the later 1290s[11] and his will was proved on 25 January 1306–7.[12] Though he is mentioned in the City of London Court Rolls for July 1307, this reference is evidently posthumous.[13] Fulk had three wives, his last, Alice, surviving him. Joan was the second wife, so she is likely to have died before the end of the thirteenth century.

STEEPLE LANGFORD, WILTSHIRE

Another heart slab, this time coffin-shaped, is at the east end of the south aisle at Steeple Langford, Wiltshire (Figure 13.6). The incised lines have red paint in them. The figure, of a similar size to that on the London Museum slab, is of a civilian in a simple ankle-length gown, with close-fitting sleeves. A hunting horn is slung from his left shoulder and a cusped line between his feet may represent a bracket. There is no inscription on this slab and it is not known whom it commemorates. Despite the small size of the figure, stylistic links can be traced with the Ashford-style slabs already discussed. The facial features and the podgy hands compare well with those of Joan de St Edmonds and the rather unconfident drawing of the hair resembles the curls on the side of the Pyrton priest's head. The curious way in which the neck emerges from the gown is similar to that shown on the Dunstable slab. Finally, the feet are placed apart, as on the Pyrton and Dunstable slabs.

TILSWORTH, BEDFORDSHIRE

At Tilsworth, Bedfordshire, where there is also a Purbeck marble slab with indents for an inscription to a member of the de Morteyne family, with two stops and a Main Group E still in situ,[14] another slab from the Ashford series lies at the west end of the south aisle. It is cracked and worn and all that now remains are the shallow indents of the inscription, formerly inlaid in Main Group size III brass letters and a few very faint traces of an incised figure. The Norman-French inscription, which runs clockwise round the

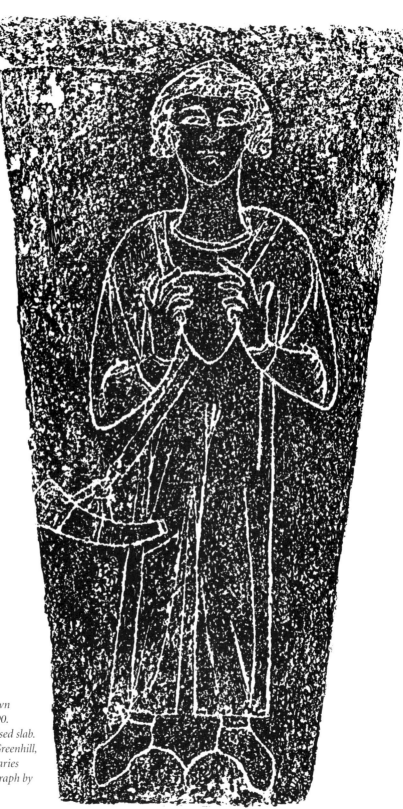

13.6 Steeple Langford, Wiltshire: unknown civilian, c 1280–90. Ashford-style incised slab. Rubbing by F A Greenhill, Society of Antiquaries collection, photograph by A C Cooper Ltd.

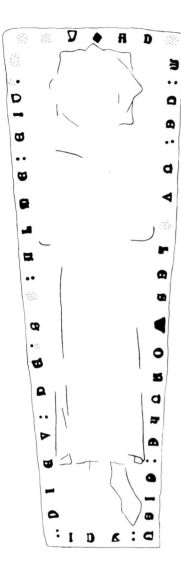

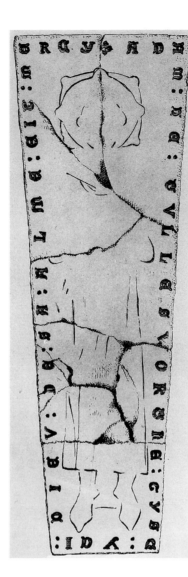

13.7 *(far left) Tilsworth, Bedfordshire: Adam de Tullesworthe, c 1280–1305. Ashford-style incised slab with indents for brass letters. Tracing from rubbing by F A Greenhill, Society of Antiquaries collection.*

13.8 *(left) Tilsworth, Bedfordshire: Adam de Tullesworthe, c 1280–1305. Ashford-style incised slab with indents for brass letters. Drawing by T Fisher, Collections Historical, Genealogical and Topographical for Bedfordshire (London, 1812–36), pl 98.*

slab, reads: '+ ADA / M: DE: TVLLESWORTHE: GIST / : YCI: / DIEV: DE: SA: ALME: EIT: M / ERCY'. Unfortunately, nothing is known of Adam de Tullesworthe. When Greenhill rubbed this slab in 1938, the hem drapery, the feet and a pair of crossed cushions at the head could still be seen (Figure 13.7). A drawing made in 1812 by Fisher shows a little more of the design, but it is not entirely accurate as to the details of the incising (Figure 13.8). Nonetheless, it is possible to assign this slab to the Ashford series. The feet are placed apart and the hem is straight across the feet, but folds back on itself at the sides, both features being paralleled on the Pyrton and Dunstable slabs.

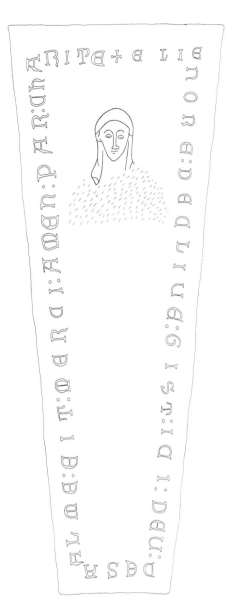 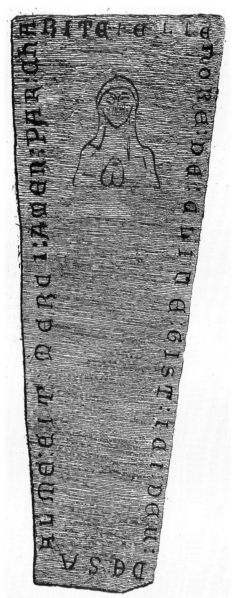

CLIFFE-AT-HOO, KENT

There is another slab from this series at Cliffe-at-Hoo, Kent, now virtually effaced. When Greenhill rubbed this coffin-shaped Purbeck marble slab to Eleanor de Clive in 1948, only part of the inscription remained. A better idea of the original composition can be gauged from a dabbing in sections dated 1810 in the Society of Antiquaries collection and a drawing made by Fisher in 1789 (Figures 13.9 and 13.10). These show the half-effigy of a lady and a marginal inscription in Norman-French, which read: '+ ELIE / NORE: DE CLIUE: GIST: ICI: DEU: / DE SA / ALME: EIT: MERCI: AMEN: PAR: CHA / RITE'. The inscription ran in a clockwise direction and the words were separated by double stops. Although the 1810 dabbing unfortunately does not include all of the figure, the face has clear Ashford-style features and is most closely related to the Pyrton priest and the London Museum lady. The letter forms are also of the distinct Ashford series script, though an unusual, quasi-Roman form of T is employed. Moreover, the lettering is unevenly sized and less well spaced than that on most Ashford series slabs. These features may suggest an early date in the Ashford chronology for this slab, but unfortunately no documentary references to Eleanor de Clive, either under this name or as Eleanor de Cliffe, have been traced.

HORTON KIRBY, KENT

Under the fixed pews in the north aisle of the church at Horton Kirby, Kent, lies a coffin-shaped Purbeck marble slab with the isolated head of a priest wearing an amice. It has been hidden from view since the 1930s, though fortunately Greenhill recorded it in 1924 (Figure 13.11). He found no signs of an inscription, but, as the sides were plastered over, he considered it just possible that there might have been a marginal inscription or that the slab had been cut down. The slab was then cracked and weathered, the

13.9 *(opposite, left) Cliffe-at-Hoo, Kent: Eleanor de Clive, c 1280–1305. Ashford-style incised slab. Reconstruction from 1810 dabbing; positioning of lettering in relation to edges of slab taken from 1948 rubbing by F A Greenhill, Society of Antiquaries collection.*

13.10 *(opposite, right) Cliffe-at-Hoo, Kent: Eleanor de Clive, c 1280–1305. Ashford-style incised slab. Drawing by T Fisher (1789) in* Gentleman's Magazine *(1794), 809.*

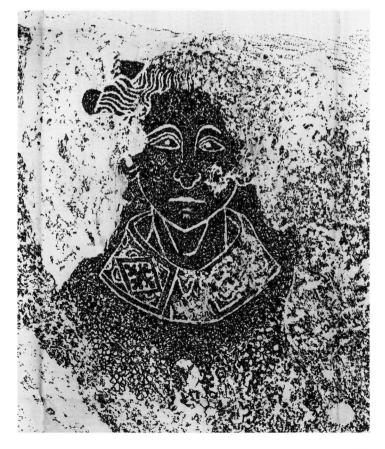

13.11 *Horton Kirby, Kent: possibly for Baldwin de Caundell, c 1300–5. Ashford-style incised slab. Rubbing by F A Greenhill, Society of Antiquaries collection, photograph by A C Cooper Ltd.*

131

damage having obliterated part of the head and hair. Fortunately, the main features are clear.

The drawing is the most accomplished in the Ashford series, and in comparison with it the other priest in this series, at Pyrton, does not show to advantage. There is a marked contrast in the treatment of the amice, which here is accurately represented and attractively decorated with lobed diamonds, each enclosing a straight-armed cross with trefoil terminals. However, the shape of the face, with its prominent pointed chin, is similar to the other slabs in this group, as are the facial features. The straight-line mouth, flaring eyebrows and almond-shaped eyes are alike, though the lobes of the nose are more pronounced on the other examples. Though sparse strands of hair straggle down over the forehead like on the Pyrton slab, the hair at the sides is much bushier, and the ears are larger and more prominent. The neck is fairly thick, but cording gives it more shape. Overall, both the design and the execution are more assured, suggesting a development beyond the other effigial slabs in the Ashford style.

Information on the rectors and vicars of Horton Kirby is very patchy in the relevant period. No candidate for this slab can be found amongst the known early rectors. The first recorded rector is Henry de Grofhurst, who was instituted in 1307.[15] However, in 1311 he exchanged the living for that of Horsmonden, where he remained until his death and where his brass is still to be seen (see Figure 10.2). His successor, William Canterey, was not instituted until after the end of the Ashford series. It is possible that the slab commemorates Baldwin de Caundell, who was instituted as vicar in 1297, but this attribution is very far from certain.[16]

FOBBING, ESSEX

13.12 Fobbing, Essex: Thomas de Crawedene, c 1290–1305. Ashford-style incised slab. Rubbing by F A Greenhill, Society of Antiquaries collection.

In addition to these seven effigial slabs, ten other incised slabs can be attributed to the Ashford series on the basis of their inscriptions in the distinctive Ashford series script. At Fobbing, Essex, is a well-preserved mural inscription to Thomas de Crawedene (Figure 13.12). It appears to have been whitewashed and, though the surface is crazed, the original stone cannot be seen.[17] Christy, who

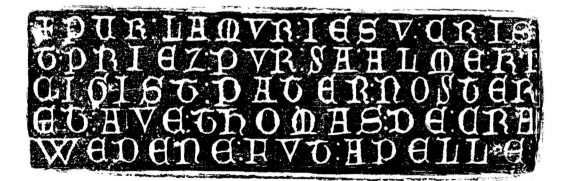

examined the slab in the late nineteenth century, described it as being 'of close-grained texture, bluish-grey in colour',[18] a description consistent with Purbeck marble. The inscription, which is set out in five lines across the slab, the words separated by double stops, reads: '+ PUR: LAMVR: IESV: CRIS / T: PRIEZ: PVR: SA: ALME: KI: / CI: GIST: PATER: NOSTER / ET: AVE: THOMAS: DE: CRA / WEDENE: FVT: APELLE'. Unfortunately, nothing is known of Crawedene.

DODDINGTON, KENT

A coffin-shaped slab with another unusually worded inscription, similarly set out in lines across the head of the slab, is at Doddington, Kent. Dug up in the churchyard in 1855,[19] it was placed first in the north aisle and then moved to its present position in the south chapel. The lettering on the dexter side of the slab is now virtually obliterated, but the entire inscription was clear when it was rubbed by Trollope in 1855 (Figure 13.13).[20] The Ashford-style inscription, which again has the words separated by double stops, reads: '+ ICI: GIST: AGNES: DE: SUTH / CESTRE PERE: UOUS: IRREZ: T / OUZ A MESON: ME: COUENT: DE: / MORERE: ORE: UOUS: PRIE: ZY / ATER: AMY: CHIER: LE: MAIE: MO / RTE: UOILLET: PENSER:'. At first sight, the idiosyncratic use of stops on this slab might lead to the impression that the name of the person commemorated was Agnes de Suthcestrepere, but in fact the first part of the inscription reads in translation 'Here lies Agnes under this stone'.[21] Clearly, in the absence of a surname nothing can be established about her.

Slabs with the inscription running in lines across the slab are comparatively rare, but the Fobbing and Doddington examples are the only ones that can be attributed to the Ashford series with any certainty. We have already discussed (in Chapter 7) the 1312 Camoys-style inscription with this layout at Little Shelford, Cambridgeshire. Two other lost incised inscriptions in lines are known from antiquarian sources, but neither appears to have been from either the Ashford or the Camoys workshop. Formerly at Robertsbridge Abbey, Sussex, was a fragment of stone, possibly

13.13 Doddington, Kent: Agnes ..., c 1290–1305. Ashford-style incised slab. Tracing from 1855 rubbing by E Trollope, Society of Antiquaries collection.

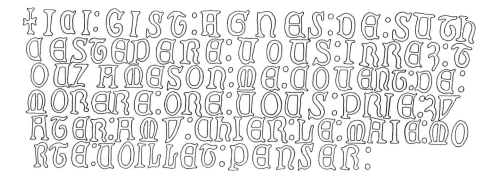

from the upper part of a coffin-shaped slab, with an inscription in Lombardic lettering in five lines to William de Bodiam.[22] It read: 'HIC: IACET / WILL'S: DE: BOD... / .. TALL: .P: OO: .. / .. IES: VENIE: P .. / ... ANTVR: EP ... '. The use of contractions indicates that it must have been incised, but the lettering looks quite unlike any of the scripts on Purbeck marble slabs known to us. William appears to have been alive as early as 1263, possibly suggesting a date of death before the Ashford and Basyng series began. Another lost fragment, this time from Chertsey Abbey, Surrey, shows parts of three lines of Lombardic lettering.[23] It read: '+ ELYS: LE ......: [GIST: I] CY / DIEV: D[E: SA: ALME:] EYT: M[ERCY: AMEN]'. The inscription appears to have been incised, but the letter shapes are not sufficiently like any of the scripts discussed in this monograph for us to attribute it to a specific series.

WHITE WALTHAM, BERKSHIRE

Another inscription in the Ashford-style lettering forms the floor of a cupboard in the south-west corner of the church at White Waltham, Berkshire (see Figure 6.2). It commemorates Joan Saddoc, the wife of Gilbert Saddoc, who was also buried at White Waltham and commemorated by a London-made brass, possibly from the same workshop (see Figure 6.1). Joan's more modest monument has only a perimeter inscription, bordered by incised fillets, set clockwise round the slab and with the words separated by double stops. Most of the letters are still fairly clear, though rather worn and partially filled with cement. The inscription reads: '+ I[OA] / [N]E: LA: FEMME: GILEBERT: SA / DDOC: GIST: / ICI: DEV: DE: SA ALM[E:] EIT: MER / CI:'. No records relating to Joan have been found, but a little is known about Gilbert. He was witness to a White Waltham deed in 1275[24] and is also mentioned in an inquisition dated 1297.[25] He gave his age then as 'forty years and more', but since he also testified that fourteen years previously he had given his daughter, Christine, in marriage, he must have been an old man by 1297, perhaps even over sixty. Since his wife had a separate monument, she may well have pre-deceased him.

LONDON MUSEUM II

Another important Ashford-style monument, on display in the London Museum, was found in 1822 beneath the Guildhall Chapel, London. The top surface is badly decayed, but Greenhill was able to get a remarkably good rubbing of it (Figure 13.14). This coffin-shaped slab, traditionally dated to the late thirteenth century, has a relief cross botonnée with a stepped base, flanked by two incised trumpets. The trumpets accurately portray trumpets of the period and are thus very like the trumpets on the shield of the brass to Sir Robert de Trumpington at Trumpington, Cambridgeshire.[26] Round the inner order of the double hollow-moulded chamfered edge of

13.14 (opposite, left) London Museum II, from Guildhall Chapel, London: Godfrey le Troumpour, c 1280–1305. Ashford-style incised slab. Rubbing of top face by F A Greenhill, Society of Antiquaries collection.

13.15 (opposite, right) London Museum II, from Guildhall Chapel, London: Godfrey le Troumpour, c 1280–1305. Ashford-style incised slab. Drawing from C Boutell, Christian Monuments in England and Wales (London, 1854), 100.

the slab are the battered remains of an incised inscription in Ashford-style lettering (Figure 13.15). It reads: 'GO / DEFREY: LE: TROVMP / OVR: / GIST: CI: DEV: DEL: EALME: EIT: M / ERCI'. The words of the Norman-French inscription are separated by triple stops and the inscription runs anti-clockwise. Unfortunately, nothing is known of Godfrey le Troumpour.[27]

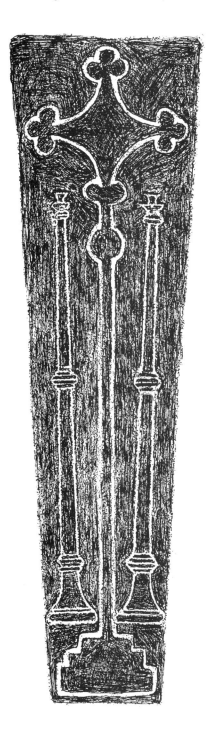
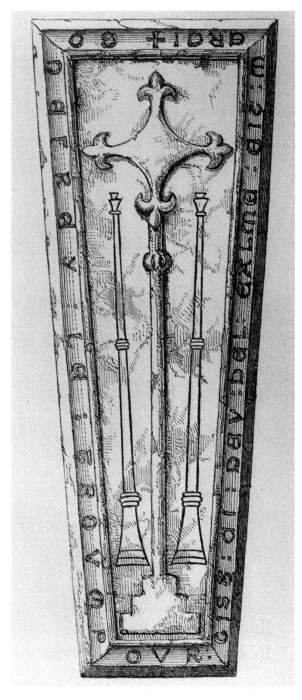

SAWBRIDGEWORTH, HERTFORDSHIRE I

13.16 Sawbridgeworth, Hertfordshire I: William de Say, ob 1295. Ashford-style slab with relief cross and incised letters. Tracing of rubbing by S F Badham of detail showing surviving lettering.

At Sawbridgeworth, Hertfordshire, is the upper half of a coffin-shaped slab, with a single hollow-moulded chamfer and a cross botonnée in relief. Running anti-clockwise round the chamfer is an incised inscription, with the words separated by triple stops. What survives reads: '+ WIL[LIAM]/ DE ..../A: ALME: EIT: M / ERCI:'. The letters are clearly of the Ashford style, with the words separated by triple stops (Figure 13.16). The manor of Sawbridgeworth was held by the de Say family.[28] In 1295, the then head of the family, William de Say, died.[29] It seems very likely that this is his monument.

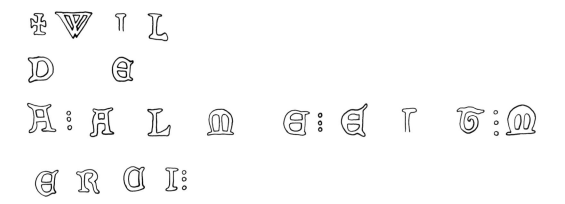

MICKLEHAM, SURREY I AND II

In the west porch of the church at Mickleham, Surrey, is a pair of Purbeck marble coffin-shaped slabs, found buried by Robinson under the church floor opposite the north door during alterations carried out in 1823.[30] His drawings show that each of the slabs had the stepped calvary of a relief cross, though the slabs are now so weathered that these features can no longer be seen. The sides of the slabs carry double hollow-moulded chamfers, with incised Lombardic inscriptions on the inner order, though most of the letters, particularly on the slab on the north side of the porch, are now indecipherable. John Blair, who saw them in 1970, suggested plausible reconstructions of the inscriptions, based in part on Robinson's drawings.[31] He read the inscription on the slab on the south side of the porch as reading: 'IHAN D[/E] . / . [?EN] . AM: GIST I: CY: DEV: DAL / ME: EIT: MERCI: AMEN'. The sections of the lettering that survive are sufficient for attribution to the

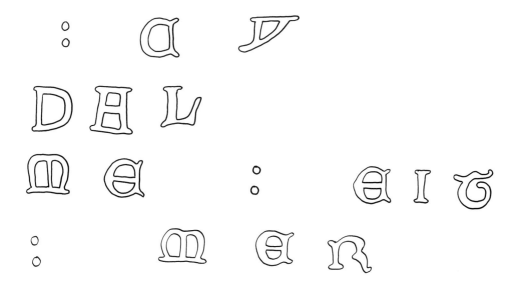

Ashford series (Figure 13.17). The slab on the north side of the porch has very little lettering left (Figure 13.18), but what traces survive are consistent with an Ashford origin. The inscription, which went round only three sides of the slab, probably originally read: '+ ALIS: DE: NE / WENHAM: GIST: ICI: DEV: DE: SA: ALME: EIT: MER / CI'.

At that very early stage into his research into such monuments, Blair suggested that these slabs dated from the middle of the fourteenth century, but the identification of the script as being of Ashford origin points to them being some fifty years earlier than that. The slab on the north side may commemorate Alice de Bocham (Bookham), called de Nywenham, who was granted lands in nearby Bookham in 1279, but of whom nothing further is recorded.[32] Far more is known of John de Newenham. He was a freeholder of Mickleham and was a witness to many local deeds from the 1280s.[33] He last appears as a witness to a deed dated 10 January 1305.[34] He was dead by 7 May 1311, when in a deed Beatrice de Newenham describes herself as 'formerly daughter of John de Newenham'.[35]

13.17 *Mickleham, Surrey II: John de Newenham, ob c 1305–11. Ashford-style slab with relief cross and incised letters. Tracing of rubbing by S F Badham of detail showing surviving lettering.*

13.18 *Mickleham, Surrey I: Alice de Newenham, ob after 1279. Ashford-style slab with relief cross and incised letters. Tracing of rubbing by S F Badham of detail showing surviving lettering.*

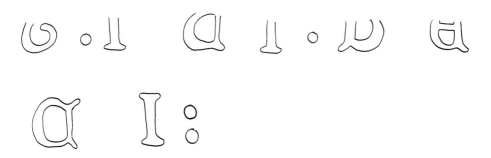

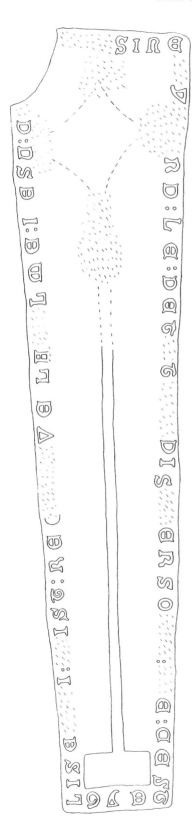
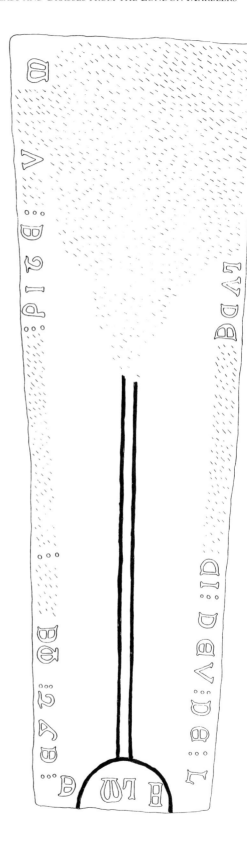

138

STOKE D'ABERNON, SURREY

At nearby Stoke d'Abernon, Surrey, under a wrought-iron screen separating the north chapel from the chancel, is a coffin-shaped slab with a double hollow-moulded chamfer (Figure 13.19). On the top surface is a relief cross botonnée with trefoil terminals, the stem ending in a rectangle.[36] The cross was badly damaged by weathering incurred when the slab was in the churchyard, but the detail of the cross has been recorded in a drawing of 1907 made by Johnston.[37] This clearly shows how the trefoil terminals had been modified to make room for the inscription in Lombardic lettering, which is incised round the perimeter of the top surface. The letters are clearly of the Ashford style, with the words separated by double stops. The inscription reads: '+ SIRE: [R]Y[CA]RD: LE: DET [I]T[: IA]DIS[: P]ERSO[NE]: [D]E: CEST / EYG / LISE[: IC]I: [G]IST: REC[EY]VE LA[: AL]ME: IESU: C[HRIS] / [T:]'. Johnston suggested that it commemorated Richard le Petit and that the slab might be dated in the period *c* 1240 to *c* 1260. Richard's name appears in the list of rectors in the church, with a date of death of 1240, but we have been unable to trace any documentary evidence for this date, or any reference to him. The list of rectors of Stoke d'Abernon is virtually non-existent before 1374 and the date of death given for Richard le Petit may be based on Johnston's dating of the slab.

ALDINGBOURNE, SUSSEX

At Aldingbourne, Sussex, is a very worn coffin-shaped slab with fragmentary remains of an incised cross, ending in a semi-circular base, with an incised inscription in Norman-French, with the words separated by triple stops (Figure 13.20).[38] Little of the inscription now remains, but more can be seen on a sketch made by Clayton in 1889.[39] It read: '+ .. / .IC.... DE .... LVDE...[:GIST :I]CI: DEV: DE: L / ALME / : EYT: ME[RCY]: ....:PITE: ..V.. [A]M / EN'. The letters that remain are of the Ashford style. The letters 'LVDE' might have formed part of the word Ludesye, an early spelling of the manor of Lidsey in Aldingbourne.[40] If that were so, the slab might commemorate a Lidsey landholder of the late thirteenth century or the early fourteenth century, but none of the names of those recorded fits with the traces of letters that are shown on Clayton's sketch.[41]

CLOTHALL, HERTFORDSHIRE

The final cross slab from this series is at Clothall, Hertfordshire, now incomplete and broken into pieces, seven of which have traces of lettering, which have been rearranged to form part of the altar step in the south chapel. It was coffin-shaped with a single hollow-moulded chamfer (Figure 13.21). On the top surface can still be

13.19 (opposite, left) Stoke d'Abernon, Surrey: Richard le Petit, c 1280–1305. Ashford-style slab with relief cross and incised letters. Tracing of rubbing by S F Badham.

13.20 (opposite, right) Aldingbourne, Sussex: unknown, c 1280–1305. Ashford-style incised slab. Tracing of rubbing by S F Badham.

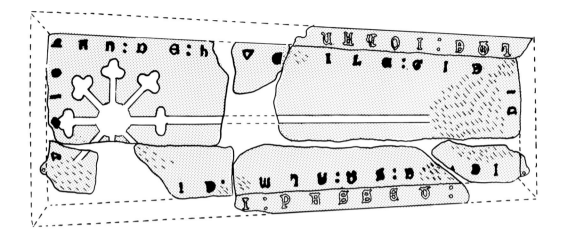

13.21 *Clothall, Hertfordshire: John de Havevile, ob c 1303–10. Reconstruction by S F Badham of Ashford-style slab with relief cross, incised letters and indents for brass letters.*

seen the very worn remains of a relief cross. The head resembles an eight-rayed wheel, each ray springing from the sides of an octagon and terminating in a trefoil. Traces of foliation can be seen part-way down the stem, but the form of the base can no longer be determined. The particular form of eight-rayed cross is unusual, but there is no reason to suggest that it was a type limited to the London workshops. Similar examples are recorded at Lesnes Abbey, Kent;[42] Great Yarmouth, Norfolk;[43] and, most significantly, at Kimmeridge and Wimborne Minster, both in Dorset. On the Clothall slab, the indent for the brass cross, which marks the beginning of the brass inscription, is cut into the uppermost portion of the relief cross. As with the Basyng-style cross slab at South Benfleet (discussed in Chapter 12), this indicates that the inscription was added to a stock relief cross slab. It again suggests that the London marblers bought in from the quarries at Corfe ready-carved cross slabs as well as plain dressed slabs, to which they would then add inscriptions, brass inlays and other details.

Running clockwise round the perimeter of the top surface of the slab is an inscription, which was once inlaid in Main Group size III brass letters. Virtually the entire text was clear when it was recorded by Salmon in 1728,[44] though some letters have since been obliterated. It reads: '+ IOH / AN: DE H[A]VE[V]ILE: GIS / [T:] IC[I:] / [D] IEV[: D]E: SA: ALM[E]: EI[T: M] / [ERC]Y'. Only part of the chamfer is now visible, the remainder being hidden within the step, but this has a second inscription, running anti-clockwise. It is of incised Lombardic letters of characteristic Ashford style, with the words separated by double stops. The traces that are visible read: '.... / .... I: PASSET: .... / : .... / LME: IOHAN .... / .... :'. A comparison with other inscriptions suggests that the full text might have read: 'VOUS / : QVI: PAR: ICI: PASSET: PVR / : SA: A / LME: IOHAN: DE: HAVEVILE: P / RIEZ:'.

The Clothall slab commemorates John de Havevile, a member of an influential Clothall family. He was a patron and benefactor of the Hospital of St Mary Magdalen at Clothall, founded by his ancestor, Hugh de Clothall.[45] In 1300 he was patron when Walter of Little Stockton was instituted master and in 1303 he and his kinsman, John de Poleye, granted land at Breda to the Hospital. However, when the next master was instituted in 1314, Havevile was no longer patron, so he was probably dead by then. The Havevile and Poleye families were also patrons of the living of Clothall, though John de Havevile is not recorded in that connection, probably because no institutions took place in the relevant period. When Robert de Havevile was instituted as vicar in 1271, Geoffrey and Emilsina, perhaps John's parents, were joint patrons.[46] Robert de Havevile died in 1310; John and Muriella Poleye acted as patrons on the institution of his successor, Elias de Poleye. This suggests that John de Havevile may well have been dead by 1310.

CHICHESTER CATHEDRAL I TO III AND WEST WITTERING, SUSSEX

Finally, mention must be made of three coffin-shaped slabs with incised crosiers at Chichester Cathedral, Sussex, and another similar slab at nearby West Wittering, Sussex, where the bishops of Chichester had a house.[47] The West Wittering slab, which has no inscription, but also incorporates a relief cross botonnée, is unattributed. Two of the Chichester slabs, in the north choir aisle, also lack inscriptions, but have been attributed by Tummers to Bishop Seffrid II, who died in 1204 (Figure 13.22), and Ralph Wareham, who died in 1222.[48] The third Chichester slab, in the south choir aisle, has indents of an inscription in Main Group Lombardic lettering (Figure 13.23). Bertram has suggested that this commemorated Gilbert de St Leofard, who died in 1305, but Tummers's analysis attributes it to Ralph Neville, who died in 1244.[49]

The designs of the crosiers on these four slabs are all very similar, suggesting that they may have been made around the same time. There are many parallels for mass provision of retrospective monuments, perhaps to enhance the status of individual cathedrals. Notable English examples include the series of relief effigies to Saxon bishops at Wells Cathedral, Somerset, all made *c* 1220–40,[50] and the series of brasses to Archbishop Thoresby and six of his predecessors in York Minster, commissioned from Robert de Patryngton in 1369–73.[51] The slab at Chichester that was singled out for the addition of a brass inscription may have commemorated either a recently deceased bishop or a bishop preparing his monument in his own lifetime; the need to provide a monument for himself may have prompted a desire to provide memorials for some of his predecessors also. If this were so, the use of Main Group brass lettering on this slab rules out a date of manufacture prior to the last quarter of the thirteenth century. Whilst the basis of Bertram's attribution was considered unconvincing by Tummers,

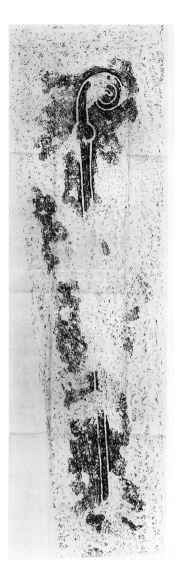

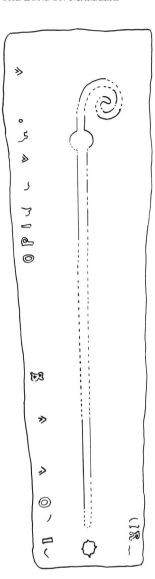

13.22 (right) Chichester Cathedral, Sussex II: possibly for Bishop Seffrid II, ob 1204, made c 1290–1305. Ashford-style incised slab. Rubbing by F A Greenhill, Society of Antiquaries collection, photograph by A C Cooper Ltd.

13.23 (far right) Chichester Cathedral, Sussex I: possibly for Gilbert de St Leofard, ob 1305. Ashford-style incised slab with indents for brass letters. Drawing by J F A Bertram.

it has to be said that a date of *c* 1305 would fit the composition very well. The use of Main Group brass lettering certainly cannot be pushed back as far as 1244. The combination of incising and brass inlay is mainly found on Ashford series slabs and we would tentatively attribute this group of crosier slabs to the Ashford workshop.

CHAPTER 14

OTHER ASHFORD-STYLE MONUMENTS

The Ashford series is unique amongst the pattern series discussed in this monograph, in the range both of brasses and of other Purbeck marble monuments that are stylistically related to the incised slabs and therefore likely to have come from the same workshop. (A full list of these monuments is in Appendix B.) That the same craftsmen produced a variety of types of Purbeck marble memorials should not come as a surprise. Documentary evidence suggests that London Purbeck marblers, such as Adam the Marbler, supplied a wide range of Purbeck marble products, including paving and architectural components, as well as monuments.[1] Research shortly to be published by Lankester and John Blair throws light on another marbler, Master Ralph of London, who dealt in brasses and other Purbeck marble products around the end of the thirteenth century.[2] From the coincidence in dates, it is tempting to speculate that he might have controlled the workshop in which the Ashford series was produced.

COTTENHAM, CAMBRIDGESHIRE

The most prestigious form of Purbeck marble monument was the carved effigy. By the end of the thirteenth century, the vast majority of such effigies were carved in full relief, but a small number show the figure carved in bas-relief. Fragmentary remains of one of these figures survive, mounted on the east wall of the south porch, at Cottenham, Cambridgeshire. The previous history of this monument is unclear.[3] Only the top and bottom sections of the coffin-shaped slab remain (Figures 14.1 and 14.2). All the decoration is on the top surface of the slab. Round the perimeter is a wide border in which are set indents for Main Group size II brass letters. The surviving letters read: '+ CRIST / E: M..........................: PRE / CE ... / ..MOT............... '. The inscription is unusual in that it begins in the top dexter corner of the slab, rather than the centre of the head of the slab, which became the conventional position by the fourteenth century. The form of the initial cross is also unusual, being a plain straight-sided cross with square terminals. Virtually all initial crosses on London brasses with Main Group inscriptions begin

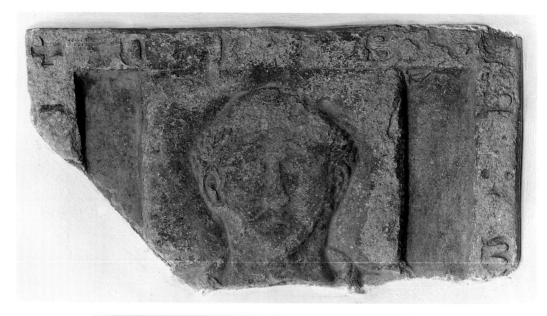

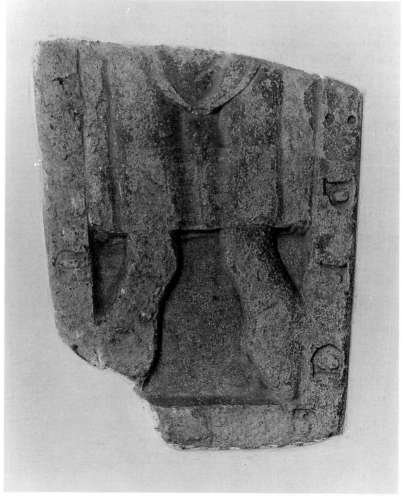

with a more elaborate straight-armed cross with fleur-de-lis terminals. Interestingly, the only other Main Group inscription known to us with a simple cross of the type shown at Cottenham is the inscription at Easton-on-the-Hill, Northamptonshire, which (as explained in Chapter 5) must date to the 1280s or earlier. These features suggest to us that the Cottenham slab holds an early date in the chronology of slabs with Main Group lettering.

The centre of the slab contains the figure of a priest in mass vestments. It is carved in sunken low relief, so that the highest points of the effigy align with the wide border around the perimeter of the slab, giving the impression that the figure lies in a coffin. As far as we can establish, this is a unique representation amongst Purbeck marble memorials. However, there are three freestone effigies, similarly shown in coffins, at Monkton Farleigh, Wiltshire, which Tummers dates to the third quarter of the thirteenth century.[4] The head of the Cottenham priest rests on a single rectangular cushion, again a feature which is normally associated with the thirteenth century.

The top surface of the slab is somewhat damaged and not all the detail is clear. Nonetheless, it cannot be doubted that the figure bears a remarkable similarity to the incised slab at Pyrton, Oxfordshire (discussed in Chapter 13). The shape of the head is the same, with a very broad brow narrowing to a pointed chin, and a thick, cone-shaped, neck. The domed head is tonsured in both cases, with the same straggly fringe and curls of hair around the ears. What can be seen of the individual facial features of the Cottenham priest mirrors the Pyrton priest; both have closely set eyes and a bulbous nose. Only a very small part of the amice can be seen on the Cottenham effigy, but this encircles the neck high at the back and appears to sweep down low at the front, in the same manner as on the Pyrton slab. Turning to the lower fragment of the Cottenham effigy, this again parallels the representation on the Pyrton slab. The large feet are fully revealed, unlike on most Purbeck marble effigies of clerics of this date, which show only the tips of the feet; they are placed apart in typical Ashford series style. The drapery is comparatively flat across the front of the figure, with indications of the distinctive Ashford-style folds at the sides. The chasuble ends at a similar level on both figures and, though the decoration on the foot apparel of the alb differs, one very significant detail is the same. On monuments to clerics the plain border of the apparel is invariably shown on all four sides of the rectangle, but on these two figures, the only two known Ashford-style full-length representations of priests, the border goes round only three sides, so that the central decorative panel extends right to the hem on the lowest side of the rectangle. In summary, the Cottenham priest is a three-dimensional representation of the pattern used for the incised slab at Pyrton, which latter probably commemorates Richard de Gretton, whom we believe to have died in the 1280s.

14.1 (opposite, top) Cottenham, Cambridgeshire: possibly for John Walerand, ob 1276. Ashford series low-relief effigy with indents for brass letters. Top section of slab. Photograph by Cambridge Reprographic Centre.

14.2 (opposite, bottom) Cottenham, Cambridgeshire: possibly for John Walerand, ob 1276. Ashford series low-relief effigy with indents for brass letters. Bottom section of slab. Photograph by Cambridge Reprographic Centre.

The parallels which we have drawn for the inscription, the representation of the effigy in a coffin, the single cushion and the detailed depiction of the figure, all point to a late thirteenth-century date for the Cottenham monument, rather than anything later. Too little of the inscription survives to give any clue to the name of the priest commemorated, so once more records of incumbents must be examined. These appear complete for Cottenham from the mid-thirteenth century; the entries for the relevant period consist of Stephen Heydon 1260–5, John Walerand 1265–76 and Thomas de Wimbise 1276–1310. Of these, John Walerand's date of vacation makes him the most likely candidate for this Ashford series memorial. It seems to us most unlikely that the series was in production as early as 1265, when Stephen Heydon ceased to hold the living. Similarly, the date of 1310, when Thomas de Wimbise vacated the living, probably falls just outside the period of the Ashford series, though he cannot be completely ruled out.

OTHER PURBECK MARBLE RELIEF EFFIGIES

It is unlikely that this would have been the only Purbeck marble relief effigy made by the Ashford workshop, but it is the only one that can be attributed with confidence to the series. It is unusual in many respects. It is the only Purbeck marble effigy that we know of with indents for brass-inlaid lettering, though there are examples in other stones. Slabs combining low-relief half-effigies with indents for brass letters of regional style are to be found at Stow, Lincolnshire,[5] Denton, Co. Durham,[6] and Valle Crucis Abbey, Denbighshire.[7] The oolitic limestone effigy of Sir John de Buslingthorpe at Buslingthorpe, Lincolnshire, lies on a slab of Purbeck marble with indents for Main Group lettering.[8] Finally, there is a full-relief effigy with indents for Main Group lettering at Sturton-le-Steeple, Nottinghamshire.[9] As mentioned above, Purbeck marble bas-relief effigies are uncommon at this date, but Tummers's seminal work on thirteenth-century secular effigies lists four thirteenth-century Purbeck marble low-relief effigies, at Faulkbourne, Toppesfield, Thruxton and Hatfield, which merit examination for links with the Cottenham figure.

The slabs at Faulkbourne and Toppesfield, both in Essex, combine an effigy with an incised inscription, the sort of combination of techniques which characterizes many Ashford series products, but on closer examination an Ashford workshop origin seems unlikely for either. The Faulkbourne monument consists of a coffin lid with a pointed top, bearing an armed figure, which is seen in profile.[10] Round the perimeter of the upper half of the slab was an incised inscription in Lombardic lettering. The slab is in a poor state of preservation, with virtually the entire top surface having exfoliated. Only two letters, 'AR', can still be detected, in the gable above the back of the helmet, and the style of the lettering is totally unrelated to that used for Ashford series products, or indeed any other pattern series discussed in this monograph. The letters are only about 25mm high and are of a very florid character.[11] As to the effigy, nothing about it, other than the fact that the carving is in low relief, resembles the Cottenham slab. At nearby Toppesfield is a slab with the effigy of a knight, partly incised and partly in low relief, with an incised inscription in Lombardic lettering. It is unfortunately now smothered in cement and hidden under the organ, but was described in detail by Hills, who thought it to have been of lias, not Purbeck marble.[12]

The other two possibly relevant bas-relief effigies which are listed by Tummers, at Thruxton, Hampshire,[13] and Hatfield, Hertfordshire,[14] appear to be related to each other and bear some resemblance to the Cottenham slab. Both show armed figures on coffin-shaped slabs, with their heads resting on large rectangular cushions like that seen on the Cottenham slab. Both were described by Tummers as having a primitive frontal representation of the figure, with a shield covering much of the body, from which straight legs protrude.[15] The lower part of the Thruxton slab is missing, but the feet of the Hatfield knight are very similar in shape and positioning to those of the Cottenham priest. However, there are no good grounds for disputing the mid-thirteenth-century date assigned to these two military figures by Tummers and, though they are in some ways similar to the Cottenham priest, they seem unlikely to have come from the Ashford workshop.

One unique Purbeck marble monument commemorating the heart burial of an unknown male or female civilian can, however, be linked with the Ashford series. Probably originally from Stone Chapel, near Faversham, Kent, this slab was found on farmland and is now in private possession at Luddenham. It is a coffin-shaped slab with a double hollow-moulded chamfer. On the top surface is a relief cross; the head is of the straight-armed type with trefoil terminals. Above it, in perfectly preserved high relief, is a pair of hands holding a heart. The position and drawing of the hands, with their supple fingers, closely resemble the depiction of the hands on the Steeple Langford and London Museum figures.

RELIEF CROSSES WITH MAIN GROUP LETTERING

Whilst both the Basyng and the Ashford workshops produced customized cross slabs, the Basyng workshop appears only to have added incised decoration to the standard quarry products from Corfe. As has been demonstrated, the Ashford workshop was more adventurous in its range of products, which include a number of mixed-media monuments, combining relief carving, incising and brass inlay. Amongst the many Purbeck marble coffin lids surviving are a small number which combine relief crosses with inlays for inscriptions in Main Group brass letters. These are broadly analogous with the Cottenham priest and some may well be Ashford products. One of the best preserved is the slab to Lucy

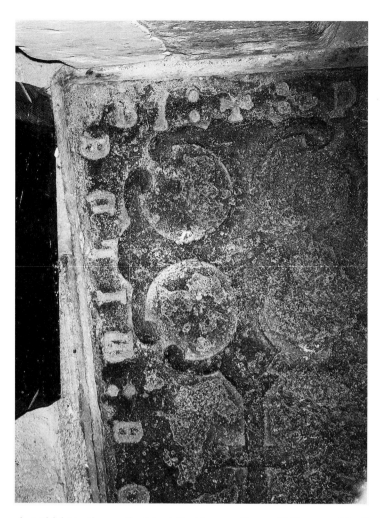

14.3 East Lavant, Sussex: Lucy de Mildebi, c 1290–1305. Possible Ashford-style slab with relief cross and indents for brass letters. Photograph by S F Badham showing indent of brass letters cut into the relief cross.

de Mildebi in the north aisle at East Lavant, Sussex.[16] The round-leaf cross with a stepped calvary, a standard Purbeck type, is carved to cover most of the top face of the slab. The spacing of the inscription has therefore had to be modified to fit round the cross (Figure 14.3). It reads: '+ PR / IEZ: QI: PASSET: PAR: ICI: / [gap] / PVR: LALME: LVCE: DE: MILDE / BI:'. Of the cross slabs discussed in this chapter, this is the most likely to have come from the Ashford workshop.

None of the remaining Purbeck marble coffin-shaped slabs that combine relief crosses with inscriptions in Main Group lettering fits so well with established Ashford types. Under semi-fixed boarding in the north aisle at Gilston, Hertfordshire, are the very worn remains of two slabs to members of the de Ros family. Both combine relief crosses with inscriptions in Main Group lettering. The names of those commemorated cannot be deciphered, but antiquarian sources record them as being Robert de Ros and Alys or Alyx de Ros.[17] Robert de Ros was alive in 1301, but no other references to him can be found.[18] References to Alice de Ros span the period 1287 to 1307.[19] These references suggest that both slabs date from the very early fourteenth century, probably in the closing years of the Ashford series. One is virtually effaced and little can be said about it. The inscription on the other is badly damaged but the beautifully carved low-relief cross is still fairly well preserved. The head is of a foliated cross patée form and the stem again ends in foliage. Originally it must have been an outstandingly fine slab. However, this form of cross is more usually associated with mid-thirteenth-century date. Whilst an Ashford origin is possible, appropriation of an earlier monument cannot be ruled out in this case.

A curious Purbeck coffin lid commemorating Brother Ralph is to be found against the north wall of the west end of the nave at Dorchester, Oxfordshire.[20] The slab is coped, with a straight-armed cross ending in a stepped calvary. Four flowers are incised round the head of the cross. The surviving traces of the inscription read: '.. W / S: E: P[AR]: ICI: D ......: / PVR: / LALME: FRERE: RAVF: I. / I .. '. Some of the letters were inlaid into the relief calvary of the cross, while others cut across the incised floral decoration.

Finally, at Willoughby, Lincolnshire, is a Purbeck marble coffin-shaped slab with a standard relief cross botonnée, ending in a stepped calvary. The inscription, which commemorates William de Ri..., is badly cut and crammed awkwardly into three lines above the crosshead; although the style of the lettering is Main Group, a mixture of sizes is used.[21] The combination of brass letters and a standard Purbeck coffin lid are characteristic of the Ashford work-shop, but the poorly designed layout is not. All five of the cross slabs discussed in this section may have originated in the Ashford work-shop, but the evidence for such an origin is by no means clear-cut.

ASHFORD SERIES BRASSES

In contrast, there is extensive evidence to indicate that the Ashford workshop also produced brasses. First, a number of the slabs we have already discussed, those at Tilsworth, Pyrton, Clothall and Cottenham, incorporate inscriptions formerly inlaid in brass Lombardic letters of the Main Group style, found on all brasses in Binski's analysis of early London brasses. Though this is not conclusive proof of common origin, it certainly suggests that the Ashford slabs and some at least of the London brasses came from the same workshop. Second, the indent to Gilbert Saddoc and the Ashford-style incised slab to his wife Joan (discussed in Chapter 13) may well have been commissioned from the same London marbler's workshop in the late thirteenth century. Finally, and crucially, there are brasses with stylistic links to Ashford slabs.

HEREFORD CATHEDRAL AND RELATED BRASSES

As previously explained in Chapter 5, the only engraved inlay from a monumental brass for which there is incontrovertible evidence of thirteenth-century date is the 100mm-high figure of St Ethelbert from the brass to Thomas de Cantilupe in Hereford Cathedral, which was laid down by 1287 (see Figure 5.4). The figure has interesting parallels with Ashford incised slabs, notably that from Steeple Langford, Wiltshire (see Figure 13.6), and the London Museum I slab (see Figure 13.5). The faces are similar, but the best comparison is in the drawing and pose of the upraised hand. The splayed fingers and fat palms are the same, the unusually thin wrists are bent back at the same impossibly sharp angle and the forearms are similarly positioned.

Although the Cantilupe brass is not assigned to a specific pattern series in *The Earliest English Brasses*, a number of other early indents appear to be linked to it stylistically. The head of Thomas de Cantilupe is depicted in semi-profile, he has a crosier in his left hand, his right hand is held in blessing and he rests his feet on an animal, possibly a wolf as on his seal. The outline thus produced is quite distinctive and can be closely paralleled on other early episcopal and abbatial indents. Those most closely related to the Cantilupe slab include the indent in Ely Cathedral, Cambridgeshire, to William de Luda, who died in 1298.[22] It should be noted that current work by Lankester and Blair on Master Ralph the Mason, whom we suggested above may have been responsible for the Ashford series products, demonstrates that he worked for Bishop de Luda, thus reinforcing the likelihood that he also made de Luda's brass.[23] Also closely related to the Cantilupe slab is the indent at St Albans Abbey, Hertfordshire, to John de Berkhamstede, who died in 1301,[24] and another indent, of a bishop under an elaborate canopy, in Ely Cathedral, now in the south choir aisle, but almost certainly originally in front of the high altar in the presbytery.[25] Rogers has suggested that John Ketton, who died in 1316,[26] is commemorated in this last indent but such a date seems to us too far removed from the other indents with figures of closely comparable outline. It may instead commemorate one of the other three bishops known to have been buried in the presbytery and commemorated by a brass. The distinctively ogival arch of the canopy rules out Hugh de Balsham, who died in 1286, but Robert Orford, who died in 1310, and possibly also Ralph de Walpole, who died in 1302, are both credible contenders. Rogers considered that the elaboration of the canopy suggested a date between the 1308 Haselshaw indent and the Beaumont indent at Durham, previously dated *c* 1333, but which we have shown in Chapter 9 may be as early as 1317. The canopy design on the Ely indent is advanced for 1310 but not unparalleled, the ogee curve being quite similar to that on the 1311 slab to Princess Eleanor at Beaulieu (discussed in Chapter 7). A date of 1302 for an ogival canopy would, however, be very unusual. The monastic mourners in the sideshaft niches of the canopy suggest it most likely commemorates a monk-bishop with close ties to the convent. Orford had been Prior of Ely, but Balsham, Walpole and Ketton also had monastic links.[27] On balance, we think the Ely slab is most likely to have commemorated

Robert Orford, putting this indent right at the end of the Ashford series.

The fourth slab with a main figure of very similar outline to the Cantilupe slab is the indent at Waltham Abbey, Essex, which most probably commemorates Robert de Elenton, who died in 1302.[28] One important additional feature is that this figure has a long, cone-shaped neck, which, as we have seen, is a distinctive feature of many Ashford series incised slabs. This feature is also seen on the large and elaborate indent in Wells Cathedral, Somerset, to Walter de Haselshaw, who died in 1308.[29] The main figure on this indent has a slightly different outline, which is also seen on indents at Bottisham, Cambridgeshire, to Elyas de Beckingham[30] and at Weekley, Northamptonshire, to Agnes de Vavasour,[31] both of whom died in 1306. Fragments from the upper portion of an indent found at Hardwick Mill, Oxfordshire, which probably commemorated Thomas de Welles, who died in 1307, may also be linked stylistically with this group of indents.[32] It is interesting to note that the Weekley indent clearly shows the head in semi-profile, as on the Hereford, Ely and St Albans indents. We suggest that all these indents should therefore be regarded as likely Ashford series products, along with other surviving and lost brasses at Gorleston, Suffolk, and Peterborough Cathedral, Northamptonshire.[33]

ASHFORD, KENT, AND RELATED BRASSES

However, these are not the only brasses to have stylistic similarities with Ashford series incised slabs. It is possible to make an even more interesting comparison between the incised slab at Pyrton, Oxfordshire, probably to Richard de Gretton and thus dating to the 1280s (see Figure 13.2), and a brass from Ashford, Kent (Figures 14.4 and 14.5). They are not identical, as the very different chin shapes show, but they are remarkably close. The head of each is inclined slightly to the side, a feature also of the main figure on the Cantilupe indent. Both the Ashford and the Pyrton figures have a lop-sided effect as if drawn freehand; for example, the hair ends at a different level on each side of the face and the amice sits crookedly on the neck. What remains of the eyes, eyebrows and nose is also alike, as is the lop-sided mouth and crescent below, defining a prominent chin. The damage on the top of the Pyrton priest's nose creates a misleading impression of eyes placed unnaturally close together. But, if the detail is studied, it can be seen that there is only one way that they could have been drawn – with a long upward curve from the outer corner, then angled sharply down to the inner corner – exactly as shown on the Ashford brass. This is shown in the reconstruction of the Pyrton priest's head in Figure 14.6. The amices too are similarly decorated and both figures have a thick inverted cone of a neck. Finally, the treatment of the hair is extraordinarily close; the wispy fringe and locks of hair at the sides of the face are

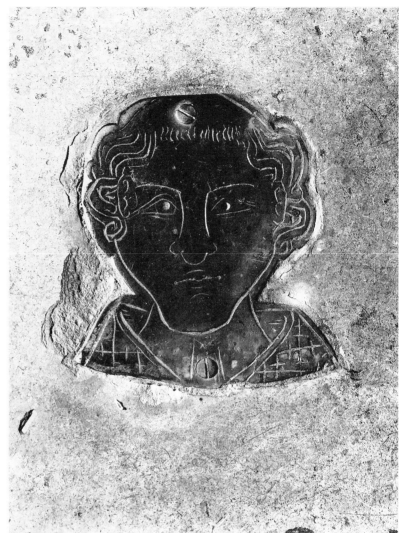

14.4 (right) Ashford, Kent:
unknown priest,
c 1282. Ashford-style
brass. The earliest
surviving English
figure brass.
Photograph by
A C Cooper Ltd.

14.5 (bottom, right)
Ashford, Kent:
unknown priest,
c 1282. Ashford-style
brass. Rubbing in the
Society of
Antiquaries collec-
tion, made before
holes were drilled in
the brass to fix it to a
new stone slab.

14.6 (bottom, far right)
Pyrton, Oxfordshire:
Richard de Gretton,
ob c 1280–9.
Ashford-style incised
slab. Detail of face
with damaged areas
reconstructed by
M W Norris.

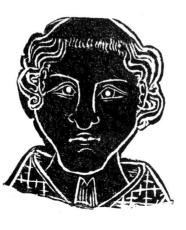

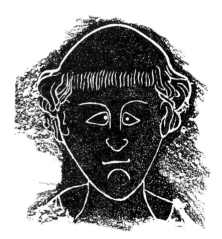

drawn the same way and, unusually, there is no line defining the tonsure. Many of the parallels drawn between the Ashford brass and the Pyrton incised slab are valid also for the Cottenham bas-relief effigy.

Unfortunately, the Ashford brass is divorced from its slab, which no longer survives, so there is no record of the form taken by the remainder of this monument. But it does seem clear that this was the only part of the figure engraved on brass. Although the bottom of the plate appears jagged on a rubbing (Figure 14.5), as if what survives has been torn from a larger plate, this impression is misleading. An examination of the brass itself reveals that the lower edge is buckled under in places, but was clearly cut straight (Figure 14.4). Moreover, the engraved lines depicting the hands do not extend quite as far as the bottom edge of the plate, which would not have been the case if this formed only part of a larger figure brass.

Although it is possible that the remainder of the figure was originally incised, it seems much more likely to us that there was never any more of the figure depicted. The head might have been placed within a crosshead, or perhaps combined with a separate cross or canopy. Three such compositions of early date are known. On the north wall of the ruined chancel of St Patrick's Cathedral, Trim, Ireland, is a coffin-shaped Purbeck marble slab with the indent of the head of a cleric under a canopy.[34] As he is wearing a cap and the plate extended slightly further down his body than that on the Ashford brass, the outline of this indent is obviously not identical with that at Ashford, but it is asymmetrical, indicating that the figure was turned slightly sideways, as on comparable Ashford series products. Round the perimeter of the Trim slab is an inscription in Main Group lettering, but unfortunately in too poor a condition to be read. It was recorded by Butler in 1854 and again by Conwell in 1872, who showed the inscription as reading: '+ WID .. / ....: HIC: RECTOR: ET: ARCH / ILEVITES: / HIC: IACET: IRA: DEI: PACIFICATV / R EI'; unfortunately, this is insufficient to provide an attribution.[35] A second example of an early demi-effigy is the lost brass from Wells Cathedral, Somerset, to Robert Burnell, who died in 1292, known only from the tiny sketch of the indent by Carter.[36]

The third indent which compares closely with the Ashford figure is in the Lady Chapel of Christ Church Cathedral, Oxford (Figure 14.7). It shows the head of a man above a cross with clustered terminals, with an animal at the base of the cross. The plate on which the head was engraved ends high on the shoulders, like the Ashford priest, and it too has a slightly asymmetrical appearance, suggesting that it was another, closely related Ashford series product. The perimeter inscription, in Main Group lettering, records that the slab commemorates John de Coleivile. The family, who gave their name variously as Colevile, Colecill or Coleshull, was very prominent in thirteenth-century Oxford. John Coleivile was a wealthy burgess. He gave rents to St Cross Church in 1268 to

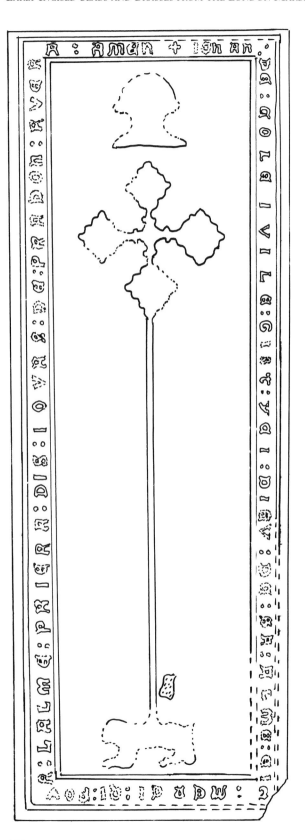

14.7 Christ Church Cathedral, Oxford: John de Coleivile, ob 1273. Ashford-style indent. The earliest known English figure brass. Drawing by J F A Bertram.

compensate them for the foundation of the Austin Friars and left a house in St John Baptist Street called Colecill Hall to St Peter-in-the-Bailey. He was provost in 1245 and 1250–1, bailiff in 1265–7 and mayor in 1269. He died in 1273.[37] John was not the only member of this family to be commemorated by a brass. His eldest son, Nicholas, who was master of St John's Hospital and died in 1323, was also buried in Christ Church Cathedral, Oxford, where his indent survives close to that of his father.[38] Firmly dated 1273, the Coleivile indent is the earliest-known London-made figure brass.

The Ashford brass has been variously dated between *c* 1320 and *c* 1340. Binski regarded it as a Camoys-style derivative and put it as *c* 1340.[39] We believe that there is overwhelming evidence to suggest it came from the late thirteenth-century workshop responsible for the products of the Ashford series and is a Camoys-style precursor of over half a century earlier. It is not an impressive brass; neither the design nor the execution is of a high standard. But both are much more the expected products of early experimentation in brass engraving than the flawless Trotton brass.

As the slab no longer survives, there is no inscription to indicate whom it commemorates. The missing inscription does not appear to have been recorded in antiquarian notes. Dering, who made an otherwise full record of the Ashford brasses in 1628, fails to refer to it,[40] as does Philpot in his notes of *c* 1613–15[41] and Scarlett in his heraldic collections of 1599,[42] though the latter is the least likely of these early sources to have included it. Possibly the brass was loose by the end of the sixteenth century; certainly by 1861 it was in the church chest.[43] Nor is there a reliable tradition as to whom it represents. Again, recourse must be had to the list of rectors. There was a priest at Ashford as early as 1086,[44] but no more names are recorded until the thirteenth century.[45] Even then the records are initially sketchy. The first rector whose institution is recorded in the registers of the Archbishops of Canterbury was the long-serving Robert de Derby, who was instituted in 1282 and resigned in 1316, nearly a decade after the Ashford workshop is thought to have ceased production. It is, of course, possible that the brass commemorated Derby and was laid down in his lifetime. However, a more likely explanation is that this brass commemorates Derby's unknown predecessor, and that the brass can be dated *c* 1282, that is about five years before the Cantilupe brass at Hereford.

Such a date may seem worryingly early when viewed against the main analyses by Binski and John Blair in *The Earliest English Brasses*, but there is unambiguous evidence for brass production in England well before 1300. Brass letters of the Westminster type were produced and incorporated in monuments from 1268.[46] The Lincolnshire A workshop was in operation from the 1270s, its products including an inscription to William de Lessington, who died in 1272, and a full-length figure to Oliver Sutton, who died in 1299, both of which indents are in Lincoln Cathedral.[47] Moreover,

Rogers has shown that evidence points to the existence of a work-shop under strong French influence operating in south-east England, most probably in London, in the 1270s and 1280s.[48] Early brasses, known only from brief documentary references, may well have been laid down in Old St Paul's Cathedral, London, to Henry of Sandwich, who died in 1273,[49] and in St Augustine's Abbey, Canterbury, Kent, to Robert de Chichester, who died in 1272.[50] Could these have been amongst the first products of the workshop responsible for the Ashford series, or were they from an even earlier workshop, for which no other evidence has yet come to light?

A date of 1282 for the Ashford brass would also sit well with our attribution of the Pyrton priest to Richard de Gretton, who prob-ably died between 1280 and 1289, and of the Cottenham bas-relief slab to John Walerand, who probably died in 1276, both of which monuments are very closely related stylistically to the Ashford brass. There can be no doubt that these three monuments were produced in the same workshop, within a very few years of each other. For each of these monuments, there is, of course, an alterna-tive possibility for the person commemorated, which would give dates of 1302 for the Pyrton slab, 1310 for the Cottenham effigy and 1316 for the Ashford brass. Whilst these alternative dates would fit more comfortably with Binski and Blair's chronologies as set out in *The Earliest English Brasses*, taken together they are at odds with the other evidence regarding the period in which the Ashford series was operational. Whilst 1302 falls within the period when other monuments which we have attributed to the Ashford series workshop were produced, 1310 is on the margin and 1316 clearly outside the operational span. It thus seems inescapable that the earlier dates for these three monuments are by far the most likely ones.

As we explained in Chapter 5, there have been a number of candidates for the 'title' of the earliest surviving English figure brass. Our conclusion is that this honour should go to the Ashford priest.

A SUMMARY LIST OF INCISED SLABS FROM THE LONDON WORKSHOPS

Notes
1. All references are to pre-1974 counties.
2. Where there is more than one slab from the same church or museum, they are numbered in chronological order with Roman numbering.
3. Slabs are listed within each series in broad chronological order, as determined by stylistic analysis.
4. Information in the date column refers to documentary evidence concerning the person commemorated; no attempt has been made to assign approximate dates of manufacture for individual slabs.

DATE	PLACE	PERSON COMMEMORATED
BASYNG SERIES		
	Wherwell, Hampshire	Not known
	Guildford Museum, Surrey	Not known
	Boreham, Essex	Henri le Marchaunt
1289	Dunstable, Bedfordshire I	Alice Duraunt
	St Cross, Winchester, Hampshire	Petrunele L...
	South Benfleet, Essex	Marcelie Pr...
1295	Winchester Cathedral, Hampshire I	Prior William de Basyng
	Winchester Cathedral, Hampshire II	Prince Edmund
	Winchester Cathedral, Hampshire III	Prince Richard
	Winchester Cathedral, Hampshire IV	Not known
1295	St Bartholomew the Great, London I	Hugh de Hendon
	Romsey, Hampshire	Johanna ...
	St Bartholomew the Great, London II	Simon de Papnei
ASHFORD SERIES		
1280–9	Pyrton, Oxfordshire	Richard de Gretton
	Cliffe-at-Hoo, Kent	Eleanor de Clive
after 1284	Dunstable, Bedfordshire II	Richard Duraunt
before 1306	London Museum I	Joan de St Edmonds
	Steeple Langford, Wiltshire	Not known
	Tilsworth, Bedfordshire	Adam de Tullesworthe
	Stoke d'Abernon, Surrey	Richard le Petit
	London Museum II	Godfrey le Troumpour
	Aldingbourne, Sussex	Not known
	White Waltham, Berkshire	Joan Saddoc
1295	Sawbridgeworth, Hertfordshire I	William de Say
after 1279	Mickleham, Surrey I	Alice de Newenham
	Fobbing, Essex	Thomas de Crawedene
	Doddington, Kent	Agnes ...
?1305	Chichester Cathedral, Sussex I	?Gilbert of St Leofard
	Chichester Cathedral, Sussex II	Bishop Seffrid II
	Chichester Cathedral, Sussex III	Ralph Wareham

Date	Place	Person commemorated
	West Wittering, Sussex	Not known
	Horton Kirby, Kent	?Baldwin de Caundell
1304–9	Clothall, Hertfordshire	John de Havevile
1305–11	Mickleham, Surrey II	John de Newenham

CAMOYS STYLE

after 1299	Sawbridgeworth, Hertfordshire II	Elizabeth de Say
	Winchester Cathedral, Hampshire V	Not known
	Hospital of St Thomas Acon, London	Not known
1305	Titchfield, Hampshire	Sir William de Pageham
1311	Beaulieu Abbey, Hampshire	Princess Eleanor
1312	Little Shelford, Cambridgeshire	Sir John de Frevile
	St Bartholomew the Great, London III	Not known
	Lesnes Abbey, Kent	Not known
1328	Barking Abbey, Essex	Martin
?1330	Stoke, Kent	?John Vaudie
1338	Snodland, Kent	John de Dennyntone

SEPTVANS STYLE

?1324	West Wickham, Kent I	?Nicholas Louseby
	Victoria and Albert Museum, London	Not known

SEYMOUR STYLE

1309	Westwell, Kent	John de la More
1309	Rothwell, Northamptonshire	William de Williamstorpe
1344	West Wickham, Kent II	Walter de Cestreford

LONDON A SLABS

1349	Newnham, Hampshire	Not known
1362	West Wickham, Kent III	John de Huntingfeld

UNCLASSIFIED EFFIGIAL SLABS

	Strood, Kent	Mariote and John Creye
	Harrow, Middlesex	Not known
	Wimborne Minster, Dorset	Not known
	Salisbury Cathedral, Wiltshire	Not known
	Elsing, Norfolk	... bourne

OTHER UNCLASSIFIED SLABS

after 1327	Christ Church Cathedral, Oxford	Edmund de Ludlow
	St Bartholomew the Great, London IV	Not known
	St Bartholomew the Great, London V	Minehele ...
	Bray, Berkshire	Alan Hereward
before 1335	Great Bookham, Surrey I	John de Pollesdene
	Southwark Cathedral, Surrey I	Not known
1327	Egham, Surrey	(Commemorative slab)
1341	Great Bookham, Surrey II	(Commemorative slab)
1349	Southwark Cathedral, Surrey II	Alein Ferthing

APPENDIX B
A SUMMARY LIST OF BRASSES, INDENTS AND RELIEF EFFIGIES ATTRIBUTED TO THE LONDON WORKSHOPS

Notes
1. All references are to pre-1974 counties.
2. Where there is more than one brass or indent from the same church, they are distinguished by the numbering system in the summary list of English-made brasses and indents in Coales 1987, 180–215.
3. Monuments are listed within each series in broad chronological order, as determined by stylistic analysis.
4. Information in the date column refers to documentary evidence concerning the person commemorated; no attempt has been made to assign approximate dates of manufacture for individual brasses or indents.

TYPE	DATE	PLACE	PERSON COMMEMORATED
BASYNG STYLE			
Brass		Chinnor, Oxfordshire	Not known
ASHFORD STYLE			
Indent	1273	Christ Church Cathedral, Oxford I	John de Coleivile
Indent	1272–8	Hook Norton, Oxfordshire	Isabel de Pleci
Relief	1276	Cottenham, Cambridgeshire	John Walerand
Brass	1282	Ashford, Kent	Not known
Indent	1284	Down Ampney, Gloucestershire	Nicholas de Villiers
Brass	before 1287	Hereford Cathedral, Herefordshire I	Thomas de Cantilupe
Indent		St Patrick's Cathedral, Trim, Ireland	Not known
Indent	1292	Wells Cathedral, Somerset I	Robert Burnell
Cross		East Lavant, Sussex	Lucy de Mildebi
Cross		Dorchester, Oxfordshire III	Brother Ralph
Cross		Willoughby, Lincolnshire	William de Ri...
Indent	1298	Ely Cathedral, Cambridgeshire I	William de Luda
Relief		Stone Chapel, Kent	Not known
Indent		Gorleston, Suffolk	Sabina de Bacon
Indent	1301	St Albans Abbey, Hertfordshire I	John de Berkhamstede
Indent	1302	Waltham Abbey, Essex I	Robert de Elenton
Indent	after 1297	White Waltham, Berkshire	Gilbert Saddoc
Cross	after 1301	Gilston, Hertfordshire II	Robert de Ros
Brass	1305	Gorleston, Suffolk	John de Bacon
Indent	1306	Bottisham, Cambridgeshire	Elyas de Beckingham
Indent	1306	Weekley, Northamptonshire	Agnes de Vavasour
Brass	1307	Peterborough Cathedral, Northamptonshire	Sir Edmund Gascelin
Indent	?1307	Hardwick Mill, Oxfordshire	?Thomas de Welles
Indent	1308	Wells Cathedral, Somerset II	Walter de Haselshaw
Cross	after 1307	Gilston, Hertfordshire I	Alyx de Ros
Indent	?1310	Ely Cathedral, Cambridgeshire II	?Robert Orford

Type	Date	Place	Person commemorated
Camoys style			
Brass		Cobham, Kent I	Joan de Cobham
Indent		Wells Cathedral, Somerset	King Ina
Indent	1309	Bindon, Dorset	Richard Maners
Indent	1310	Saltwood, Kent	William Archer
Brass	1311	Old St Paul's Cathedral, London IV	Ralph de Hengham
Brass		New College, Oxford (palimpsest)	Not known
Indent	1314	Aston Rowant, Oxfordshire	Sir Hugh le Blount
Indent	1315	Milton Abbas, Dorset	Walter de Sydelinge
Brass	before 1318	Trotton, Sussex I	Margaret de Camoys
Brass	before 1318	Stoke-by-Nayland, Suffolk I	Sir John Peytone
Brass		Stanton St John, Oxfordshire (palimpsest)	Not known
Indent		Dunwich, Suffolk	Not known
Brass		Pitstone, Buckinghamshire	Not known
Brass	1322	Merton College, Oxford I	Richard de Hakebourne
Indent		Beaulieu Abbey, Hampshire II	?Isabel Marshall
Indent	1326	Stoke-by-Nayland, Suffolk II	Christine de Peytone
Brass	1326	Trumpington, Cambridgeshire	Sir Roger de Trumpington
Brass	1327	Stoke d'Abernon, Surrey I	Sir John d'Abernon II
Indent	after 1326	Redenhall, Norfolk	William de Neuport
Brass	after 1327	Oulton, Suffolk	Adam de Bacon
Indent		Walgrave, Northamptonshire	Not known
Brass		Clifton Campvile, Staffordshire (palimpsest)	Not known
Brass		Pettaugh, Suffolk (palimpsest)	Not known
Indent		Emneth, Norfolk I	Not known
Brass	1331	Acton, Suffolk	Sir Robert de Bures
Indent	1332	Hollesley, Suffolk	William de Gaytone
Indent	1332	Harpley, Norfolk	John de Gernay
Brass	1331–8	Pebmarsh, Essex	Sir William FitzRalph
Indent		Hanslope, Buckinghamshire	Not known
Septvans style			
Brass	1306	Chartham, Kent	Sir Robert de Septvans
Ghost		Canterbury Cathedral, Kent I	Not known
Brass		Cople, Bedfordshire (palimpsest)	Not known
Brass		All Hallows Barking, London (palimpsest)	Not known
Brass		St John Maddermarket, Norwich (palimpsest)	Not known
Brass		Ingham, Norfolk (palimpsest)	Not known
Indent	1320	Letheringham, Suffolk	Sir William de Bovile
Seymour style			
Indent	1317–33	Durham Cathedral IV	Louis de Beaumont
Brass		Great Brington, Northamptonshire	Not known
Indent		Westleton, Suffolk	Not known

TYPE	DATE	PLACE	PERSON COMMEMORATED
Brass		Westley Waterless, Cambridgeshire	Sir John de Creke
Brass	1333	Denchworth, Berkshire (palimpsest)	(Commemorative plate)
Brass	1336	St Albans Abbey, Hertfordshire III	Richard de Wallingford
Brass	1337	Higham Ferrers, Northamptonshire	Lawrence Seymour
Brass	1339–50	Stoke d'Abernon, Surrey II	Sir John d'Abernon III
Brass	1348	Bowers Giffard, Essex	Sir John Gifford

HASTINGS STYLE

Indent	1346	Connington, Huntingdonshire	John and Margaret de Brus
Brass	1347	Elsing, Norfolk	Sir Hugh Hastings
Brass	1347	Wimbish, Essex	Sir John de Wautone
Brass		Checkendon, Oxfordshire (palimpsest)	Not known

Notes

Chapter 1 Introduction and methodology

1 Greenhill 1958, 15; Greenhill 1976, 1, 15 and 18–19.
2 Dru Drury 1949; Leach 1978; Sadler 1975–86; J Blair 1987.
3 C Blair 1991.
4 Greenhill 1958, 1; Greenhill 1976, 1, 3–4.
5 For Dorset coffin-shaped Purbeck marble cross slabs, see Gittos and Gittos 1994a. Lists of incised cross slabs in other stones and of incised inscription slabs of any stone type in Dorset have yet to be published. For Lincolnshire, see Greenhill 1986. Posthumous publication of Greenhill's studies of incised slabs in Oxfordshire, Northamptonshire and Warwickshire is in preparation. In addition, the inventories of the Royal Commission on Historical Monuments (RCHM) (England) include incised slabs amongst other monuments listed; for slabs discussed in this monograph, see in particular RCHM 1923, RCHM 1924 and RCHM 1984.
6 Harding 1992, 129.

Chapter 2 Common sources of brasses and incised slabs

1 Greenhill 1958, 6.
2 Ibid, 16.
3 Norris 1978, 81–2.
4 Trivick 1969, 32–3.
5 Greenhill 1958, 15.
6 Norris 1978, 48.
7 Preserved in the Bibliothèque Nationale, Paris, and the Bodleian Library, Oxford. Those of the period relevant to this monograph are illustrated in Adhémar 1974. See also Coales 1997.
8 Illustration of the Boncourt slab is in Norris 1988, fig 183. Illustrations of the St Omer slab are in Nys 1993a, fig 26, 294 (whole slab), and Nys 1993b, fig 12, 106 (detail).
9 Illustrated in Norris 1988, fig 13. We are grateful to Jerome Bertram for pointing out that the absence of stole-ends showing at the right wrist rule out a deacon as being commemorated by this slab and for suggesting that the long-sleeved, tight-wristed garment is more like a tunicle than a dalmatic, thus indicating that the deceased was a subdeacon.
10 van Belle 1992, Item 47, 26.
11 Hocquet 1924, 25–7, and English translation in Norris 1978, 94–5.
12 Page-Phillips 1989.

13 Nys 1993b. The evidence in relation to Ghent and Tournai contracts has been summarized by several writers, including H K Cameron, F A Greenhill, M W Norris and L Nys. The primary sources, however, remain de la Grange and Cloquet 1887 and van der Hagen 1914.
14 de la Grange and Cloquet 1887, 130.
15 Nys 1993b, 116.
16 The Walsokne brass is illustrated in Norris 1977, 2, pl 31. The Smalenburgh slab is illustrated in Greenhill 1986, pl 3.
17 Norris 1977, 1, 124.
18 The Gadebusch brass is illustrated in Edleston 1932, pl 4. The Doberan slab is illustrated in Greenhill 1976, 2, pl 67a.
19 Illustrated in Norris 1956, pl 14 (1).
20 The Lübeck slabs are illustrated in Baltzer and Bruns 1920, 245, 250 and 257. The Riga slab is illustrated in Greenhill 1976, 2, pl 21b.
21 Illustrated in Norris 1977, 2, pl 62.
22 The Gassmann and Mengershausen slabs are illustrated in Becker *et al* 1929, figs 290 and 291.
23 Illustrated in Norris 1977, 2, pl 142.
24 Illustrated in Norris 1978, pl 203.
25 Illustrated in Edleston 1949, pl 42.
26 Illustrated in Nadolskeigo 1990, fig 57, 511.
27 Kębłowski 1971, 72–85, and especially pls 1 and 22.
28 Illustrated in Norris 1988, pl 405.
29 Illustrated in Greenhill 1976, 2, pl 98a.
30 Ibid, 1, 25–6.
31 Greenhill 1958, 12.
32 This brass was for a time at Monk Hopton, Shropshire, but has been returned to Upton Cressett.
33 Bayliss 1990; Bayliss 1991.
34 Bayliss 1993, 50 and fig 10.
35 Badham 1989a.
36 Badham 1994.

Chapter 3 The development of effigial slabs to 1400 in England and Wales

1 Illustrated in Dark 1992, 23.
2 J Blair 1988a.
3 The Carisbrooke slab is illustrated in Bertram 1972, 32, fig 5.
4 Illustrated in Greenhill 1976, 2, pl 16b.
5 Ryder 1985, figs 29a–b.
6 Illustrated in Norris 1988, fig 427.
7 Illustrated in Fryer 1926, pl 10, though this does not show all the traces of the canopy.

8 Illustrated in Cresswell 1918. This slab, which was temporarily housed in Exeter Museum, has been returned to Hawkridge. We are grateful to John Coales for bringing this slab to our attention; it was the last effigial slab seen and added to his corpus by Greenhill, though too late to be published in Greenhill 1976.

9 Badham 1994.

10 Ryder 1991, 5.

11 Dru Drury 1949, 89, pl 22.

12 Fryer 1925; Gittos and Gittos 1997.

13 C Blair 1991, 5–6; Saul 1992.

14 Roper 1931, 184.

15 Illustrated in Greenhill 1976, pl 46c.

16 Ellacombe 1881, 35–6.

17 Ibid, 11 and Appendix.

18 Hills 1945, 259–62. It is hoped that the organ will be temporarily moved in the near future to enable a further examination of this slab and the removal to elsewhere in the church of the 1534 brass also currently underneath the organ.

19 Illustrated in Coales 1987, 50, fig 38.

20 Illustrated in Fryer 1926, pl 7.

21 The two drawings of this lost slab are illustrated in Fryer 1926, fig 1, and Greenhill 1976, 2, pl 47c.

22 Illustrated in Paul 1882, pl 2, fig 3.

23 Illustrated in Lysons 1791, pl 3.

24 Illustrated in Gittos 1985, pl 5.

25 J Blair 1979.

26 Cresswell 1918.

27 Hamilton-Rogers 1877, 125–6.

28 Illustrated in Greenhill 1976, 2, pl 52b.

29 Illustrated ibid, pl 134a.

30 Illustrated in Greenhill 1958, pl 4b.

31 Illustrated in Chatwin 1921–3, 44, pl 12, fig 1.

32 King and Russell 1913, 65.

33 Illustrated in Badham 1996, fig 17.

34 We are grateful to Nicholas Rogers and Lynda Dennison for advice on the dating of this slab.

35 J Blair 1987, 142–4 and 153–8.

36 Illustrated in Greenhill 1986: Harpswell pl 18, Buslingthorpe pl 19, Lincoln Cathedral pl 15b and Tetney pls 14 and 15b.

37 We are grateful to Brian and Moira Gittos for drawing this parallel to our attention.

38 Illustrated in Greenhill 1986, pl 2.

39 Illustrated ibid, pl 23.

40 Illustrated in RCHM 1984, 55, fig 69.

41 Illustrated in Greenhill 1976, 2, pl 29b.

42 Illustrated in Edleston 1939–40, opp 18.

43 Illustrated in Greenhill 1976, 2, pl 64a.

44 Gittos and Gittos 1989, 102.

45 Gittos and Gittos 1978.

46 For an analysis of brasses from the York workshops, see Badham 1989b.

47 Farman 1992.

48 Badham 1989b, 166.

49 Badham 1994, 220. For Yorkshire Series 0 brasses, see Badham 1989b, 167–71 and 180.

50 The earliest group of brasses from the Yorkshire 1 series, dating from c 1388 to c 1400, also have sideways-turned hands; Badham 1989b, 171–4 and 180–1.

51 Illustrated in Edleston 1939, fig 11.

52 The date has been left incomplete on the inscription.

53 Illustrated in Knowles 1880, fig 33.

54 Illustrated in Greenhill 1976, 2, pl 138a.

55 Illustrated in Edleston 1939–40, fig 2.

56 Gresham 1968, 1–3.

57 Illustrated in Gresham 1968, 217, fig 88.

58 Illustrated in Coales 1987, 55, fig 44.

59 Illustrated in Gresham 1968, pl 17.

60 Illustrated ibid, 236, fig 94.

61 Illustrated ibid, pl 17.

62 Illustrated ibid, pl 17.

63 Illustrated ibid, 242, fig 96.

64 Illustrated ibid, 172, fig 73.

65 A study of incised slabs and related monuments in south Wales by Sally Badham is in preparation.

66 In the Greenhill collection of rubbings, now at the Society of Antiquaries, is a rubbing of the St Dogmael slab taken in 1963 by H W Catling, annotated to explain that it was found that year during excavations, doing duty as a drain cover. The slab was not found in St Dogmael's in 1995, either on the Abbey site or at the nearby parish church.

Chapter 4 The Purbeck marble industry

1 J Blair 1988b; J Blair 1991.

2 J Blair 1991; Badham 1985, 475–7; Firman 1994.

3 We are grateful to Jerome Bertram for detailed information on this point.

4 J Blair 1991; Lankester and J Blair forth-coming.

5 Dunning 1949; Calkin 1960.

6 J Blair 1991; Kusaba 1993.

7 Illustrated in Dru Drury 1949, 76–7, pls 9 and 10.

8 Illustrated in Badham 1996, fig 24; we are grateful to Brian and Moira Gittos for bringing this slab to our attention.

9 We are grateful to Jerome Bertram for bringing the Durford Abbey slab to our attention.

10 Illustrated in Clapham 1915, 65, fig 10.

11 Tummers 1988, 29–30.

12 We are grateful to Jerome Bertram for bringing the Stoke Poges and Bray slabs to our attention; to Jon Bayliss and Les Smith for details of the Wingham slab; and to Brian Gittos for information on the St Martin, Canterbury slab.

13 J Blair 1991, 43–4; Leach 1978, 3.

14 Gittos and Gittos 1981.

15 New discoveries relating to the use of Purbeck marble in Ireland, specifically Dublin, are discussed in Gittos and Gittos forthcoming.

16 J Blair 1991, 44.

17 Ibid; Gittos and Gittos 1992a.

18 Conwell 1872–3, 400; King 1994, 123–4. We are grateful to Jerome Bertram for pointing out that the Trim slab is of Purbeck marble.

19 Firman 1991, 18.

20 C Blair 1991, 7.

21 Firman 1991, 18.

22 J Blair 1991, 45–6.

23 Ibid, 45; Leach 1978, 81, maps 14 to 16.

24 J Blair 1987, 140.

25 Lankester and J Blair forthcoming.

26 Harvey 1984, 47.

27 Ibid.

28 Ibid, 53.

29 Ibid.

30 J Blair 1987, 46.

31 Harvey 1987, 9; Badham forthcoming 2.

32 Ibid, 167–8.

33 J Blair 1991, 46.

34 J Blair 1980, 67.

35 Ibid; Emmerson 1990, 146.

Chapter 5 The dating of pre-Black Death London brasses

1 J Blair 1987, 136–40.

2 Foster 1991. The surviving letters are illustrated on pages 82–3, figs 72 to 78.

3 John de Valence's slab is illustrated in Binski 1995, 100, fig 137.

4 For an account of the changing views on the dating of early brasses, see Norris 1987.

5 Ward 1965.

6 Spittle 1970.

7 Coales 1987.

8 J Blair 1987, 134.

9 Ibid, 140 and fig 148.

10 Illustrated in J Blair 1981a, 258, pl 50c.

11 J Blair 1987, 140.

12 Illustrated in Norris 1988, fig 281.

13 J Blair 1987, 144–53.

14 Binski 1987.

15 For an account of Cantilupe's life and the Cantilupe–Pecham controversy, see Jauncey 1982, 15–19, 57–72 and 103–23.

16 Emmerson 1980.

Chapter 6 Evidence linking London brasses and incised slabs

1 J Blair 1987, 142.

2 Binski 1987, 113.

3 J Blair 1987, 146.

4 Ibid, 144.

5 Greenhill 1976, 1, 17.

6 Ibid, 18.

7 J Blair 1987, 144.

8 Ibid.

9 Badham 1989b; Gittos and Gittos 1989, 101.

10 Badham 1989a.

11 Weever 1631, 413.

12 Emmerson 1978a.

13 Greenwood 1996.

14 Binski 1987.

Chapter 7 The Camoys style

1 Illustrated in Coales 1987, 177, fig 216.

2 Illustrated ibid, fig 217.

3 Blatchly 1982.

4 Illustrated in Coales 1987, 76, fig 58.

5 Burnett 1974.

6 Pepys 1984 suggests that Margaret's husband, Ralph, had remarried, to Elizabeth Rogate, in 1311–12, but this is based on an erroneous reading of VCH 1905–87, 4, 24–5. In fact, this gives no clue as to the date of the marriage, but refers only to a sale of land to the Rogate family, which probably later belonged to the Camoys family and may have been brought to them through Ralph Camoys's subsequent marriage to Elizabeth Rogate. Cockayne 1910–59, 2, 507, reveals that the marriage took place by 1319, but is no more specific. We are grateful to Brian and Moira Gittos for this information.

7 Illustrated in Coales 1987, 81, fig 64.

8 Binski 1987, 82.

9 Ibid.

10 Rogers 1987, 30.

11 Illustrated in Coales 1987, 71, figs 51 and 53.

12 VCH 1902–14, 3, 339.

13 We are grateful to Nigel Saul for information on this point.

14 PRO 1912, 23 Edward I, no. 271, 170.

15 Moor 1929–32, 4, 220.

16 Cockayne 1910–59, 6, 475–7.

17 PRO 1893, 310.

18 Elliston-Erwood 1947.

19 Pers comm, Elliston-Erwood to Greenhill.

20 Illustrated in Coales 1987, 85, fig 70.

21 He is referred to in a document of 1327, and was therefore still living; PRO 1968, 235.

22 Dru Drury 1934, 3–4.

23 Bodleian Library, Oxford, MS Gough Kent 36, interleaved between fos 192–3.

24 Clapham 1911, 19.

25 Badham 1986.

26 C Blair 1994, 37–8; C Blair 1995a.

27 We are grateful to Claude Blair for advice on this point.

28 VCH 1900–11, 2, 506; 3, 137; 4, 492.

29 Moor 1929–32, 4, 3–4.

30 Hanna 1988–9, 1, 258–9, and 2, 48–9. We are grateful to Nigel Saul for bringing these references to our attention.

31 PRO 1912, 22 January 1305, no. 290, 196–7.

32 Wrottesley 1893, 85.

33 Neither the family nor these arms is recorded in Ryland 1913, Squibb 1991, Bannerman 1905 or Berry 1833.

34 We are grateful to Claude Blair and to Brian and Moira Gittos for information on this slab.

35 Franks 1848, Appendix.

36 C Blair 1995a.

37 Thanks are due to Philip Whittemore and Les Smith for alerting Sally Badham to the excavation on the site of the Hospital of St Thomas Acon and to Portia Askew, Museum of London Archaeology Service, for access to the finds.

38 Gough 1786–1802, 1, 42.

39 Greenhill 1976, 1, 14–15.

40 Fowler undated, 28.

41 Tanner 1953, 25–6.

42 Devon 1837, 124.

43 PRO, Dorset Pipe Roll, 38 Henry III, m 9.

Chapter 8 The Septvans style

1 Blatchly 1974, 176–8 and pl 19.

2 Binski 1980.

3 Binski 1987, 88–90 and 102.

4 Rogers 1996.

5 C Blair 1993, 8–9. For a discussion of the evidence, see C Blair 1995b and Gittos and Gittos 1995.

6 C Blair 1995b.

7 C Blair 1994, 36.

8 Gittos and Gittos 1992b; Gittos and Gittos 1994b, 25–7; Badham, Gittos and Gittos 1996.

9 Illustrated in Coales 1987, 43, fig 27.

10 Illustrated ibid, 44, fig 29.

11 Alexander and Binski 1987, 289.

12 Williamson 1988, 78.

Chapter 9 The Seymour style

1 Binski 1987, 110–13 and fig 104; Norris 1977, 1, 2.

2 Illustrated in Greenhill 1976, 1, fig 28a.

3 Adhémar 1974, no. 460.

4 Ibid, no. 597.

5 Ibid, nos 41, 119, 567, 596, 843 and 854.

6 Binski 1987, 130, n. 69.

7 Illustrated in Coales 1987, 125, fig 127.

8 Illustrated ibid, 105, fig 98.

9 Binski 1987, 104.

10 Fowler 1903, 105.

11 Binski 1987, 113.

12 We are grateful to Col Frank Robson for considerable help in compiling a list of the rectors of Westwell.

13 Emden 1957, 1, 112–13.

14 Ibid.

15 Bridges 1762–91, 2, 62.

16 Society of Antiquaries of London MS 423, 3, fol 78.

17 d'Elboux 1948, 119–20.

18 Illustrated in Coales 1987, 118, fig 119; Lack et al 1993, 130.

19 Badham 1990.

20 Kent 1949; Emmerson 1978b; Emmerson 1990.

21 J Blair 1987, 168.

Chapter 10 Post-Seymour-style brasses and incised slabs

1 Kent 1949.

2 Badham forthcoming 2.

3 Society of Antiquaries of London, 'Kent Illustrations: Prints and Drawings', 3, fol 61.

4 VCH 1902–12, 4, 158.

5 Ibid, 2, 68; in 1346 the Prior of Bermondsey complained that Alain (sic) Ferthyng of Southwark and twelve others broke and threw down a close and dykes at Bermondsey.

6 Ibid, 4, 158.

Chapter 11 Unclassified fourteenth-century Purbeck marble incised slabs

1 In Greenhill's unpublished notes he records an extract from a letter of 21 October 1947 from the then incumbent of Strood church: 'The vandals who were here about a hundred years ago, pulled down the beautiful twelfth-century church . . . filled the crypt with rubble, and then built an oblong box on top of it, which is the building we have today. In the course of destroying the church, they must have destroyed the ancient monuments, for none remain.'

2 Society of Antiquaries of London, 'Kent Illustrations: Prints and Drawings', 3, fol 42.

3 Bodleian Library, Oxford, Gough Maps 226, fol 240v.

4 We are grateful to Jane Houghton and George Bradbury for establishing the present location of this slab.

5 Bodleian Library, Oxford, Gough Maps 6, fol 18v; Hutchins 1796–1815, 3, 205.

6 Illustrated in Greenhill 1976, 2, 109a.

7 We are grateful to Nicholas Rogers for this suggestion.

8 Description from Greenhill's unpublished notes.

9 Manning 1864, 205.

10 Clark 1889–99, 2, 468–9.

11 Bodleian Library, Oxford, MS Top Oxon d460, fol 19.

12 Coales 1987, 182.

13 J Blair 1971. In this article, the Great Bookham I slab, together with slabs at Mickleham and Stoke d'Abernon, are described as being of Sussex marble. Having examined them all, we conclude that the small fossil size strongly suggests that the stone employed is Purbeck marble.

14 We are grateful to Claude Blair for bringing this slab to our attention.

15 Amongst other pre-Black Death incised inscriptions commemorating building work is an early fourteenth-century inscription beneath the external sill of the east window at North Crawley, Buckinghamshire. This reads: '+ PETRUS CANCELLVM TIBI DAT FIRMINE NOVELLVM UT CVM LAUDERIS DEO PETRI MEMORERIS'. However, we have excluded from our study inscriptions that are neither on Purbeck marble slabs nor have script relating to the lettering discussed in this monograph.

Chapter 12 Basyng-style incised slabs

1 British Library, Add MS 29926, fos 14–15. An engraving in Gough 1786–1802, 1, 63, is based on one of these drawings. See also Quirk 1954, 13 and pls 7a and 7b.

2 Liveing 1906, 120.

3 We are grateful to Brian and Moira Gittos for this suggestion and for first drawing this slab to our attention.

4 Hunt 1974, 2, pl 104.

5 Pevsner 1958, 231–2.

6 Styan 1902, 40–1. Illustrated in Newman 1976, pl 19.

7 Rogers forthcoming.

8 Spence 1841, 96–9.

9 Worthington Smith 1905–7; Bagshaw 1936.

10 Luard 1866, 313.

11 Webb 1921, 1, 139; Boutell 1854, 38.

12 Details of Prior Hugh's life are in Webb 1921, 1, 133–9.

13 We are grateful to Martin Stuchfield for providing detailed information on this slab.

14 RCHM 1923, 138.

15 We are grateful to Stephen Freeth for this information.

16 Binski 1987, 74.

17 We are grateful to Brian and Moira Gittos for bringing this slab to our attention.

18 Atkinson 1940.

19 Clutterbuck undated, 1, 9.

20 Suckling 1845, 32.

21 Christy 1900, 383–4.

22 J Blair 1973.

23 Biddle 1993, 298, n. 44.

24 Ibid, n. 51.

25 It is hoped that fuller information on features associated with Purbeck marble coffin-shaped slabs will emerge from a survey of these monuments currently in progress: Badham *et al* 1994–8.

26 Butler 1964; Butler 1957.

27 Ryder 1985; Ryder 1991.

28 Gittos and Gittos 1994a.

29 Norris 1978, 82.

30 We are grateful to Nicholas Rogers for this suggestion.

31 Smith 1981.

32 J Blair 1991, 44.

33 Ibid.

34 Blair 1981b.

Chapter 13 Ashford-style incised slabs

1 The first letter of the inscription should be a P, but a D was used instead.

2 Leach 1978, 33.

3 Hill 1948, xiii.

4 Bodleian Library, Oxford, MS Top Oxon d460, fol 124; Lincoln Record Office, Dalderby 2/145d.

5 Bodleian Library, Oxford, MS Top Oxon d460, fol 124; Lincoln Record Office, Dalderby 2/147d.

6 Davis 1925, 221.

7 Bodleian Library, Oxford MS Top Oxon d460, fol 124; Lincoln Record Office, Dalderby 2/145d.

8 Bridges 1762–91, 1, 360, records that Robert (*sic*) de Gretton was instituted to the living of Hardingstone, Northamptonshire, at some date between 1281 and 1314. It is conceivable, though perhaps not likely, that this was the same man as the vicar of Pyrton; that when he was instituted to the living of Pyrton his name was mistakenly recorded as Richard instead of Robert; and that he planned to be buried at Pyrton and prepared his monument while vicar of that parish. Certainly the name Roberd most easily fits the traces of lettering that are recorded on the Pyrton slab. We are grateful to John Coales for bringing this reference to our attention and for pointing out that Richard de Gretton and Roger de Corby may well have come from the adjoining parishes of Gretton and Corby in Northamptonshire, which also formed part of the Diocese of Lincoln, and that this may well have a bearing on the problem of whom the Pyrton slab commemorates.

9 Worthington Smith 1905–7; Bagshaw 1936.

10 Luard 1866, 313; Bagshaw 1936, 176–7.

11 Calendar of Early Mayors' Court Rolls for the Corporation of London, 24.

12 Sharpe 1889–90, 1, 184.

13 Calendar of Early Mayors' Court Rolls for the Corporation of London, 259–60.

14 The E and two stops are illustrated in J Blair 1987, 145, fig 149. See also Blaydes 1886.

15 Bannerman 1918, iv–viii.

16 Hasted 1788–99, 2, 509.

17 We are grateful to Martin Stuchfield for this information.

18 Christy 1899.

19 Trollope 1855; Trollope 1874.

20 We are grateful to Derrick Chivers for bringing Trollope's rubbing of this slab in the main collection of incised slab rubbings in the Society of Antiquaries to our attention, and to Les Smith for information on the present position and condition of the slab.

21 The inscription may be translated as: 'Here lies Agnes under this stone; you will all go to this house in the course of death. Now pray a Pater, dear friend, and be good enough to think of your dead friend'. It appears that the marbler may have made errors in incising the lettering. It has been assumed that the Y at the beginning of 'yater' is intended for a P and that 'maie' should have been rendered 'amie'. We are grateful to Jerome Bertram for considerable help with this inscription.

22 Lower 1857, 280.

23 Pocock 1858, illustration on second unpaginated insertion after p 114.

24 Surrey Record Soc 1933, 156.

25 PRO 1912, 330.

26 Illustrated in Norris 1977, 2, pl 15 (upper part), and Coales 1987, fig 86, 93 (whole fig).

27 Bullock-Davies 1986 throws no further light on his identity.

28 VCH 1902–14, 3, 239.

29 PRO 1912, no. 271, 169–70.

30 Robinson 1824, 18.

31 J Blair 1971, 142.

32 Ibid.

33 J Blair 1975, will dated 1295; J Blair 1974, 226–9, undated rental but *c* 1286–1306; J Blair 1978–84, 4, 33, deed dated 1293; ibid 4, 37, deed *c* 1280–90; ibid, 4, 93–4, agreement dated 1303; ibid, 4, 95, grants *c* 1286–95; ibid, 4, 172, grant *c* 1280–90; ibid, 4, 203, deed dated 1303; ibid, 4, 210, deed *c* 1290; ibid, 4, 211; deed *c* 1290–1300; ibid, 4, 214, two deeds dated 1300.

34 J Blair 1978–84, 4, 203.

35 Ibid, 4, 271.

36 The slab has been described by J Blair 1971, 141, and VCH 1902–12, 3, 461, as being of Sussex marble, but the small size of the fossils indicates that the stone is Purbeck marble. The latter source furthermore erroneously describes the crosshead as being of the cross crosslet type, whereas the drawing in Johnston 1907, 45, and the surviving traces clearly show it is of the cross botonnée type.

37 Johnson 1907, 45. Whilst the drawing of the cross may be accurate, the transcription of the inscription contains a number of errors.

38 We are grateful to Jerome Bertram for bringing this slab to our attention.

39 Clayton 1889.

40 We are grateful to Nicholas Rogers for this information.

41 VCH 1905–87, 4, 135, records landholders of Lidsey in the relevant period as including George de Barenton, Nicholas de Barenton, John de Palyng, Simon Ferryng, Alice att Setene, Nicholas Avenel, Geoffrey de Gates, John Daundevill, Roger Daundevill, Ralph Pesson, Geoffrey Brown, Robert de Ernesberne, Geoffrey de Ernesberne, Peter de Ernesberne and John de Ernesberne.

42 Elliston-Erwood 1947, 121.

43 Styan 1902, pl 56.

44 Salmon 1728, 333.

45 Cusssans 1870–81, 1, 61–2.

46 Clutterbuck 1815–27, 3, 504.

47 Bertram 1984, 387–9.

48 Tummers 1988, 6, fig 2, and 36–7, n. 3; Tummers 1994.

49 Bertram 1984, 387–8; Tummers 1988, 36–7, n. 3.

50 Stone 1972, 106–7.

51 Badham 1989b, 167.

Chapter 14 Other Ashford-style monuments

1 J Blair 1991, 45–6.

2 Lankester and J Blair forthcoming.

3 The church guide says: 'The slab seems to have been used as a paving stone, face downwards, for a long time; at some modern restoration it was removed to the Museum of Archaeology at Cambridge, and its fragments have now been restored to the church.' Neither the Museum of Archaeology and Anthropology at Cambridge nor the Fitzwilliam Museum can find any reference to the fragments having been in their care, nor can we find any other records corroborating the story given in the church guide.

4 Tummers 1980, 140 and 145, and illustrated in pls 40 and 41.

5 J Blair 1981b, 86–7.

6 Ibid.

7 Illustrated in Gresham 1968, 187, fig 78.

8 J Blair 1978, 266 and fig 1.

9 We are grateful to Jon Bayliss for this information.

10 Hills 1945, 253–5.

11 We are grateful to Martin Stuchfield for providing us with detailed information on this slab.

12 Hills 1945, 259–62.

13 Illustrated in Tummers 1980, pl 45.

14 Illustrated ibid, pl 48.

15 Ibid, 43 and 90.

16 We are grateful to Jerome Bertram for bringing this slab to our attention.

17 Noted British Library, Add MS 27766, fol 67.

18 Clutterbuck 1815–27, 3, 175.

19 VCH 1902–14, 3, 320.

20 Illustrated in Coales 1987, 167, fig 212.

21 J Blair 1981b, 86.

22 Illustrated in Coales 1987, 46, fig 30.

23 Illustrated ibid, 42, fig 26.

24 Lankester and J Blair forthcoming.

25 Illustrated in Coales 1987, 46, fig 31.

26 Ibid, 45–7.

27 We are grateful to Nicholas Rogers for information on this point.

28 Illustrated in Coales 1987, 42, fig 25.

29 Illustrated ibid, 52, fig 40; see also Connor 1924–6.

30 Illustrated in Coales 1987, 74, fig 54.

31 Illustrated ibid, fig 55.

32 Illustrated ibid, fig 56.

33 Badham forthcoming 1.

34 Illustrated in King 1994, fig 6b, though not accurately. We are grateful to Jerome Bertram for pointing out that this slab is of Purbeck marble.

35 Butler 1854, 155; Conwell 1872–3, 400–1.

36 British Library, Add MS 29943, fos 124–5.

37 Clark 1889–99, 1, 182, 217 and 300; 2, 104, 447–8 and 461; 3, 9–12. We are extremely grateful to Jerome Bertram for references to the Coleivile family.

38 Oxford Historical Soc 1905, 8, 33 and 63.

39 Binski 1987, 116.

40 Society of Antiquaries of London MS 497, fos 12–18.

41 British Library, Egerton MS 3310A.

42 British Library, Harleian MS 1366.

43 Haines 1861, cxxxv and 92.

44 Pearman 1886, 72.

45 We are grateful to Nigel Ramsay for his help in checking the Ashford entry in Frampton's manuscript list of incumbents in the Kent Record Office.

46 J Blair 1987, 136–40.

47 Ibid, 142–4.

48 Rogers 1987, 29–34.

49 Dugdale 1658, 45.

50 Rogers 1987, 30; Hasted 1788–99, 4, 197; Weever 1631, 257.

Bibliography

Adhémar, J 1974. 'Les tombeaux de la collection Gaignières: dessins d'archélogie du XVIIe siècle', *Gazette des Beaux-Arts*, July–September 1974, Paris

Alexander, J and Binski, P 1987. *The Age of Chivalry: Art in Plantagenet England 1200–1400*, London

Atkinson, T D 1940. 'Fragments of architecture and sculpture at Werewell church', *Proc Hampshire Fld Club Archaeol Soc*, 14, 369–70

Badham, S F 1985. 'An interim study of the stones used for the slabs of English monumental brasses', *Trans Monumental Brass Soc*, 13, 475–83

— 1986. 'A fourteenth-century composite slab from the Newcastle Blackfriars', *Trans Monumental Brass Soc*, 14, 44–9

— 1989a. 'The Fens 1 series: an early fifteenth-century group of monumental brasses and incised slabs', *J Brit Archaeol Ass*, 142, 46–62

— 1989b. 'Monumental brasses: the development of the York workshops in the fourteenth and fifteenth centuries', in *Medieval Art, Architecture and Archaeology in the East Riding of Yorkshire* (ed C Wilson), Brit Archaeol Conference Trans (for 1983), 165–85, Leeds

— 1990. 'London standardisation and provincial idiosyncrasy: the organisation and working practices of brass-engraving workshops in pre-Reformation England', *Church Monuments, J Church Monuments Soc*, 5, 3–25

— 1994. 'Simon de Wudston's incised slab at Hemsworth, Yorkshire', *Trans Monumental Brass Soc*, 15, 215–21

— 1996. 'Status and salvation: the design of medieval English brasses and incised slabs', *Trans Monumental Brass Soc*, 15, 413–65

— forthcoming 1. 'The Bacon brass at Gorleston, Suffolk', *Trans Monumental Brass Soc*, 15, Part 6

— forthcoming 2. 'Monumental brasses and the Black Death: a re-appraisal', *Trans Monumental Brass Soc*

Badham, S F, Gittos, B and Gittos, M 1996. 'The fourteenth-century monuments in the Saltmarshe chapel at Howden, Yorkshire', *Yorkshire Archaeol J*, 68, 113–55

Badham, S F, Gittos, B, Gittos, M and Lankester, P 1994–8. 'Survey of Purbeck marble coffin-lids',

Church Monuments Soc Newsletter, 10, 4–11 and 34–7; 11, 18–21 and 45–50; 12, 25–8 and 53–4; 13, 13–18 and 44–9; and continuing

Bagshaw, T W 1936. 'Two inscribed stones in St Peter's church, Dunstable', *Antiq J*, 12, 175–7

Baltzer, J and Bruns, F 1920. *Die Bau und Kunstdenkmäler der Freien und Hansestadt Lübek*, Lübeck

Bannerman, W B (ed) 1905. *Visitation of Sussex 1530 and 1663–4*, Harleian Soc, 53, London

— 1918. *The Parish Register of Horton Kirbie, Co. Kent*, Parish Register Soc, Croydon

Bayliss, J 1990. 'Robert Parker, the alabasterman', *Church Monuments, J Church Monuments Soc*, 5, 39–56

— 1991. 'Richard and Gabriel Royley of Burton-upon-Trent, tombmakers', *Church Monuments, J Church Monuments Soc*, 6, 21–42

— 1993. 'A Dutch carver: Garrett Hollemans in England', *Church Monuments, J Church Monuments Soc*, 8, 45–56

Becker, K, Brückner, M, Haetge, E and Schürenberg, L 1929. *Die Kunstdenkmäler der Provinz Sachsen*, Burg

Berry, W 1833. *County Genealogies: Hampshire*, London

Bertram, J 1972. *Brasses and Brass Rubbing in England*, Newton Abbot

— 1984. 'Incised slabs in Sussex', *Trans Monumental Brass Soc*, 13, 387–96

Biddle, M 1993. 'Early renaissance at Winchester', in *Winchester Cathedral: Nine Hundred Years* (ed J Crook), 257–304, Chichester

Binski, P 1980. 'Chartham, Kent, and the Court', *Trans Monumental Brass Soc*, 13, 73–9

— 1987. 'The stylistic sequence of London figure brasses', in *The Earliest English Brasses* (ed J Coales), 69–132, London

— 1995. *Westminster Abbey and the Plantagenets*, New Haven and London

Blair, C 1991. 'The Conington effigy: fourteenth-century knights at Conington, Doddington and Tollard Royal', *Church Monuments, J Church Monuments Soc*, 6, 3–20

— 1993. 'The de Vere effigy at Hatfield Broad Oak', *Church Monuments, J Church Monuments Soc*, 8, 3–11

— 1994. 'The wooden knight at Abergavenny', *Church Monuments, J Church Monuments Soc*, 9, 33–52

— 1995a. 'An identified early fourteenth-century military effigy at Little Shelford,

Cambridgeshire', *Church Monuments Soc Newsletter*, 11, 36–8

1995b. 'Yorkshire effigies and ring scabbard attachments', *Church Monuments Soc Newsletter*, 11, 4–5

Blair, J 1971. 'A mediaeval grave slab in Great Bookham church', *Proc Leatherhead Dist Local Hist Soc*, 3, 139–45

1973. 'A reused medieval grave slab in Guildford Museum', *Surrey Archaeol Collect*, 69, 200

1974. 'The early manorial records of Leatherhead', *Proc Leatherhead Dist Local Hist Soc*, 3, 218–43, 268–97 and 329–46; 4, 12–18

1975. 'The will of William de Arundel, rector of Mickleham', *Proc Leatherhead Dist Local Hist Soc*, 3, 266–7

1978. 'The Buslingthorpes and their monuments', *Trans Monumental Brass Soc*, 12, 265–70

1978–84. 'Mediaeval deeds of the Leatherhead district', *Proc Leatherhead Dist Loc Hist Soc*, 4, 30–8, 58–62, 86–96, 118–25, 150–7, 172–81, 203–19 and 268–74

1979. 'An early fourteenth-century incised slab at Odstock, Wiltshire', *Trans Monumental Brass Soc*, 12, 370–2

1980. 'Harry Lakenham, Marbler of London, and a tomb contract of 1378', *Antiq J*, 60, 66–74

1981a. 'English monumental brasses before the Black Death', in *Collectanea Historica: Essays in Memory of Stuart Rigold* (ed A P Detsicas), Kent Archaeol Soc, 256–72, Maidstone

1981b. 'Grave slabs in early fourteenth-century England with added inscriptions in separate brass letters', *Bull Int Soc Study Church Monuments*, 5, 86–8

1987. 'English monumental brasses before 1350: types, patterns and workshops', in *The Earliest English Brasses* (ed J Coales), 133–74 and 185–215, London

1988a. 'An early 12th-century Purbeck marble grave slab from St Frideswide's Priory', *Oxoniensia*, 103, 266–8

1988b. 'A bishop orders his brass: buying a slab from the Purbeck quarries *c.* 1400', *Trans Monumental Brass Soc*, 14, 243–6

1991. 'Purbeck marble', in *English Medieval Industries* (ed J Blair and N Ramsay), 41–56, London

Blatchly, J 1974. 'The lost and mutilated monuments of the Bovile and Wingfield families at Letheringham', *Proc Suffolk Inst Archaeol Hist*, 33, 168–94

1982. 'Early 14th-century indents from the seabed at Dunwich, Suffolk', *Trans Monumental Brass Soc*, 13, 260–3

Blaydes, F A 1886. 'Tilsworth', *Bedfordshire Notes and Queries*, 1, 3

Boutell, C 1854. *Christian Monuments in England and Wales*, London

Bridges, J 1762–91. *History and Antiquities of the County of Northamptonshire*, 2 vols, Oxford

Bullock-Davies, C 1986. *A Register of Royal and Baronial Domestic Minstrels 1272–1327*, Woodbridge

Burnett, M 1974. 'The FitzRalph brass at Pebmarsh', *Essex Archaeol Hist*, 6, 99

Butler, L A S 1957. 'Medieval gravestones of Cambridgeshire, Huntingdonshire and the Soke of Peterborough', *Cambridge Antiq Soc*, 50, 89–100

1964. 'Minor medieval monumental sculpture in the east Midlands', *Archaeol J*, 121, 111–53

Butler, R 1854. *Some Notices of the Castle of Trim* (3rd edn, reprinted 1978), Meath Archaeol Hist Soc, Trim

Calkin, J B 1960. 'Some archaeological discoveries in the island of Purbeck: Part II', *Proc Dorset Natur Hist Archaeol Soc*, 131, 121–2

Chatwin, P B 1921–3. 'Monumental effigies in the county of Warwick', *Trans Birmingham Warwickshire Archaeol Soc*, 42, 35–88; 43, 136–68; 44, 36–53

Christy, M 1899. 'On a late thirteenth-century inscription in Fobbing church', *Essex Review*, 8, 34–6

1900. 'Some Essex coffin slabs', *Trans Essex Archaeol Soc*, 7, 369–95

Clapham, A W 1911. *The Benedictine Abbey of Barking*, London

1915. *Lesnes Abbey*, London

Clark, A 1889–99. *Survey of the Antiquities of the City of Oxford by Antony Wood*, 3 vols, Oxford Historical Soc, 15, 17 and 37, Oxford

Clayton, G E 1889. 'Aldingbourne church, Sussex', *Sussex Archaeol Collect*, 37, 191–2

Clutterbuck, R 1815–27. *The History and Antiquities of the County of Hertford*, 3 vols, London

undated. *The Story of Werewell Abbey*, 2 vols, Winchester

Coales, J 1997. 'The drawings of Roger de Gaignières: loss and survival', *Church Monuments, J Church Monuments Soc*, 12, 14–34

Coales, J (ed) 1987. *The Earliest English Brasses*, Monumental Brass Society, London

Cockayne, G E 1910–59. *The Complete Peerage* (new edn, revised V Gibbs, H A Doubleday, D Warrand, Lord Howard de Walden, G H White and R S Lea), 12 vols (new edition published in 13 volumes, with volume 12 divided into two parts), London

Connor, A B 1924–6. 'Bishop Haselshaw's brass at Wells Cathedral', *Somerset Dorset Notes and Queries*, 18, 214–15

Conwell, E A 1872–3. 'A ramble round Trim', *J Roy Soc Antiq Ir*, 12, 361–430

Cresswell, B F 1918. 'Sepulchral slabs with crosses in Devon churches', *Devon Cornwall Notes and Queries*, 10, 65–7

Cussans, J E 1870–81. *History of Hertfordshire*, 3 vols, London

Cutts, E L 1849. *A Manual for the Study of Sepulchral Slabs and Crosses of the Middle Ages*, London

Dark, K R 1992. *The Inscribed Stones of Dyfed*, Llandysul

Davis, F N (ed) 1925. *Rotuli Ricardi Gravesend, diocesis Lincolniensis*, Lincoln Record Soc, 20, Lincoln

de la Grange, A and Cloquet, L 1887. 'Etudes sur l'art à Tournai et sur les anciens artistes de cette ville', in *Mémoires de la Société historique et littéraire de Tournai*, 20, Tournai

d'Elboux, R H 1948. 'Some Kentish indents II', *Archaeol Cantiana*, 111, 119–20

Devon, F 1837. *Issue Roll of Edward II*, London

Dru Drury, G 1934. 'The Abbots of Bindon', *Proc Dorset Natur Hist Archaeol Soc*, 55, 3–4

1949. 'The use of Purbeck in mediaeval times', *Proc Dorset Natur Hist Archaeol Soc*, 70, 74–98

Dugdale, W 1658. *History of St Paul's Cathedral*, London

Dunning, G C 1949. 'The Purbeck marble industry in the Roman period', *Archaeol Newsletter*, I.II, 15

Edleston, R H 1932. 'Monumental brasses', *Peterborough Natur Hist Sci Archaeol Soc*, 1–3 (pamphlet, reprinted from 60th Annual Report)

1939. 'Incised monumental slabs in Northumberland and Durham', *Archaeol Aeliana*, 4th ser, 15, 71–86

1939–40. 'Monumental brasses and incised slabs', *Teesdale Record Soc*, 5, 17–18

1949. *Illustrations of Incised Monumental Slabs on the Continent of Europe*, 2 vols, Darlington

Ellacombe, H T 1881. *The History of the Parish of Bitton in the County of Gloucester*, Exeter

Elliston-Erwood, F C 1947. 'Two incised slabs from Lesnes Abbey, Erith, Kent', *Archaeol Cantiana*, 60, 119–21

Emden, A B 1957. *A Biographical Register of the University of Oxford to AD 1500*, 3 vols, Oxford

Emmerson, R 1978a. 'Margaret Paston's brass', *Bull Monumental Brass Soc*, 17, 13

1978b. 'Monumental brasses – London design *c.* 1420–85', *J Brit Archaeol Ass*, 131, 50–78

1980. 'St Thomas Cantilupe's tomb and brass of 1287', *Bull Int Soc Study Church Monuments*, 2, 41–5

1990. 'Design for mass production: monumental brasses made in London *c.* 1420–85', in *Artistes, Artisans et Production Artistique au Moyen-Age 3: Fabrication et consommation de l'oeuvre*, 133–71, Rennes

Farman, P 1992. 'Yorkshire', *Bull Monumental Brass Soc*, 59, 538–9

Firman, R 1991. 'Geological comments on Claude Blair's paper on the Conington effigy', *Church Monuments, J Church Monuments Soc*, 6, 17–20

1994. 'Purbeck marble: some east Midlands examples of mistaken identity', *Church Monuments Soc Newsletter*, 10, 30–4

Fisher, T 1812–36. *Collections Historical, Genealogical and Topographical for Bedfordshire*, London

Foster, R 1991. *Patterns of Thought: The Hidden Meaning of the Great Pavement of Westminster Abbey*, London

Fowler, J undated. *Guide to Beaulieu Abbey*, 2nd edn, London

Fowler, J T (ed) 1903. *The Rites of Durham*, Surtees Soc, 107, Durham

Franks, A W 1848. 'The genealogical history of the Frevile family, with some account of their monuments in Little Shelford church, Cambridgeshire', *Quarto Publications of the Cambridge Antiquarian Soc*, 4, 21–31

Fryer, A C 1925. 'Monumental effigies made by Bristol craftsmen', *Archaeologia*, 74, 1–72

1926. 'Incised effigies in Somerset', *Somerset Archaeol Natur Hist Soc*, 121, 38–56

Gittos, B and Gittos, M 1978. 'An incised slab at Burgwallis, Yorkshire', *Trans Monumental Brass Soc*, 12, 319–21

1981. 'A military effigy at Welton, North Humberside', *Yorkshire Archaeol J*, 103, 129–31

1989. 'A survey of East Riding monuments', in *Medieval Art, Archaeology and Architecture in the East Riding of Yorkshire* (ed C Wilson), Brit Archaeol Conference Trans (for 1983), 91–108, Leeds

1992a. 'Purbeck marble cross slab in Normandy', *Church Monuments Soc Newsletter*, 7, 30

1992b. 'Yorkshire effigies *c.* 1300 and their place in English sculpture', in *Medieval Europe 1992: Art and Symbolism Pre-printed papers*, 2, 209–15, York

1994a. 'List of Purbeck marble cross slabs in Dorset', *Church Monuments Soc Newsletter*, 10, 6–11

1994b. 'The Goldesborough effigies', *Church Monuments, J Church Monuments Soc*, 9, 3–32

1995. 'Yorkshire effigies and the ring attachment of sword-belt to scabbard', *Church Monuments Soc Newsletter*, 11, 38–40

1997. 'Alfred Fryer's "Monumental effigies by Bristol craftsmen": a reassessment', in *'Almost the richest city': Bristol in the Middle Ages* (ed L Keen), Brit Archaeol Conference Trans (for 1996), 88–96, Leeds

forthcoming. 'Irish Purbeck', *Church Monuments, J Church Monuments Soc*, 13

Gittos, M 1985. 'A survey of East Coker churchyard', *Chronicle*, 3, 54–7, Yeovil Archaeol Loc Hist Soc, Yeovil

Gough, R 1786–1802. *Sepulchral Monuments in Great Britain*, 2 vols (in 5 parts), London

Greenhill, F A 1948. 'An incised slab at West Wickham, Kent', *Archaeol Cantiana*, 61, 106–8

1958. *The Incised Slabs of Leicestershire and Rutland*, Leicester

1976. *Incised Effigial Slabs*, 2 vols, London

1986. *Monumental Incised Slabs in the County of Lincoln*, Newport Pagnell

Greenwood, R 1996. 'Wills and brasses: some conclusions from a Norfolk study', in *Brasses as Art and History* (ed J Bertram), 82–102, Stroud

Gresham, C A 1968. *Medieval Stone Carving in North Wales*, Cardiff

Haines, H 1861. *Manual of Monumental Brasses*, London

Hamilton-Rogers, W W 1877. *The Antient Sepulchral Effigies of Devon*, Exeter

Hanna, K A (ed) 1988–9. *The Cartularies of Southwick Priory, Part 1*, Record Series 9, Hampshire; *Part 2*, Record Series 10, Hampshire

Harding, V 1992. 'Burial choice and burial location in later medieval London', in *Death in Towns* (ed S Bassett), 119–35, Leicester

Harvey, J 1984. *English Mediaeval Architects*, 2nd edn, Gloucester

1987. *Supplement to Revised Edition of English Mediaeval Architects*, Isle of Wight

Hasted, E 1788–99. *The History and Topographical Survey of the County of Kent*, 4 vols, Canterbury

Hill, R M T (ed) 1948. *The Rolls and Register of Bishop Oliver Sutton* 1280–99, Lincolnshire Rec Soc, 39, Lincoln

Hills, A 1945. 'Three military coffin slabs in Essex', *Trans Essex Archaeol Soc*, 7, 251–62

Hocquet, A 1924. *Le Rayonnement l'Art Tournaisien*, Tournai

Hunt J 1974. *Irish Medieval Figure Sculpture 1200–1600*, 2 vols, Dublin

Hutchins, J 1796–1815. *The History and Antiquities of the County of Dorset*, 4 vols, 2nd edn, London

Jauncey, M (ed) 1982. *St Thomas Cantilupe, Bishop of Hereford*, Hereford

Johnston, P R 1907. 'Stoke d'Abernon church', *Surrey Archaeol Collect*, 20, 1–89

Kębłowski, J 1971. *Pomniki Piastów Slaskich W Dobie Sredniowiecza*, monographie Slaskie Ossolineum, 20, Warsaw

Kent, J P C 1949. 'Monumental brasses – a new classification of military effigies *c.* 1360–1485', *J Brit Archaeol Ass*, 3rd series, 12, 70–97

King, H A 1994. 'Irish Memorial Brasses to 1700', *Proc Royal Ir Acad*, 94, 111–40

King, R W and Russell, J 1913. *History of Arnold*, Nottingham

Knowles, E H 1880. 'Fragments at St Bees', *Trans Cumberland Westmorland Antiq Archaeol Soc*, 2, 27–30

Kusaba, Y 1993. 'Henry of Blois, Winchester and the twelfth-century renaissance', in *Winchester Cathedral: Nine Hundred Years* (ed J Crook), 69–79, Chichester

Lack, W, Stuchfield, M and Whittemore, P 1993. *The Monumental Brasses of Berkshire*, London

Lankester, P and Blair, J forthcoming. 'The Purbeck marble industry at London and Corfe: some new discoveries'

Leach, R 1978. *An Investigation into Purbeck Marble in Medieval England*, 2nd edn, Crediton

Liveing, H 1906. *Records of Romsey Abbey*, Winchester

Lower, M A 1857. 'Bodiam and its lords', *Sussex Archaeol Collect*, 9, 275–302

Luard, H R (ed) 1866. *Annales Monastici*, PRO Chronicles and Memorials, Rolls Series 3, 36, London

Lysons, S 1791. *Etchings of Gloucester Antiquities*, London

Manning, C R 1864. 'Elsing church', *Norfolk Archaeol*, 6, 200–12

Moor, C 1929–32. *Knights of Edward I*, 5 vols, Harleian Soc, London

Nadoloskeigo, A 1990. *Uzbrojenie W Polsce Sredniowiecznej 1350–1450*, Polska Akademia Nauk, Lodz

Newman, J (ed) 1976. *West Kent and the Weald*, Buildings of England series, 2nd edn, Harmondsworth

Norris, M W 1956. 'The schools of brasses in Germany', *J Brit Archaeol Ass*, 3rd series, 19, 34–52

1977. *Monumental Brasses: The Memorials*, 2 vols, London

1978. *Monumental Brasses: The Craft*, London

1987. 'Views on the early knights, 1786–1970', in *The Earliest English Brasses* (ed J Coales), 1–7, London

1988. *Monumental Brasses: The Portfolio Plates of the Monumental Brass Society 1894–1984*, Woodbridge

Nys, L 1993a. *La pierre de Tournai*, Tournai

1993b. 'Incised wall tablets in Tournai stone', *Trans Monumental Brass Soc*, 15, 90–118

Oxford Historical Society 1905. *Collectanea*, 4th series, 47

Page-Phillips, J 1989. 'Three Flemish Fragments', *Trans Monumental Brass Soc*, 14, 324–8

Paul, R W 1882. *An Account of some of the Incised and Sepulchral Slabs of North-West Somerset*, London

Pearman, A J 1886. *Ashford: Its Church, Vicars, College and Grammar School*, Ashford

Pepys, N 1984. 'Who lies here? The Camoys brass in Trotton church', *Bull Monumental Brass Soc*, 37, 110–13

Pevsner, N 1958. *Shropshire*, Buildings of England series, Harmondsworth

Pocock, W W 1858. 'Chertsey Abbey', *Surrey Archaeol Collect*, 1, 97–114

PRO 1893. *Calendar of Patent Rolls, Edward III, 1330–4*, London

1912. *Inquisitions Post Mortem Edward III*, London

1968. *Calendar of Memoranda Rolls, Edward III, 1326–7*, London

Quirk, R N 1954. 'The monuments of Prior Basyng and "the old bishop in marble" ', *Winchester Cathedral Record*, 23, 12–21

RCHM 1923. *An Inventory of Historical Monuments in South-East Essex*, London

1924. *London: Westminster Abbey*, London

1984. *An Inventory of Historical Monuments in North Northamptonshire*, London

Robinson, P R 1824. *An Attempt to Ascertain the Age of the Church of Mickleham in Surrey*, London

Rogers, N 1987. 'English episcopal monuments 1270–1350', in *The Earliest English Brasses* (ed J Coales), 8–68, London

1996. 'Brasses in their art-historical context', in *Brasses as Art and History* (ed J Bertram), 146–59, Stroud

forthcoming. 'Monuments to monks and monastic servants', in *Monasteries and Society in Medieval England* (ed B Thompson), Harlaxton Medieval Studies 6, Stamford

Roper, I 1931. *Monumental Effigies of Gloucestershire and Bristol*, Gloucester

Ryder, P F 1985. *The Medieval Cross Slab Grave Cover in County Durham*, Architect Archaeol Soc Durham Northumberland Res Rep, 1, Durham

1991. *Medieval Cross Slab Grave Covers in West Yorkshire*, West Yorkshire Archaeol Service Res Rep 1, Durham

Ryland, H (ed) 1913. *Visitation of Hampshire 1530, 1575 and 1622–34*, Harleian Soc, 64, London

Sadler, A G 1975–86. *The Indents of Lost Monumental Brasses in Southern England*, Worthing

Salmon, N 1728. *History of Hertfordshire*, London

Saul, N 1992. 'The slab of John le Botelier at St Brides, Glamorgan', *Church Monuments Soc Newsletter*, 7, 4–7

Sharpe, R R 1889–90. *Calendar of Wills for the Corporation of London*, 2 vols, London

Smith, D M 1981. *Guide to Bishops' Registers of England and Wales*, Royal Hist Soc, London

Spence, C 1841. *An Essay Descriptive of the Abbey Church at Romsey*, Romsey

Spittle, S D T 1970. 'The Trumpington brass', *Archaeol J*, 127, 223–7

Squibb, G D (ed) 1991. *Visitation of Hampshire 1686*, Harleian Soc, new series, 10, London

Stone, L 1972. *Sculpture in Britain: The Middle Ages*, London

Styan, K 1902. *History of Sepulchral Cross Slabs*, London

Suckling, A 1845. *Memorials of the Antiquities and Architecture of Essex*, London

Surrey Record Society 1933. *Chertsey Cartularies 1*, 12

Tanner, J D 1953. 'Tombs of royal babies in Westminster Abbey', *J Brit Archaeol Ass*, new series, 16, 25–40

Thomas, A H (ed) 1924. *Calendar of Early Mayors' Court Rolls for the City of London AD 1298–1307*, Cambridge

Trivick, H 1969. *The Craft and Design of Monumental Brasses*, London

Trollope, E 1855. 'Note', *Archaeol J*, 12, 280
   1874. 'St John the Baptist, Doddington', *Archaeol Cantiana*, 9, xxxi

Tummers, H 1980. *Early Secular Effigies in England*, Leiden
   1988. 'The medieval effigial tombs in Chichester Cathedral', *Church Monuments, J Church Monuments Soc*, 3, 3–41
   1994. 'Church monuments', in *Chichester Cathedral* (ed M Hobbs), 203–24, Chichester

van Belle, R 1992. *Catalogue of Exhibition of Brass Rubbings of Incised Slabs and Memorial Brasses from West Flanders*, Bruges

van der Hagen, V 1914. *Enquête sur les dalles, lames de cuivre et autre monuments funéraires provenant d'ateliers de tombières Gantois XVIe–XVe siècles (d'apres les documents d'archives)*, Ghent

VCH 1900–11. *Hampshire*, 4 vols, London
   1902–12. *Surrey*, 4 vols, London
   1902–14. *Hertfordshire*, 4 vols, London
   1905–87. *Sussex*, 9 vols, London

Ward, J 1965. 'Sir Robert de Bures', *Trans Monumental Brass Soc*, 10, 144–50

Webb, E A 1921. *The Records of St Bartholomew's, Smithfield*, 2 vols, Oxford

Weever, J 1631. *Ancient Funeral Monuments*, London

Williamson, P 1988. *Northern Gothic Sculpture 1200–1450*, London

Worthington Smith, J 1905–7. 'Note', *Proc Soc Antiq*, 21, 314–16

Wrottesley, G 1893. 'Pedigrees from the Plea Rolls', *The Genealogist*, new series, 34, 79–86

Index